THE UNIVERSITY OF MICHIGAN
CENTER FOR JAPANESE STUDIES

MICHIGAN PAPERS IN JAPANESE STUDIES
NO. 9

THE NEW RELIGIONS OF JAPAN:
A BIBLIOGRAPHY
OF WESTERN-LANGUAGE MATERIALS

H. Byron Earhart

Second Edition

Ann Arbor

Center for Japanese Studies
The University of Michigan

1983

ISBN 0-939512-13-0

Library of Congress Cataloging in Publication Data

Earhart, H. Byron.
    The new religions of Japan.

    (Michigan papers in Japanese studies ; 9)
    Bibliography: pp. 23-176
    Includes index.
    1. Japan—Religion—1868-   —Bibliography.
I. Title.   II. Series.
Z7834.J3E2   1983   [BL2207.5]   016.291'0952   83-2054
ISBN 0-939512-13-0

Printed in the United States of America

to my parents

CONTENTS

THE AUTHOR

H. Byron Earhart received his Ph.D. in history of religions from the University of Chicago after study at Columbia University and Tōhoku University (Sendai, Japan). He spent three years in Japan for research on his dissertation, which was published as *A Religious Study of the Mount Haguro Sect of Shugendō* (Sophia University, *Monumenta Nipponica* Monograph). He has written a widely used text, *Japanese Religion: Unity and Diversity*, and a companion sourcebook, *Religion in the Japanese Experience* (Wadsworth). A translation from the Japanese of Shigeyoshi Murakami's *Nihon Hyakunen no Shūkyō* was published in English as *Japanese Religion in the Modern Century* (University of Tokyo Press). He has traveled and studied extensively in Japan and published numerous articles and reviews on the subject of Japanese religion. His present work includes the writing of a general introduction to Japanese religion and the preparation of a book on the New Religion Gedatsu-kai. Dr. Earhart is professor of religion at Western Michigan University, which in 1981 honored him as Distinguished Faculty Scholar.

PREFACE TO THE FIRST EDITION

The Japanese New Religions have probably attracted more attention from a wider group of Western scholars than any other aspect of Japanese religious history. They are of interest not only for the understanding of Japanese history, Japanese religion, and contemporary Japan in general, but also for such comparative study as modernization and cultural change. Thus, they have gained the attention of anthropologists, sociologists, and political scientists, as well as specialists in the field of religion and Japanese studies.

As a student of Japanese religion I was interested in this remarkable phenomenon long before I had time to pursue the subject. When I finally began a closer study of the subject, I made it a practice to keep a file of all Western references. As this file grew in size, it occurred to me that, if compiled thoroughly and systematically, a bibliography of this kind could be quite valuable for Western scholars and students. For, although many scholars of various disciplines are interested in the New Religions, few of them are able to read the Japanese materials on the subject. Most will have to depend on Western-language materials, but these materials are scattered in widely diverging and often obscure publications. With the intention of making a comprehensive bibliography available for Western scholars have I undertaken this work.

References were compiled mainly during the period 1967–69. Entries were gained first from my own files, then from secondary works on the New Religions, from numerous bibliographical works on Japan and religion, from systematic searching of academic journals, and from library catalogs. A form letter (in Japanese) requesting denominational publications in Western languages was sent to the headquarters of about 200 New Religions. This letter offered payment for publication and shipping cost, but it should be noted that many New Religions kindly sent materials without fee. To confirm complete references to denominational publications I traveled to some of the headquarters of New Religions in the spring of 1969. A number of people familiar with the New Religions have kindly checked the contents of the bibliography at one stage or another. However, in spite of all these precautions, the admission that this work is subject to omissions and errors is an inevitable if unfortunate fact; the compiler apologizes for such deficiencies and begs to be informed of the same. Even as this work goes to press, references have appeared that cannot be printed in the present edition. It is my hope that, after a few years, these and later publications may be included in another edition.

If the making of a bibliography is a thankless task, it is so because there is not sufficient space to thank all those who assisted in its compilation. This incomplete list includes the libraries (and their staffs) at: Western Michigan University, the University of Michigan, the University of Chicago, Notre Dame University, Columbia University, Union Theological Seminary in the City of New York (Missionary Research Library); in Japan: Japanese Diet Library, Kokugakuin University, Sophia (Jōchi) University, Tenri University, Tokyo University, International House of Japan, Kokusai Bunka Shinkōkai (The Society for International Cultural Relations), International Institute for the Study of Religion, Ministry of Education (Religious Affairs Section), and Oriens Institute for Religious Research.

For preliminary help in searching journals thanks are due to Mr. Michael Perrone, undergraduate assistant, under special arrangement with Dr. Samuel I. Clark, Director, Honors College, Western Michigan University. A number of Japanese scholars helped me in obtaining materials and in organizing the bibliography. Mr. Shūten Ōishi, Executive Secretary of the Union of New Religious Organizations of Japan, kindly offered advice, materials, and introductions to headquarters of New Religions. Mr. Yuiken Kawawata of the Religious Affairs Section, Ministry of Education, aided in obtaining and verifying information about the New Religions. Professor Fujio Ikado of Tsuda College helped in clarifying the Introduction. While collecting materials in Japan, I was provided office space in the Institute for Japanese Culture and Classics, Kokugakuin University, thanks to Professor Kenji Ueda, Executive Secretary of the Institute. Secretarial help in typing the manuscript was provided by Western Michigan University.

For financial aid I acknowledge a Faculty Research Grant from Western Michigan University and a Travel and Study Grant from the Institute of International and Area Studies, Western Michigan University. A 1969 summer stipend from the National Foundation for the Humanities allowed time to organize the bibliography for publication.

PREFACE TO THE SECOND EDITION

A decade has passed since the appearance of the first edition of this work, making it appropriate to comment briefly on the current status of the New Religions, the procedures in compiling the materials for the second edition, the nature of these materials, and some changes in the format of the bibliography.

The simplest generalization one can make about the Japanese New Religions is that they continue today, much as they did ten years ago, as one of the most powerful and conspicuous forces on the Japanese religious scene. In fact, the New Religions are more powerful and better organized than they were in the 1960s. The present situation of the New Religions is a result of the continuous process of "growth" they have experienced: the New Religions have advanced in organizational development as they have increased in age, and now most New Religions have rather elaborate bureaucratic structures.

Of course, the level of development and extent of change depends greatly on the relative age of the particular movement. For example, Tenrikyō, founded in 1838, has had about a century since the death, in 1887, of its foundress, Mrs. Miki Nakayama, to systematize its teachings, branch organization, administrative headquarters, and overseas mission, and even to found a major private university. As can be expected from its more lengthy history, Tenrikyō achieved a highly developed organizational structure much earlier and has not changed that much during the past decade. On the other hand, Sōka Gakkai, whose founding in 1937 followed by a century that of Tenrikyō's, and which gained momentum only in the 1950s through the effort of several dynamic leaders (after the death of the founder, Tsunesaburō Makiguchi, during World War II), has developed more recently and more rapidly. The relatively shorter history of Sōka Gakkai is reflected in the fact that it has undergone more dramatic changes during the past decade: the 1970s saw the opening of Sōka University; the relationship of Sōka Gakkai to its political arm, Kōmeitō (the Clean Government Party), has been seriously challenged; and even the relationship of Sōka Gakkai to its formal parent organization, Nichiren Shōshū (a Buddhist denomination in the Nichiren line), has experienced serious difficulties.

A somewhat different case is that of the New Religions whose founders are still living and are actively directing the course of development and organization of their movements: these religions may continue to undergo significant shifts of energy and direction throughout the coming decades. One interesting change in the overall situation of New Religions is that recent years have not seen many founders (or foundresses) appearing to set up new movements. It seems that the most important developments are the expansion, consolidation, and elaboration of existing New Religions. The newly formed organizations tend to be more in the nature of secessions or splinters from existing organizations than based on the fresh inspiration of charismatic founders. (This is a matter of degree, for many of the earlier "founders" borrowed from previous New Religions; the point is that the day of powerful founding figures seems to be on the wane, and the time of organizing geniuses is at hand.)

This is not the place to analyze and document the status of the Japanese New Religions. It is enough to show that they continue to be important aspects of social and religious change in contemporary Japan. Therefore, the original purpose of this bibliography is renewed in the second edition: to make available to students of social and religious change a comprehensive list of Western-language materials on the Japanese New Religions.

Some more specific remarks may be directed to the new materials in this edition. A serious attempt was made to broaden the geographical scope of the coverage for this edition, particularly for Hawaiian and South American materials. Two days spent in the library and special collections of the University of Hawaii resulted in more complete coverage of Japanese New Religions in Hawaii, as indicated under the topic "Hawaiian branches" in the Topical Index. In fact, several Hawaiian movements that may be considered New Religions of Japanese origin did not appear in the first edition but are included in this edition: Bodaiji Mission, Chōwadō Henjōkyō Mission of Hawaii, and Tōdaiji of Hawaii. However, such a brief excursion into Hawaiian culture, far from ensuring complete coverage, only serves to indicate that more thorough work needs to be done in this area. Several other movements might have been included if reliable information about them could have been obtained. It is hoped that other scholars will collect and publish this information on religion in Hawaii,[1] a task that goes beyond the limits of this bibliography. It seemed better to publish these items on Hawaiian branches and admit their incompleteness than to accept the less desirable alternatives: either exclude Hawaiian branches from the bibliography or delay publication of this second edition until more comprehensive coverage of Hawaiian movements became possible.

---

1. See the Japanese-language work of Yanagawa and Morioka (entry 253), which includes some English-language materials and is planned for translation into English. More work of this nature would greatly improve our knowledge of Japanese religion in Hawaii, including new religious movements.

South American materials were searched by using the leads in *The Japanese and Their Descendants in Brazil: An Annotated Bibliography*,[2] by searching the Library of Congress, and through interlibrary loan. Some materials were also sent in by Rev. Kjell Nordstokke. The same note of caution, however, applies to both the Hawaiian and South American materials: although more comprehensive coverage is included in the second edition, more work needs to be done. Until the above-mentioned bibliography is updated, or another work is produced, a 1979 article by Robert J. Smith (entry 210) provides a quick overview of the South American situation.

Some new materials in European languages, notably German and French, are included in this edition, but no European libraries were searched, and it is to be expected that there are other works on Japanese New Religions in these languages.

It may be well at this point to make a general disclaimer: the present bibliography, while attempting to be comprehensive, is certainly not exhaustive. Out of the hundreds of New Religions in Japan, surely more than those represented in this bibliography have produced Western-language materials. And obviously there are publications about the New Religions, articles and books not found in standard bibliographies and periodical indexes, that are not included in this edition. I have already begun to file such materials as they become known to me, and I will continue to actively search citations with the intention of preparing a third edition. (As this edition goes to press, the file includes more than a hundred entries.) Corrections and additions to this bibliography will be greatly appreciated; they can be sent to me at the Department of Religion, Western Michigan University, Kalamazoo, Michigan 49008, U.S.A.

The only subject that was deliberately limited while searching was Kōmeitō (the Clean Government Party), the political arm of Sōka Gakkai. So many general works on Japan, particularly works on Japanese history and politics, briefly mention Kōmeitō that to include all such works would have inordinately expanded that section of the bibliography without adding to its value. Only articles and books dealing with Kōmeitō at greater length have been added to this bibliography. For additional references, please consult Kōmeitō or Clean Government Party in the indexes of general books on Japan.

The general nature and quality of works on Japanese New Religions has not changed remarkably during the past decade. Works issued by the New Religions (referred to herein as "denominational" materials) have increased in number, but they still deal mainly with doctrine and propagation, while moving somewhat into

2. Robert J. Smith, John B. Cornell, Hiroshi Saito, and Takashi Maeyama (São Paulo: Centro de Estudos Nipo-Brasileiros, 1967), viii + 188 pp.

the cultural area. Secondary materials are still focused mainly on a few well-known movements such as Sōka Gakkai and Tenrikyō. Looking only at these two movements, we find that Sōka Gakkai spans entries 778 to 878 for denominational materials and 879 to 1094 for secondary materials; Tenrikyō spans entries 1101 to 1269 for denominational materials and 1270 to 1357 for secondary materials. The total of almost 600 entries about these two groups constitutes well over a third of the 1,450 entries in the bibliography. The extensive denominational materials demonstrate the size, organizational development, and dynamics of the two New Religions; the many secondary materials show that scholars publishing in Western languages are drawn mainly to the larger and more controversial New Religions. More often than not these secondary materials are the rephrasing and reinterpretation of previous Western-language publications rather than the presentation of new information and new interpretations. Some of the best works listed in both the first edition and the present edition are the results of doctoral dissertations, published and unpublished. For this reason, not only unpublished doctoral dissertations but also master's theses and some undergraduate papers have been included, insofar as possible, since they often include information not available elsewhere.

Recent dissertations on specific movements have helped improve our knowledge of the development, activities, and nature of individual movements, but more monographs are needed in this area. For example, even the extremely important Oomoto and Tenrikyō have elicited only three serious monographs in the last decade (two are dissertations in German). By contrast, more than ten doctoral dissertations on Sōka Gakkai were completed between 1969 and 1979. The area of Shinto, which has always been underrepresented in Western scholarship as compared with Buddhism, is also slighted in connection with New Religions. Except for the two monographs on Oomoto and one on Tenrikyō, no major work on any of the former members of Sect Shinto (Kyōha Shintō) has appeared in the last decade. Perhaps the closest candidate is the work of Lokowandt (entry 130), which deals with legal matters rather than with religion as such. Davis's work on Sūkyō Mahikari (entry 1095) is a welcome exception to the general fact that smaller New Religions tend to be ignored. The conclusion concerning monographs on New Religions is the same today as ten years ago: more monographs are needed, with greater use of Japanese materials and first-hand study in Japan.

Studies published during the last decade have helped advance our general understanding of the New Religions, but it is safe to say that there is still no widely accepted synthetic interpretation of the New Religions. With the continuing publication of specialized monographs, it is likely that the next decade will usher in better synthetic studies. One hopeful sign is the enthusiastic activity of a relatively younger group of Japanese scholars, the Shūkyō Shakaigaku Kenkyūkai (sociology of religion society), which is very active in the study of New

Religions and is increasingly publishing Japanese materials on this subject.[3] These works are just now appearing in English; see entries 166, 207, and 759. Many previous studies have tended to use the New Religions as convenient material for proving older theories about social change, but the younger scholars of this society have been more creative in taking a fresh look at the New Religions and attempting to arrive at their own interpretations. This tendency is a good sign for future studies of Japanese New Religions.

Comments on the procedures for obtaining the new entries in the second edition, and the different arrangement of entries, are now in order. Even before the first edition was published in 1970, a file was begun for subsequent materials. Cards have been gathered systematically since 1970 at every opportunity, with some more intensive periods of bibliographic searching, especially during summers and while traveling in the vicinity of research libraries. Procedures for collecting the entries have been essentially the same as for the first edition, with a few minor innovations.

Most of the secondary citations were acquired through continued research on the New Religions. Every time a new work was encountered, a card was typed and placed in the file. An attempt was made to locate every item, verify the citation, and inspect the item for footnotes and bibliography in order to discover new citations. Many of the denominational publications were kindly sent to me by the headquarters of the various religious organizations.

Systematic searching was carried out at various libraries in the United States. Initial searching began at my home university, Western Michigan University, and then moved to the closest research libraries at the University of Michigan and the University of Chicago. In addition to the university libraries mentioned in the first edition, I have had the opportunity of using libraries at the University of California, Los Angeles; the University of Hawaii (including special collections); the University of California, Berkeley; and the Graduate Theological Union (including the Center for the Study of New Religious Movements). Two days were spent at the Library of Congress in the spring of 1979. While in Japan during 1979 and 1980, I systematically searched bookstores and the Diet Library. The procedure during these searches was to follow up all leads developed from previous reading and examination of other bibliographies; also searched in the card catalog were names of New Religions, names of founders, and general subjects such as Japanese religion. The main purpose of systematic searching was to verify previously recorded citations and discover new entries for scholarly (secondary)

---

3. For one example of the work of the members of this society, see the convenient handbook of essays outlining the problems for studying Japanese New Religions: Nobutaka Inoue et al., *Shinshūkyō Kenkyū Chōsa Handobukku* (Handbook for study and field research of the New Religions), listed in Appendix B.

articles and books. These searches also turned up some pamphlets and "ephemera" published long ago by Japanese New Religions, for which there is no record in their respective headquarters. Many books and articles were obtained through interlibrary loans with the assistance of the Interlibrary Loan staff of Western Michigan University.

In early 1980, after most new entries had been gathered, searches were carried out for three computerized data bases: names of New Religions and the term "New Religion" (or "New Religious") for *Comprehensive Dissertation Abstracts* (1861-1979) and *Social Scisearch* (1972-1979), and only the term "New Religion" (or "New Religious") for *Magazine Index* (1977-1979). Relatively few works were discovered through these searches, and most of these were already included in the second-edition materials. This negative result is mentioned here to save readers the time and expense of initiating this particular kind of search (by title of New Religion and the term "New Religion") for these data bases.[4]

The main source of denominational materials has been the headquarters of New Religions. Many complimentary copies of denominational publications were sent to me by New Religions during the past decade, and others were located in scholarly publications and libraries. The procedure for checking denominational publications while I was in Japan (in late 1979 and early 1980) was to duplicate printed pages from the first edition and the accumulated file cards for each New Religion, and send the copies to each headquarters (with a letter in Japanese) asking for corrections and additions to this checklist. The headquarters of most New Religions not only returned the corrected checklists but also sent free copies of their recent publications.   The accuracy and comprehensiveness of the denominational sections were greatly improved by this invaluable help.

The 810 entries from the first edition (with a few corrections and some supplemental information) form the basis for the second edition, together with the more than 600 new entries inserted in appropriate sections. Thus, the combined total of approximately 1,450 entries, almost twice the size of the first edition, actually results in a new work in its own right. To avoid confusion, however, it has seemed best to retain the original title and to designate this a second edition. At the same time, it has seemed fitting to improve the work wherever possible, and this had led to a change in the arrangement of the New Religions in Part II. In the first edition, I followed the practice of the Ministry of Education (now the Ministry of Education, Science and Culture) in grouping New Religions

4. The difficulty in locating materials about New Religions is that often such articles and books do not include in the title the name of the particular New Religion but focus on a more general topic such as social change or "The Popular Religion of a Japanese Village." Of course, other types of searches, such as by works cited, are possible for these and other data bases; the required time and expense did not seem justified for the present bibliography.

according to the major tradition from which they derived: Shinto-derived, Buddhist-derived, Christian-derived, and "Other Religions" (sho-kyō).   The major change in the organization of materials in the second edition has been to drop this pattern of grouping by derivation and to arrange the New Religions simply by alphabetical order of their names.   The reason for this change is twofold: first, the determination of a single tradition as the source of derivation is rather ambiguous, since all New Religions arise out of a complex background of diverse influences[5]; second, the matter of derivation is not a practical and efficient manner of arranging New Religions.   It seems much easier for the user to locate New Religions through a simple alphabetical ordering.   Note, however, that those categorized as "Utopian Groups" appear under that heading at the end of the bibliography.   An attempt has been made in this edition to give more complete citations and to conform more closely to Library of Congress style.   For example, where material and references were available, prefatory pagination of books has been provided.   Books have been listed in as many editions as known (except for some standard works), and reprintings have been noted for both books and articles.   Doctoral dissertations have been cited in full, with the publication in which they are abstracted, and the microfilm order number, when available. Other unpublished materials have been listed by the collection where they are located or the work in which they are cited.   Titles of works in languages other than German, French, Spanish, and Italian have been translated.   Russian works have been transliterated according to the Library of Congress style.   Standard abbreviations for places of publication and publishers have been adopted.

One exception to this quest for greater bibliographical completeness is the mention of illustrations (indicated by "Illus." at the end of the citation); although many of the works in this bibliography are listed by the Library of Congress as illustrated, I have used "Illus." only for works that illustrate Japanese New Religions.   Unfortunately, some references still are not as complete as desired, but it has seemed better to provide partial citations than to omit those works. For more information on the materials contained in this bibliography, and how to obtain them, see Appendix A, "Suggestions for Locating Western-Language Materials on the Japanese New Religions."

Several other changes should make the bibliography easier to use.   All cross-references within the bibliography provide the entry number of the reference.   Also, the topical index has been expanded to include subdivisions for

---

5.   The rather arbitrary character of "derivation" is revealed in the fact that a New Religion is asked to designate the category in which it is placed in the Religion Yearbook (Shūkyō Nenkan) published by the Ministry of Education, Science and Culture.   New Religions may decide to change their designation, as when Tenrikyō asked to be removed from the category of Shinto-derived and placed in the category of Other Religions (sho-kyō).

general materials and then for each New Religion. This enables the reader to recognize immediately under each topic the general publications on that topic, and then the publications on that topic dealing with individual New Religions. For example, the topic "Founders and foundresses" is followed by "(General)," and the entry numbers for those works dealing generally with founders and foundresses; next, this topic is subdivided alphabetically by New Religions for works treating the founding figure of that New Religion: "(Ananaikyō)," "(Dōtoku Kagaku)," "(Gedatsu-kai)," through "(Tenshō-Kōtai-Jingū-Kyō)." Utopian movements are given last. For this or any other topic the reader can tell at a glance which entries are general and which deal more specifically with one New Religion.

My sabbatical in Japan 1979-80 came just ten years after my trip to Japan to research the first edition of the bibliography, and for various practical reasons it has seemed best to take the end of this decade as the cutoff point for this edition: insofar as possible, the bibliography is comprehensive through 1979. Upon my return from Japan in early 1980, materials collected in Japan were added to the ongoing file, recently published Western works were noted (including some items for 1980), and the second edition was organized and entries were renumbered.

The process of compiling bibliographies never ends, however, and much of the summers of 1980 and 1981 was spent checking and completing citations. This resulted in not only more complete and corrected citations but also the inclusion of additional entries. It has seemed best to incorporate as much of this new information as possible, and to do so, some changes in the numbering system have been necessary. Newly discovered items published in 1979 or earlier have been inserted in the appropriate place in the bibliography, with a letter following the entry number (see Prebish, entry 1040A). In some cases, works already listed in the bibliography have been shifted in order to conform to Library of Congress style (for example, different listing of multiple-author works; see Arutiunov, entry 12A). In addition, authorship was confirmed for some works that had been listed without author. In order to shift these works to their proper place (and to avoid renumbering almost 1,500 items), some numbers appear without entries and are labeled "no entry." In a subsequent edition my file of post-1979 entries will be added to the present list and all works will be numbered consecutively.

It is worth noting that several other kinds of information were considered for inclusion in this edition but excluded, mainly due to limitations of time and space. For example, in the first edition there was a table listing "Approximate Derivation of New Religions." This table has been omitted from the present edition because these derivations are problematic, and to expand and clarify these derivations would go beyond the scope of a bibliographic work. Those who wish to explore the ambiguities of the derivation of these movements can refer to the first edition of this work[6] or consult Japanese works such as Shigeyoshi Murakami, *Kindai Minshū Shūkyōshi no Kenkyū*, or Nobutaka Inoue et al., *Shinshūkyō Kenkyū Chōsa Handobukku* (cited in full in Appendix B).

Another possibility considered was the listing of brief information for each movement—founding figure and date, development, clerical and membership figures, etc. But however useful such information might be, it seemed to go beyond the scope of a bibliography. My primary objective has been to compile and have published a comprehensive bibliography before it went out of date. Already this task has consumed an inordinate amount of time, and it seemed better to send forth an up-to-date bibliography than to devote more time and energy to the even larger project of a handbook on the Japanese New Religions. Those interested in statistical information may refer to "Statistics on Religious Organizations in Japan, 1947-1972" (entry 216A), or the Japanese work of Nobutaka Inoue et al. in Appendix B. In the future I may work on a more general treatment of the Japanese New Religions that includes such features as derivation and statistics of these movements.

For ease in composition, all Sino-Japanese characters have been removed from the body of the bibliography. Those interested in the Sino-Japanese forms of the names of the New Religions may refer to Table 1 and the Contents.

---

6. H[arry] Byron Earhart, *The New Religions of Japan: A Bibliography of Western-Language Materials*, Monumenta Nipponica Monograph Series (Tokyo: Sophia University, 1970), pp. 21-22.

ACKNOWLEDGMENTS

It is a pleasure to acknowledge the many sources of assistance in compiling this edition of the bibliography.

No specific grant was received to support this work on the second edition, but several grants indirectly helped make possible the completion of this book. Much of the final checking of the new items, particularly the denominational materials, was done in Japan during 1979-80. This research trip (for a study of Japanese New Religions, especially Gedatsu-kai) was supported by a grant from the Japan Society for the Promotion of Science (Nihon Gakujutsu Shinkōkai) in a joint study with Professor Hitoshi Miyake of Keiō University. Keiō University kindly provided office space. The Faculty Research Fund of Western Michigan University supplied additional funds, and Mr. Kōjirō Miyasaka, Chief of the International Division of Risshō Kōsei-kai, kindly provided housing.

A Fulbright housing grant in Korea during the summer of 1973 provided a valuable opportunity to study Korean New Religions and gain insights on the comparative study of Japanese and Korean New Religions.

The headquarters of many New Religions kindly provided complimentary copies of their publications and corrected my checklists of their publications. Without their enthusiastic cooperation this work would hardly have been possible.

The staff of many libraries and their special collections helped locate materials that otherwise would not appear in this work. The library staff of my home university, Western Michigan University, should be singled out for special thanks: they helped complete obscure citations, and the Interlibrary Loan service secured many volumes needed to prepare this edition.

A number of colleagues were good enough to submit citation information, often unsolicited, and occasionally on request. There is no space to thank each one individually, but one name that should not remain unmentioned is Harold W. Turner, himself an indefatigable bibliographer: he has contributed many cards (particularly from European journals) ever since the preparation of the first edition.

The following persons translated foreign-language titles: Professor Larry ten Harmsel (Dutch), Professor Larry Syndergaard (Norwegian and Swedish), Professor Emanuel Nodel (Polish), Maria Helena Crandall (Portuguese), Professor Irene Storoshenko (Russian), all at Western Michigan University; and Donald J. Harlow (Esperanto), of the Esperanto League for North America, El Cerrito, California.

Dr. Michael Cooper, Editor of *Monumenta Nipponica*, kindly arranged for the printing of the Sino-Japanese characters used in this volume.

The tedious task of completing a manuscript was greatly facilitated by the help of a research assistant, Mr. William W. McCall. Through the generosity of Dean Laurel Grotzinger and the Graduate College of Western Michigan University, Mr. McCall spent part of the summer of 1980 searching citations and editing the manuscript. My sons Paul and David helped in arranging the citations, compiling the two indexes, and completing and checking many citations. Mrs. Dolores Condic did all the necessary typing for the draft submitted to the publisher.

The entire manuscript was read by a professional bibliographer in Asian Studies, Professor Frank Joseph Shulman, of the University of Maryland, College Park. His extensive suggestions, corrections, and additions have helped eliminate a number of errors and omissions and generally improved the format of the bibliography. The staff of G.K. Hall & Co., especially Mr. Ara Salibian, helped prepare the manuscript for publication. Special thanks are due to Dr. John Campbell, Director, Bruce E. Willoughby, Associate Editor, and Cindi Larson, Word Processor, of the Center for Japanese Studies, the University of Michigan for their prompt, efficient, and careful production of this book.

INTRODUCTION

The New Religions in the Light of
Japanese Religious History

Although the Japanese New Religions have attracted much attention and have served as the subject for many publications in Japanese and Western languages, they are not yet fully understood. Even for a specialist in Japanese studies, the New Religions present a number of enigmas. For the person not specializing in Japanese studies or Japanese religions, these phenomena are especially difficult to understand without some general introduction. For this reason, and to facilitate utilization of the bibliography, a brief interpretation of the origin and nature of the New Religions is offered here.[1]

The term "New Religions" is misleading, for these movements do not present much novel religious content. Rather, they are new in the sense of being new socioreligious movements. "New Religions" is the commonly accepted translation for the Japanese *shinkō shūkyō*, which means literally "newly arisen religions." This term was apparently coined by newspaper reporters and has the disparaging nuance of upstart religions. The new religious groups themselves favor the term *shin shūkyō*, which translates directly as "New Religions" without any pejorative sense. Since the term New Religions has gained widespread usage, there seems to be no point in adding to the confusion by proliferating terminology. We should be careful of the way in which we use the term, however, and this writer prefers to use it in the descriptive sense of new religious movements. In order to understand these New Religions, or new religious movements, we must know something about the general religious context of which they are a part, the general circumstances of their emergence, and their general religious character.

The general context of the New Religions is the fabric of Japanese religion. The New Religions are of recent design, but the design is stamped on the

---

1. Those more familiar with Japanese religions and Japanese studies may proceed directly to the discussion "Western-Language Materials on the New Religions," and "Organization and Utilization of the Bibliography." Those wishing to use the bibliography before referring to any introductory material may turn immediately to "Suggestions for Convenient Use of the Bibliography."

warp and woof of Japanese religion. The earlier or "old" Japanese religion provides the background against which the New Religions are set in relief. Japanese religion is at least several thousand years old, featuring indigenous and borrowed religious elements intermixed through the course of history, resulting in a distinctive Japanese religious worldview. There are at least five major traditions in Japanese religion: folk religion, Shinto, Buddhism, Confucianism, and Taoism; six if we count the recent addition of Christianity. With the passage of time these traditions interacted to such a high degree that not one of them remains free from mutual influence. Of the five major traditions, only Shinto and Buddhism emerged as religious organizations with strong institutional structures, while the other traditions remained important covert influences. Thus, Japanese religion reveals a plurality of religious traditions without the notion of exclusive affiliation to one ecclesiastical body. In fact, in Japanese religion informal practices are just as important as institutionally organized activities.

What constitutes Japanese religion is not just the totality of these individual traditions, but also their mutual contribution toward a common religious worldview sharing a number of persistent themes. These persistent themes include: the closeness of man, "gods" (kami), and nature; the religious significance of the family (living and dead), and the home as a religious center; the importance of purification, discipline, rituals, and charms; the prominence of local festivals and individual cults; the intimate relationship between religious practice and daily life; and the natural bond between Japanese religion and the Japanese nation. These persistent themes pervade almost every individual tradition and every specific historical period.

In general, Japanese religious history can be understood in terms of three major periods: (1) the period of formation, from prehistory to the ninth century A.D., when all the major traditions first came into contact with each other; (2) the period of development and elaboration from the ninth to the seventeenth century, when these traditions became intricately interrelated; and (3) the period of formalization and renewal, from the seventeenth century to the present, when the older "established" religions became formalized and New Religions began to appear.[2]

The New Religions arose at a time when the two major "established" religions, Shinto and Buddhism, became so rigidly formalized that they tended to lose their religious vitality and retreat from the needs of the people. The New Religions appeared out of a complicated interrelationship between prior religious

---

2. This interpretive framework of persistent themes and historical periods forms the basis of my general introduction, *Japanese Religion: Unity and Diversity*, 3d ed. (Belmont, CA: Wadsworth, 1982). For a more complete one-volume history, see Joseph M. Kitagawa, *Religion in Japanese History* (New York: Columbia University Press, 1966).

history, socioeconomic conditions, and personal inspiration. The stagnation of established religions opened the door to external innovations, while the prior Japanese religious tradition provided the content for the new groups: socioeconomic conditions of severe hardship stimulated or precipitated the formation of the groups, and to a certain extent socioeconomic conditions influenced the pattern of their formation; the personal inspiration of the founders initiated the movements and became the religious orientations around which the groups of believers could organize their corporate life. Although institutional religion became formalized, there were still vital religious elements within institutional religion and informal religion. The New Religions may be best understood as renewals of the older tradition in somewhat different form. The New Religions revitalized the slumbering religious heritage by reviving its vital elements in the garb of divine inspiration and creative restructuring.[3]

What distinguishes the New Religions is not their novelty of religious content but their existence as new socioreligious organizations. In particular they present a strong contrast to the established religions of Shinto and Buddhism. In general, the established religions are more concerned with preserving the heritage of the past, while the New Religions are directly engaged in the life and salvation of the populace. The vitality of the New Religions is reflected in their dynamic origin and active character. These new movements usually were initiated by founders (or foundresses) who received the special inspiration or revelation which resulted in the formation of a new socioreligious group. The founder was considered as semidivine or even as a "living god" (iki-gami) in the Japanese sense. Usually through the combined power of the founder's charisma and the revealed (or renewed) set of religious resources, a sufficient following was attracted to form a permanent group. The existence of "living gods," charismatic leaders, and powerful religious sources is nothing new to Japanese religion—the remarkable thing is that such leaders and their messages resulted in new socioreligious bodies. With the increase of followers came a structuring of the movement into a unified religious organization. For example, if a previously existing scripture was not revered, the founder often dictated a set of scriptures. Other aspects of organization that appeared were priestly offices, doctrine, ritual life, and the like. Sometimes they developed wedding and memorial rites, but they were usually willing to share religious devotion and practice with other religious institutions. Therefore, the New Religions are not necessarily "religions"

3.   The interpretation of the New Religions presented in this brief introduction is treated in greater detail in my article, "The Interpretation of the 'New Religions' of Japan as Historical Phenomena," *Journal of the American Academy of Religion* 37, no. 3 (September 1969): 237-48. In subsequent articles I have treated other theoretical aspects of Japanese New Religions; see entries 50-59 in Part I, General Bibliography, especially entry 59, "Toward a Theory of the Formation of the Japanese New Religions: A Case Study of Gedatsu-kai."

in the ordinary Western sense of the Judaeo-Christian tradition or Protestant sects and denominations. Many of the New Religions encourage their members to continue their attendance at Shinto shrines and Buddhist temples. Indeed, a prevalent feature of the New Religions is their syncretistic character, which has led some groups to include aspects of Western thought. All the New Religions promise an immediate contact with sacred power, either personal or embodied in a sacred resource (such as a sutra), which is able to solve personal and social problems. Some groups feature creative forms of individual and group counselling (or blending of confession and guidance). These practices shade off into forms of faith-healing.

These groups prospered, especially after 1945, when the New Religions were free to organize, and their membership increased. They have plunged into the modern world more quickly and deeply than the older religions, using mass media, developing extensive publication facilities, erecting elaborate modern buildings, and setting up their own schools and facilities with emphasis on lay participation. In the immediate postwar years, when severe control of religion was removed, a great number of short-lived religions arose, some with questionable intentions. But at present the older and larger of the New Religions are so efficiently organized and stable that already they have assumed the status of established religions. This is attested by the several religious federations that they have set up.

Definition of the New Religions

Definition of the New Religions is beset by a number of difficulties: the complex and syncretistic nature of Japanese religion, the sudden changes in political and religious history, and the large number of New Religions. We may review some of the alternatives for defining the New Religions before outlining the particular usage followed in this bibliography. It has been suggested that there are three ways of focusing on the definition of the New Religions: (1) in terms of those religions such as Tenrikyō and Konkōkyō that formed around charismatic leaders about the time of the Meiji Restoration (1868) and came to possess well-established, large religious orders; (2) in terms of those religions such as Seichō-no-Ie, PL Kyōdan, and Sekai Kyūsei-kyō, which were legally considered spurious or "pseudo-religions" (ruiji-shūkyō) when they originated about 1910 to 1920 (but experienced their major growth after World War II); and (3) in terms of those religions such as Sōka Gakkai and Tenshō-Kōtai-Jingū-Kyō, whose development and expansion occurred mainly after World War II.[4] Each of these ways of defining the New Religions is based on an important aspect of their

4. *Shūkyō Nenkan, Shōwa* 37 [Religion Yearbook, 1962] (Tokyo: Ministry of Education, 1963), p. 206.

development.   For example, Tenrikyō and Konkōkyō are important because they were among the first new religious groups to emerge as large religious bodies: chronologically they are landmarks in the rise of New Religions, and practically they served as prototypes for the organization of later emergents.   Some scholars, however, feel that the status of Tenrikyō and Konkōkyō as officially recognized members of Sect Shinto (Kyōha Shintō) already at the beginning of the twentieth century separates them from the truly "New Religions" that existed outside of officially recognized organizations.   In this sense Tenrikyō and Konkōkyō are forerunners or pioneers of the New Religions which later arose.   This is one reason why Japanese scholars tend to see Oomoto (and other prewar groups) as indicative of the rise of New Religions, since these groups arose and continued outside officially recognized channels, providing the model for new socioreligious organization.   Kyōha Shintō may be seen partly as an extension of the prior established religions, but Oomoto and its contemporaries were clearly labeled as "pseudo-religions" (ruiji-shūkyō).   Here we see the clear legal distinction between officially sanctioned sects and spurious religions.   The third possibility for defining the New Religions, in terms of postwar developments, emphasizes chronologically the tremendous significance of postwar expansion in the New Religions and their success in realizing the ideal of drawing the masses into these movements.   This is the general pattern usually employed to bring the several hundred New Religions into some semblance of order.

Another means of arranging the New Religions is to trace them back to their primary derivation.[5]   Japanese religion is syncretistic, and this is even more true of the New Religions, but many of them owe heavy debts to particular branches of Shinto and Buddhism.   These are the two major categories of derivation, and those which have no explicit denominational point of departure are placed in the category of "other" or "various" religions (sho-kyō).[6]   In fact, some scholars prefer to limit the term "New Religions" to the sho-kyō, on the grounds that they alone present a distinctively new blend of religious life which cannot be placed in the camp of Shinto or Buddhism.   These are the major alternatives for defining the New Religions; further discussions of these alternatives may be found by consulting the General Bibliography.[7]

It will be seen that the author's interpretation of the New Religions as "new religious movements" is more inclusive than any of the previous alternatives.   The present definition recognizes the value of these previous attempts and incorporates them within a systematic framework.   Thus, there seem to be three

5.   Ibid., pp. 213-26 contains a valuable chart of derivation and lineage for all major Japanese religious groups.
6.   Ibid., pp. 206-13.
7.   See items listed under "New Religions, definition of" in the Topical Index.

major criteria for distinguishing new religious movements: (1) chronologically, those movements that appeared from late Tokugawa or early Meiji to the present; (2) in origin, those movements that arose as renewal or "revitalizing"[8] forces; and (3) in formation, those movements that led to permanent socioreligious organizations. This tentative definition is helpful in compiling a bibliographical work since its criteria are both chronological and typological. This definition allows the inclusion of any movements from late Tokugawa times to the present that are revitalistic in character and have resulted in socioreligious organization. Such usage embraces all the religious groups mentioned in the major definitions of the New Religions, without insisting on either a specific derivation or independent origin (lack of clear derivation). Thus, it grasps both the sho-kyō and the New Religions directly related to a prior established religion. For example, it includes Sōka Gakkai, which technically is a lay organization within the Buddhist sect called Nichiren Shōshū. At the same time, such a criterion makes possible the exclusion of various movements that did not result in socioreligious organizations, as well as the exclusion of splinter groups that are schismatic in character rather than new religious movements. The author's interpretation of New Religions in the sense of new religious movements will become clearer by noting some specific exclusions and inclusions.

Excluded from this work, for example, are the various ethicoreligious movements such as Shingaku, which have been quite influential since late Tokugawa and early Meiji times. They are excluded because, even though they may represent revitalizing forces which exerted considerable influence (even on the New Religions), they did not result in major socioreligious organizations. Their main activity was ethical and educational training.[9] The boundary between religion and ethical instruction is quite hazy in both China and Japan, where a "teaching" (chiao in Chinese, kyō or oshie in Japanese) can be the basis for a religious movement just as well as a divine revelation. While recognizing their considerable importance, we exclude ethical movements for the reason that they do not in themselves constitute significant socioreligious organizations. The group Dōtoku Kagaku or Moralogy, however, which legally is organized as a foundation rather than a religion, can be considered a New Religion in terms of our criteria for new religious movements. (See entries 297-301 under Dōtoku Kagaku in Part II.)

---

8. See Anthony F.C. Wallace, "Revitalization Movements," *American Anthropologist* 58 (1956): 264-81, for a general anthropological treatment of this concept. Wallace's theoretical framework for revitalization and especially its application to religious movements raise problems which cannot be discussed here. Some of these problems were mentioned indirectly in my "The Interpretation of the 'New Religions' of Japan as Historical Phenomena" and were discussed more directly in my "The Interpretation of the 'New Religions' of Japan as New Religious Movements" (entry 52).
9. See Robert N. Bellah, *Tokugawa Religion* (Glencoe, IL: Free Press, 1957) and the bibliography therein. Reprint. Boston: Beacon Press, 1970.

Also excluded are many groups which first achieved independent status from higher ecclesiastical control in postwar times. Many groups in this category represent schismatic splits that had long been thwarted by political control. The formation of both new denominational patterns and new religious groups was strictly controlled by the government, with increasing suppression, up until 1945. Then, with the enactment of complete religious freedom, shrines and temples were free to break former lines of authority and either become independent or form new associations.[10] These groups represent changes in polity and finances, but they do not constitute new religious movements. What confuses the picture is that the enactment of religious freedom in 1945 opened the floodgates to a simultaneous outpouring of repressed religious currents which flowed originally from several different sources: new religious movements that had existed in prewar times either in expedient submission to a recognized sect or as nonreligious associations, which after 1945 were able to express their true character; groups that desired independence of polity (but not a new religious orientation) in prewar times, which were able to gain independent or revised status; and New Religions which arose for the first time in the surge of unsuppressed activity after 1945. These groups achieved independence simultaneously, but that does not mean that they are identical in character. The most numerous of these postwar denominational or schismatic splits are found within Buddhism. Some groups stand on the borderline between schismatic splits and the formation of new religious movements, but no attempt is made to include them in this bibliography.

This definition also excludes a number of cults that, although quite important in religious activities in Japanese history, are usually neither revitalizing forces nor formally organized socioreligious institutions. In some cases these cults may take on the character of new religious movements, but most often they simply continue the prior tradition of loosely organized cultic devotion. The cult of Kannon, a Buddhist saint or *bodhisattva*, has apparently been influential in some New Religions such as Risshō Kōsei-kai; other Buddhist cults like that of Jizō have not resulted in new religious movements. The widespread (Shinto) faith in Amaterasu (Sun Goddess) has been an important aspect of some New Religions. At the same time the cult of Inari, the so-called fox deity, seems to retain the status of a cult. In some cases even the Inari cult centers have been considered as New Religions, but this deserves further consideration.[11]

---

10. See Kitagawa, pp. 290-91.
11. See Harry Thomsen, ed., *A Religious Map of Japan* (Kyoto: Christian Center for the Study of Japanese Religions, 1959), p. 9. The famous center of Inari worship, Fushimi Inari Taisha, is treated as Shinto, while several other Inari groups are treated as New Religions: Inari Shin-kyō and Inari-kyō. Concerning

The present interpretation of New Religions as new religious movements entails the inclusion of several developments that may be seen as being on the periphery of *shinkō shūkyō*: these are the members of Sect Shinto (Kyōha Shintō) and several communal or "utopian" groups. For even if they should not be considered identical with *shinkō shūkyō*, they do represent important attempts at revitalization resulting in socioreligious organizations. Sect Shinto was recognized by the government in the Meiji era partly as a countermeasure when, in 1882, most Shinto shrines were declared to be integral to state Shinto, and therefore "nonreligious." By contrast, those Shinto shrines that had gathered many followers through the work of historical "founders" and had disseminated teachings were designated as Sect Shinto, of which thirteen members were eventually recognized. In the eyes of the government these sects were "religious" and accordingly treated apart from nonreligious state Shinto. For example, Sect Shinto was required to use the term *kyōkai* (religious meeting or "church") instead of the traditional Shinto term *jinja* (shrine). This sort of official recognition was observed until 1945, when religious freedom was enacted.[12]

The problem in treating Sect Shinto is that, in spite of the uniform government recognition, the members represent diverse phenomena in terms of religious history. Two of its original members, Tenrikyō and Konkōkyō, are sometimes considered the first major New Religions, while other members exhibit strong Shinto, Confucian, or mountain pilgrimage influences. Even though it is widely agreed that Tenrikyō and Konkōkyō are important New Religions, the other groups maintain Shinto practices to such an extent that it is difficult to judge whether or not they actually left the established religion of Shinto. The interpretation of Kyōha Shintō will be left for future research, but their members are included in this bibliography because they are socioreligious groups seeking revitalization, and because they are directly involved in the history of the New Religions.

Also included in this bibliography are four groups which are communal or "utopian" in character: Atarashiki Mura, Ittōen, Shinkyō, and Yamagishi-kai.[13]

Inari see D.C. Buchanan, "Inari: Its Origin, Development, and Nature," *Transactions of the Asiatic Society of Japan*, 2d ser. 12 (December 1935): 1-191.

12. See Daniel C. Holtom, *The National Faith of Japan: A Study in Modern Shinto* (London: Kegan Paul, Trench, Trubner & Co., 1938), pp. 189-286, for a study of the original thirteen members. See also Table 2. As many as 82 movements are listed in the "Sect Shinto line" (Kyōha Shintō-kei, literally "Sect Shinto-derived") in the 1979 government publication for religion. See *Shūkyō Nenkan, Shōwa 54* [Religion Yearbook, 1979] (Tokyo: Ministry of Education, Science and Culture, 1980), pp. 58-62.

13. See David W. Plath, "The Fate of Utopia: Adaptive Tactics in Four Japanese Groups," *American Anthropologist* 85, pt. 2 (1966): 1152-62; also references listed under each group in the section "Utopian Groups," entries 1409-1447.

These groups are certainly attempts at revitalization and have produced distinctive organizations, but their avowed purpose for organization is more social or communal than explicitly religious. (One may remark that in spite of this avowed purpose there is a great deal of religious content in them.) It may be best, as with Sect Shinto, to recognize that these groups, too, stand on the periphery of the *shinkō shūkyō*. But they stand so close that it seems appropriate to include them in this bibliography.

A problem that will interest many Western readers is whether there are any Japanese New Religions that can be considered as "Christian"—either by virtue of deriving from Christian movements or by virtue of containing considerable Christian content. If this question is directed to Korean New Religions, an affirmative answer can be given without hesitation, for Korean new religious movements such as the Unification Church (Tongilgyo, known widely in the United States as "the Moonies") and Chondogwan (sometimes translated as the "Evangelical Church") are clearly Christian both in derivation and content.[14] But the role of Christianity has been much more limited in Japan than its expansive role in Korea, such that its contribution to Japanese New Religions has been slight.[15] There are no Christian-derived New Religions in Japan comparable in scope and dynamics to Korean movements such as the Unification Church and Chondogwan.

Some Christian movements may be considered as quite similar to new religious movements. For example, at least one Christian group, the Omi Brotherhood, has a long history as a communal movement. It is probably best to consider it in relationship to the previously mentioned utopian movements because of its communal character, but it seems to be a Christian development with no peculiar Japanese features. It does not seem to correspond to the criteria of a New Religion and, therefore, is not listed in this bibliography.[16] It is sometimes claimed that Christianity exerted influence on a number of Japanese New

14. See my "The New Religions of Korea: A Preliminary Interpretation," *Transactions of the Korea Branch of the Royal Asiatic Society* 49 (1974): 7-25.
15. For a general interpretation of the role of Christianity in Korea, with comparative remarks concerning China and Japan, see Spencer J. Palmer, *Korea and Christianity: The Problem of Identification with Tradition* (Seoul, Korea: Hollym Corporation, 1967).
16. Since these references did not seem to fit into the present bibliography they are noted here: Grace Niles Fletcher, *The Bridge of Love* (New York: E.P. Dutton & Co., 1967), 220 pp.; Winburn T. Thomas, "Faith Working by Love in Japan: The Story of the Omi Brotherhood," *Missionary Review of the World* 60, no. 12 (December 1937): 584-86; William Merrel Vories, *A Mustard Seed in Japan* (Omi-Hachiman: Omi Mission, 5th ed., 1925), 129 pp.; William Merrel Vories (pseud. Hitotsuyanagi), *Poems of the East and West*, ed. Frederica Mead Hiltner (Omi-Hachiman: Omi Brotherhood, 1960), 169 pp.

Religions,[17] but this indirect Christian influence (whatever it may be) is only a small facet of the multiple influences upon the New Religions and would not be sufficient to label them "Christian." Only two Japanese New Religions appearing in this bibliography can be called Christian: Iesu no Mitama Kyōkai Kyōdan (The Spirit of Jesus Church) and the movement called either Genshi Fukuin Undō (Original Gospel Movement) or Makuya (Tabernacle of Christ). There is still insufficient information on these groups, particularly in Western languages, and we will have to wait for scholars of Japanese Christianity to assess more fully the nature of these movements. But it does appear they meet the criteria of new religious movements and are Christian in derivation and content. Makuya, which arose out of the well-known non-church movement (Mukyōkai), has been closely compared to the New Religions: "It is clear that the Makuya movement resembles many of the new religions in Japan, and it performs the same social function. . . ."[18]

In general, the definition and classification of the New Religions requires further study, which I hope will be encouraged by this bibliography.[19]

Western-Language Materials on the New Religions

Just as the New Religions are rather recent developments, so the study of these developments is still in its infancy. And it is to be expected that Western-language materials will remain well behind the number, quality, and importance of Japanese-language materials. A safe generalization is that all works on the New Religions by Western scholars are the initial steps into a new and difficult field. It may be remarked, parenthetically, that Western study of the Japanese New Religions can best be advanced by three kinds of study: (1) solid monographs on individual New Religions, utilizing Japanese sources; (2) an overview of the New Religions as a phenomenon in Japanese history and society, utilizing both Japanese sources and Western monographs; and (3) comparison of the Japanese New Religions with other new religious movements, utilizing Western materials on both Japanese and other movements. This bibliography may help in achieving these goals, particularly the second and third.

17. See "Christian influence on New Religions" in the Topical Index.
18. Carlo Caldarola, *Christianity: The Japanese Way* (Leiden: E.J. Brill, 1979), p. 208. He goes on to say that "The Makuya is the only movement to indigenize Christianity—traditionally an upper-class religion—in the Japanese lower classes," a statement full of significance for understanding both the extensive development of the New Religions and also the rather slight impact of Christianity in Japan. On p. 3, Caldarola mentions other independent Christian movements arising within the last few decades which might be compared to new religious movements.
19. See the materials in Appendix D.

Western-language materials on the New Religions may be divided roughly into two kinds: (1) denominational publications, written and often published by denominational personnel; and (2) secondary publications, produced by people outside the denomination (both Japanese and non-Japanese). Even if the present bibliography is rather comprehensive in both categories, it should be noted that these materials still represent a limited sector of the New Religions. For example, starting with denominational materials, we should recognize that those New Religions that publish in Western languages exhibit some general features not necessarily shared by all the New Religions. There is a contrast between those New Religions that publish many Western-language materials, and those that publish few or none. This contrast can be charted as follows:

NEW RELIGIONS WITH MANY WESTERN-LANGUAGE PUBLICATIONS	NEW RELIGIONS WITH FEW OR NO WESTERN-LANGUAGE PUBLICATIONS
1. Longer history	1. Shorter history
2. Rather large	2. Rather small
3. Rather affluent	3. Less affluent
4. National in scope	4. Local in scope
5. Dissemination international in scope or intention	5. Dissemination limited mainly to Japan
6. More open to outside religious and cultural influence	6. More closed to outside religious and cultural influence

This chart represents the kind of contrasts within the history and nature of the New Religions that has led to different publishing records. It will be evident from looking at either column that the reasons for publishing or for not publishing are not universal; usually two or three outstanding features will suffice to explain the case for any New Religion. For example, on the left side of the chart, Tenrikyō (which has produced by far the most denominational materials in Western languages) is exceptional in that it displays all six features. Sōka Gakkai has also published considerable Western-language materials, but in contrast to Tenrikyō manifests strength only in points two through five, having a shorter history and being less open to outside influences. Seichō-no-Ie, like Sōka Gakkai, has a shorter history but is still a frequent publisher of Western-language materials; however, Seichō-no-Ie seems to publish partly due to its emphasis on point six and its international contacts with spiritualists. These are just a few examples of the varying factors which lead New Religions to publish Western-language materials.

On the other hand, it is important to ask the question of omission: what kind of groups are not likely to be represented by Western-language denominational publications? A glance at the right column of the chart will give some immediate if tentative answers. Those groups with a shorter history, even if they would want to publish Western-language materials, may not have had time to produce and translate them. Likewise, those that are small and local in scope do not have the organizational and financial resources for such publication. Those that are local in scope or limited to Japan have no reason for publishing Western-language materials; those groups closed to outside influence may even be opposed to the notion of such publications. On this side of the chart, moreover, one or more of the factors, and not necessarily all of them, will suffice to explain a New Religion's publishing record. For example, Nyorai-kyō,[20] which has a longer history than Tenrikyō, has published no Western-language materials, apparently because of the preponderance of points two through six. Some of the New Religions that fall in this category of few or no Western-language publications represent local, particularistic faiths, which are important for understanding current Japanese religion. Some of these groups present different attitudes than will be found in New Religions producing abundant Western-language publications. Such publications often make much of international cooperation and world peace, or at least insist on a worldwide faith; to read these materials one might think that it was a universal trait of the New Religions. But those groups that present a more particularistic (and sometimes nationalistic) viewpoint often do not publish in Western languages. These points should be remembered when utilizing the denominational materials in this bibliography; they do not necessarily provide the basis for sweeping generalizations. (See Table 1 for a list of groups belonging to the Union of New Religions.)

Secondary publications (especially those by Western writers) tend to follow the pattern of more works for those New Religions that produce Western publications. Original interpretations of the New Religions are few, the bulk of those Western works being based on translated denominational materials and Western scholarly works. In general, there are more secondary publications on the New Religions falling in the left side of the chart—especially abundant are works on the older and larger groups. There are more secondary treatments of Oomoto because it has a long history, of Tenrikyō because it has a long history and a large following, and of Sōka Gakkai because of its large size and controversial character. Secondary publications are limited not only in their coverage of the entire field of New Religions but also in their interpretation of individual religions. The gap that needs most attention is the placing of the New Religions in their natural context of Japanese history and Japanese religion. The

20. See the secondary references Nyorai-kyō (entries 439-443) listed in Part II of this bibliography.

temptation to try to understand the New Religions in their most recent form, without fully tracing their background and formation, is too often not resisted. Also, the tendency to try to interpret the New Religions in the categories of Western religion (especially Christian theology) is a hindrance rather than an aid in the task.[21] While acknowledging our debt to all earlier works on the New Religions, we must use them critically so as to advance our understanding of the subject.

Organization and Utilization of the Bibliography

A brief description of the practical organization and scope of the bibliography will facilitate its most efficient use. The scope of the bibliographical references encompasses: all books, pamphlets, essays, and magazine articles dealing directly with the New Religions or one New Religion; those parts of books (and longer articles) that deal with the New Religions; longer book reviews and reviews of Japanese books on the New Religions that introduce new material or important insights; and unpublished theses and dissertations. Some unpublished materials have been included, with mention of their location, or the works in which they were cited. Materials to be excluded are shorter book reviews, newspaper articles, and other brief notices (some brief notices have been included on subjects for which little information is available). The Western languages covered most completely are English, French, and German: I have tried to search out and verify these references comprehensively through 1979, including some 1980 publications. References in other Western languages are included but have not always been searched out and verified.

References have been divided into two major parts: Part I, General Bibliography, materials describing the general phenomenon of the New Religions without being limited to one specific New Religion; and Part II, Bibliography of Individual New Religions, materials limited mainly to one New Religion. Materials in Part I have all been arranged alphabetically by author's name. In Part I it has been the compiler's intention to further introduce the New Religions to general readers by annotating all available references in English, French, and German. (Those items listed with an asterisk "*" preceding the entry number indicate materials not available to the compiler.) Realizing that, for the newcomer, having too many references is as frustrating a dilemma as having too few references, I have placed a plus sign "+" before items that are recommended for primary consultation.

21. For elaboration see the review by Werblowsky (entry 244) in the General Bibliography; also my review article "Recent Publications on the Japanese New Religions" (entry 57).

For all available materials, the following publication information is cited: complete author's name (family name first); title of article or book; for articles, title of journal, volume and issue number, date and year, followed by page citation; for books, place published and date, followed by prefatory pagination and total pages (with reference to specific pages if part of a book), and indication of illustrations. Incomplete citations (such as no indication of place of publication or page numbers) are given for works not available for direct verification; these citations are preceded by an asterisk.

In Part II, Bibliography of Individual New Religions, materials have been listed under the name of each New Religion, with the New Religions arranged in alphabetical order. Under each New Religion, materials have been subdivided into "Denominational" and "Secondary" headings. Denominational materials are those published by a New Religion or written by persons identified as leaders or members of a New Religion. Under denominational materials, those with no known authors are listed first, followed by those with known authors; periodicals published by this New Religion are listed at the end of the denominational materials. Secondary materials are those materials written and published by persons outside of a New Religion, about that particular New Religion. Secondary materials are arranged alphabetically by author (and by title when the author is unknown). Materials in Part II are not annotated, but plus signs before entries (especially secondary materials) indicate those recommended for primary consultation.

Many items are listed both in Parts I and II. In this case full citation will be given only in the General Bibliography, and later references will mention name and title, followed by a cross-reference to the number of the entry in the General Bibliography. For denominational materials, the most common place of publication and publisher will usually be given but once, with exceptions being noted as they occur. Every entry is preceded by a number, which serves to identify materials in the indexes.

All Japanese names in the bibliography are treated in the Western bibliographical fashion: family name, followed by a comma, and then given name. Long vowels have been indicated as listed in the original publication. Otherwise, the Hepburn system of romanization has been followed. In some cases where the published form of the name varies significantly from the Hepburn system, alternate readings are listed in parentheses.

Transliteration of the names of New Religions presents special problems because each group tends to favor its own style of transliteration. My practice has been to follow the transliteration favored by the New Religions, with several exceptions: e.g. Sōka Gakkai instead of Sōkagakkai (because the former has passed into Western usage).

Translation of these names is not attempted since direct translations are difficult and sometimes meaningless. Some common terms frequently appearing in the names of New Religions are: *kyō* (also read *oshie*), "teaching" in the sense of a way of life or religion; *kai*, meeting or association; and *kyōdan*, religious organization. In transliteration these terms may be directly joined to a previous term, separated by a hyphen, or stand as a separate word.

Suggestions for Convenient Use of the Bibliography

The following suggestions are offered to help the reader use this bibliography to the best advantage, finding as much information about the desired subject as quickly as possible. These suggestions move from a more general to a more specific concern with New Religions.

1. *Those interested in general information on the New Religions,* such as articles interpreting the nature of the New Religions or books surveying the New Religions, will benefit by first turning to Part I, General Bibliography. Entries preceded by a plus sign (throughout the entire bibliography) are recommended for first reading. Readers with no previous knowledge of Japanese New Religions may want to scan the titles in the General Bibliography that are preceded by a plus sign to find entries that are most relevant to their study (and readily available).

2. *Those interested in a specific New Religion* may turn directly to Part II, Bibliography of Individual New Religions. Materials in Part II are grouped by specific New Religion, with the New Religions alphabetized according to their most widely used names. (Some New Religions are known by more than one name; see Table 2, "Alternate Names of New Religions.") Under each New Religion, such as Ananaikyō, the first to appear in Part II, materials are separated into "denominational" (published by the New Religion) and "secondary" (published by scholars and writers outside of the New Religion). Denominational materials will be harder to find in libraries, but where available, they will give an "inside" view of the New Religion by its own representatives. Secondary materials provide an "outside" view of the New Religion from the viewpoint of journalists and scholars not members of that New Religion.

3. *Those interested in a particular topic or aspect of the New Religions* should first refer to the Topical Index. For example, to find out about activities of Japanese New Religions in a geographical area such as the continental United States, refer to "American (continental) branches of New Religions" in the Topical Index (or "Hawaiian branches" or "South American branches"). Readers more interested in the social aspect of the New Religions can refer to "Social background and social change"; for the political aspect, "Political activity and elections." All references in the indexes are to entry numbers of citations (*not* page numbers).

The Topical Index is subdivided according to the format of the bibliography: first come "General" references, if there are any, and then entries for each New Religion, arranged alphabetically (with "Utopian Groups" last). For example, under the broad topic "Social background and social change," first comes a large number of entries for "General" works, then entries for specific works about Ananaikyō, works on Gedatsu-kai, works on Genshi Fukuin Undō, etc. Those wanting to know about social aspects of Tenrikyō can look up "Social background and social change" and scan the alphabetical listing of references down to "Tenrikyō," which is followed by entry numbers 1280, 1303, 1312, etc. These entry numbers will help the reader quickly find the needed citation. Unfortunately, Western-language treatments for many aspects of many New Religions are not available, but this process enables the reader to quickly check availability without having to scan long lists of citations.

4. *Those interested in a particular presentation of a New Religion* by a denominational author or a particular interpretation of a New Religion by a secondary writer can check for the presence of the author's name in the alphabetical listing of authors under the individual New Religion. For convenience, all works authored or coauthored by any person are listed in the Author Index. Sōka Gakkai has more citations than any other New Religion, with denominational materials spanning entries 778 through 878 and secondary materials 879 through 1091. Out of the hundred denominational materials one can choose materials written by earlier Sōka Gakkai leaders such as Makiguchi, Toda, and Ikeda. Out of the more than two hundred secondary materials one can choose materials written by a scholar known to the reader (or first scan the items marked with a plus sign).

To facilitate access to individual New Religions and individual authors, a single article or book has been listed under as many New Religions as it deals with. Such works usually are listed first in Part I, where they are cited in full; subsequent citations in Part II simply identify author and title followed by the entry number of the full citation in parentheses. This refers the reader to the General Bibliography for full citation. Books (and some lengthy articles) with separate chapters or sections on individual New Religions will also include page numbers to help locate the specific pages of the work treating that New Religion.

5. *Those interested in materials related to the Japanese New Religions* may wish to refer to additional citations. A separate category for "Utopian Groups" has been added at the end of Part II (entries 1409 through 1447) because these groups, even if not considered New Religions, are very closely related.

Some readers may want related materials to help interpret the Japanese New Religions. Toward this end three bibliographical appendixes have been included: Appendix B, "Western-Language Materials on Japanese Religion," to help place these New Religions within the context of Japanese religious history;

Appendix C, "Japanese-Language Materials on the New Religions," to indicate some preliminary materials on the New Religions published in Japanese; and Appendix D, "Comparative Materials for the Study of New Religious Movements," to provide some comparative and theoretical works on new religious movements in cultural areas outside Japan.

Table 1: Members of Shin Nihon Shūkyō Dantai Rengō-kai (Shin-shū-ren), Union of New Religious Organizations of Japan

Founded in 1951, this Union is a legal foundation composed of religious groups who choose to participate. (These religious groups are all "religious juridical persons," as defined and registered according to Japanese law.) Although Sect Shinto (Kyōha Shintō) has its own federation, and although some religious groups do not choose to participate in the Union, it is still the major spokesman for "New Religions" (shin shūkyō). The large number of groups that participate in the Union and the fact that they designate themselves as New Religions are important considerations in assessing their significance. This list is offered here to indicate the number of such groups still flourishing in Japan, many of which do not appear in this bibliography.

The basis for this list is a 1966 publication of the Union, Shin-shū-ren Yōran [Union of New Religions Directory], rev. and enlarged ed. (Tokyo: Shin-shū-ren, 1966), pp. 68-75. Mr. Shūten Ōishi provided information to bring this list up to date as of 1979. New memberships and withdrawals are noted as follows:

(w)   withdrew prior to 1969;
(w1)   withdrew between 1969-1979;
(n)   new member, entered prior to 1969; and
(n1)   new member, entered between 1969-1979.

Ananaikyō 三五教
A-un-a-kyō 阿吽阿教
Amaterashimasu Tenshu-kyō Honchō   天照坐天主教本庁
Bussho-Gonen Kai (w1) 仏所護念会
Byakkō Shinkō-kai (n) 白光真宏会
Daie-kai Kyōdan 大慧会教団
Daihizen-kyō 大日然教
Daishizen-kyō 大自然教
Daiuchū Daishizen Kyōdan 大宇宙大自然教団
Daiwa Kyōdan 大和教団
Dōhō Kyōdan Byōdō-in 同朋教団平等院

Table 1 (continued)

Ennō-kyō　円応教
Enjōshū Giken-in　円浄宗義堅院
Enshō-in (w)　延照院
Gedatsu-kai　解脱会
Goō-in　護王院
Heiwa Kannon Myōan　平和観音妙庵
Higashiyama Kyōkai　東山教会
Hikari Kyōkai (w1)　ひかり教会
Hikawa Kamiichi-jō　日月神一条
Hi no Oshie　日之教
Hōraizan Seishin-kai (w1)　蓬莱山精神会
Iōzan Risshū　医王山立宗
Ishin-kai (w)　惟神会
Ichigen no Miya　一元ノ宮
Ichijō-in　一乗院
Isson-kyō　一尊教
Izumo Shintō Yakumo-kyō Shinjin-kai Kyōdan　出雲神道八雲教神人会教団
Jishō Kyōdan　璽照教団
Kami Ichijō-kyō　神一条教
Kannagara-kyō　神ながら教
Kikuei-kai Kyōdan　揃営界教団
Kishin-kai　希心会
Kōmyō Kyōkai (n)　光明教会
Kyūseishu Hikari no Michi Honbu (n)　救世主光の道本部
Makoto no Ie (n1)　⊛の家
Meiji Kyōdan　明治教団
Meirin-kyō　明倫教
Minetaka Inari Taisha-kyō　峰高稲荷大社教
Miwa Shintō Hiromitsu-kyō　三輪神道宏充教
Myōchi-kai Kyōdan　妙智會教団
Myōdō-kai Kyōdan　妙道会教団
Muryō-ji　無量寺
Nanayō-kai　七曜会
Naobi-kyō　直日教
Nihon Jingū Honchō　日本神宮本庁
Nikkō-kyō　日光教
Ōmiwa-kyō　大神教
Ōmiwa-kyō　大三輪教
PL Kyōdan　ピーエル教団　(or PL　教団)
Risshō Kōsei-kai　立正佼成会
Ryōben-kyō Honbu-Kyōkai　良弁教本部教会

Table 1 (continued)

Seichūdō-kai (n1)   聖中道会
Seigi-kai Kyōdan   正義会教団
Seihikari Kyōkai   聖ヒカリ教会
Seikyō Jikaku-in   生教自覚院
Seishin Myōjō-kai   誠心明生会
Sekai Heiwa Kyōdan   世界平和教団
Sekai Kyūsei-kyō (w)   世界救世教
Sekai Shindō-kyō   世界心道教
Shidai-dō Honchō (w1)   四大道本庁
Shinkakuhō-ji   新覚法寺
Shinkō-en   神光苑
Shinkōmyō En   神光明苑
Shinnyo-en (w1)   真如苑
Shinri Jikkō no Oshie   真理実行の教
Shinshin Kyōkai*   神真教会
Shishin-kai   思親会
Shintō Funi-kai (n1)   神道不二会
Shintōryū Yōgen Shin-kyō   神統流養源心教
Shintō Tenkō-kyo   神道天行居
Shaka Danjikidō Kōmyō-ji   釈迦断食堂光明寺
Shōroku Shintō Yamato-yama   松緑神道大和山
Shūyodan Hōsei-kai   修養団捧誠会
Soshindō Kyōdan   祖神道教団
Taireidō   大霊道
Taiyō-kyō Tenchikai Manseidō   太陽教天地開万生洞
Tamamitsu Jinja   玉光神社
Tengen-kyō Kokoro no Ie   天元教心の家
Tenjō-kyō   天壌教
Tenken-kyō   天顕教
Tenkō-kyō   天光教
Ten-on-kyō   天恩教
Tenshin-kyō   天心教
Tenso Kō-kyō Kanazawa Shibu   天祖光教金沢支部
Tenchi Genrei Kyōdan   天地玄霊教団
Uchū Moto Hajime Shin-kyō (w1)   宇宙元始神教
Wakōdō Kyōdan   和光道教団
Zenrin-kai   善隣会

* Name has changed to Kōbōen Shinshin Kyōdan.

Table 2: Alternate Names of New Religions

Materials for each New Religion are grouped under the most common name for that New Religion, with the names of the New Religions arranged alphabetically. Western readers may have encountered alternate names for the New Religions; for convenience such names are listed here, with indication of the more common name used in this bibliography. Most of these names are variants accepted by the New Religions: alternate pronunciations, alternate names, and abbreviated or more formal names. The term Odoru Shūkyō (Dancing Religion) is a label applied by outsiders and is not accepted and used by this New Religion.

ALTERNATE NAMES FOR THE NEW RELIGIONS	MORE COMMON NAMES USED IN THIS BIBLIOGRAPHY
Hikari-kyō	Kagami no Hongi
Izumo Ōyashiro-kyō	Izumo Taisha-kyō
Kegon Shū Tōdaiji Hawaii Bekkaku Honzan	Tōdaiji of Hawaii
Kōmeitō (Clean Government Party)	Sōka Gakkai
Makuya	Genshi Fukuin Undō
Mitake-kyō	Ontake-kyō
Moralogy	Dōtoku Kagaku
Nichiren Shōshū	Sōka Gakkai
Odoru Shūkyō (Dancing Religion)	Tenshō Kōtai-Jingū-Kyō
Perfect Liberty	PL Kyōdan
Shintō Honkyoku	Shintō Taikyō
Taisei-kyō	Shintō Taisei-kyō
Sōkagakkai	Sōka Gakkai
Tenchi Kōdō Zenrin-kai	Zenrin-kai

PART I

GENERAL BIBLIOGRAPHY

[+]1. ABE, YOSHIYA. "Religious Freedom under the Meiji Constitution." *Contemporary Religions in Japan* 9, no. 4 (December 1968): 268-338; 10, nos. 1-2 (March-June 1969): 57-97; nos. 3-4 (September-December 1969): 181-203; 11, nos. 1-2 (March-June 1970): 27-97; nos. 3-4 (September-December 1970): 223-96.

Treats the general problem of religious freedom for all groups, but especially in the last installment deals with the denial of full freedom of practice for the "newly emerging popular sects" (New Religions).

2. AKIYAMA, AISABURO. *Shinto and Its Architecture.* Kyoto: Japan Welcome Society, 1936. Reprint. Tokyo: Tokyo News Service, 1955, 217 pp. See pp. 35-46.

Brief comments on Sect Shinto.

[+]3. ANESAKI, MASAHARU. *History of Japanese Religion.* London: Kegan Paul, Trench, Trubner & Co., 1930. Reprint. Rutland, VT: Charles E. Tuttle Co., 1963, xxii + 423 pp. See pp. 309-16, 370-74, 395-403.

A brief mention of "The Rise of Popular Theism" and popular religion in the light of recent Japanese religious history.

[+]4. _____. *The Religious and Social Problems of the Orient.* New York: Macmillan Co., 1923, xi + 77 pp. See pp. 52-73.

An analysis of the socioeconomic factors causing "religious agitation." Description of the new religious groups Oomoto and Ittōen, and of the Christian leader Kagawa.

[+]5. _____. *Religious Life of the Japanese People.* Tokyo: Kokusai Bunka Shinkokai (The Society for International Cultural Relations), 1938. Revised by Hideo Kishimoto, 1961, 105 pp. See pp. 93-102.

In the context of "The Prewar and Postwar Situations," the reviser Kishimoto concludes that "The 'new religions' . . . are the most conspicuous religious phenomena of postwar Japan."

+6.   _____. "Social Unrest and Spiritual Agitation in Present-day Japan."
       Harvard Theological Review 15, no. 4 (October 1922): 305-22.
       Reprinted in Anesaki, *Katam Karaniyam; Lectures, Essays and
       Studies.* Tokyo: Herald Press, 1934; Boston: Marshall Jones Co., 1936,
       pp. 132-52.

       A discussion of the rise of the New Religions out of the troubled social
       and economic conditions in the 1920s; mentions Oomoto and Ittōen.

+7.   ANZAI, SHIN. "Catholicism in an Isolated Village." In *The Sociology
       of Japanese Religion.* Edited by Kiyomi Morioka and William H.
       Newell. Leiden: E.J. Brill, 1968, pp. 44-53. Printed simultaneously in
       Journal of Asian and African Studies 3, nos. 1-2 (January-April 1968):
       44-53.

       Documents peaceful coexistence in one Japanese village of three
       groups: Oomoto, Nichiren Shōshū (Sōka Gakkai), and Catholicism.

8.   _____. "Newly-Adopted Religions and Social Change on the Ryukyu
       Islands (Japan) (With Special Reference to Catholicism)." *Social
       Compass* 23, no. 1 (1976): 57-70. See pp. 64-70.

       Comparison of recruitment and experience in Catholicism with two
       New Religions: (Christian) Iesu no Mitama Kyōkai and Sōka Gakkai in
       the Ryukyu Islands.

9.   AOKI, TAMOTSU. "Some Remarks on the New Religion Movements in
       Contemporary Japan." In *The Symposium on Family and Religion in
       East Asian Countries.* Edited by Chie Nakane and Akira Goto. Tokyo:
       Center for East Asian Cultural Studies, 1972, pp. 106-12. Reprinted
       from *East Asian Cultural Studies* 11, nos. 1-4 (March 1972): 106-12.

       An attempt to present the "special characteristics of the New Religion
       movement."

+9A.   ARAI, KEN. "New Religious Movements." In *Japanese Religion: A
       Survey by the Agency for Cultural Affairs.* Edited by Ichirō Hori et
       al. Tokyo and Palo Alto: Kodansha International, 1972, pp. 89-104.

       A good general introduction to Japanese New Religions, focusing on
       their general characteristics and distinctive features. (Other articles
       in this volume provide introductions to the various religious traditions
       in Japan.)

10. ARIGA, TETSUTARŌ. "The Non-Christian Religions." In *The Japan Christian Yearbook*, 1953. Edited by B.L. Hinchman and Robert W. Wood. Tokyo: Kyo Bun Kwan (The Christian Literature Society), 1953, pp. 47-67. See pp. 59-67.

A description of the growth and decline of several New Religions.

11. ____. "The So-called 'Newly-Arisen Sects' in Japan." *Occasional Bulletin* (Missionary Research Library, Union Theological Seminary in the City of New York) 5, no. 4 (March 1954): 1-6.

A Japanese Christian defines a New Religion as "a living contemporary religion or religious movement that has spontaneously arisen and grown rather recently on Japanese soil" in the "religious vacuum" following World War II.

12. ARMSTRONG, ROBERT CORNELL. "Modern Revivals of Ancient Religions in Japan." *Japan Evangelist* 31 (July 1924): 43-48.

Modern revivals have been attempted both within established religions and recent sects (New Religions).

12A. ARUTIUNOV, SERGEI ALEKSANDROVICH and SVETLOV, GEORGII EVGEN'EVICH [pseud. of Georgii Evgen'evich Komarovskii]. *Starye i novye bogi IAponii* [Old and new gods of Japan]. Moscow: Nauka, 1968, 200 pp.

In Russian. Chapters on the classification and nature of New Religions.

13. BACH, MARCUS. *Strangers at the Door*. Nashville: Abingdon Press, 1971, 189 pp. See pp. 96-128.

A popular account of contacts with seven Japanese New Religions.

+14. BAIRY, MAURICE A. *Japans neue Religionen in der Nachkriegszeit*. Bonn: Ludwig Röhrscheid Verlag, 1959, 135 pp.

A general analysis of the Japanese context of the New Religions, a survey of the chief religious and social characteristics of the New Religions, and a description of PL Kyōdan.

15. BALLOU, ROBERT O. *Shinto: The Unconquered Enemy. Japan's Doctrine of Racial Superiority and World Conquest, With Selections from Japanese Texts*. New York: Viking Press, 1945, xi + 239 pp. See pp. 200-7. Reprinted from Daniel C. Holtom, *The National Faith of Japan* (entry 85).

"Doctrines of Sectarian Shinto" includes quotations from Japanese sources.

16. BASABE, FERNANDO M. *Japanese Religious Attitudes*. Maryknoll, NY: Orbis Books, 1972, vii + 94 pp. Illus. See pp. 12, 68-69.

A brief summary of two surveys by the author and collaborators; contains some general statistics and survey information regarding New Religions.

17. ____; ANZAI, SHIN; and LANZACO, FEDERICO. *Religious Attitudes of Japanese Men: A Sociological Survey*. Tokyo: Sophia University; Rutland, VT: Charles E. Tuttle Co., 1968, 135 pp. See pp. 6-8, 25-45, 51-53.

Results of detailed sociological surveys of religious beliefs and practices, including comparisons of established religions and New Religions in Japan.

18. ____; ANZAI, SHIN; and NEBREDA, ALPHONSO M. *Japanese Youth Confronts Religion: A Sociological Survey*. Tokyo: Sophia University and Charles E. Tuttle, 1967, vi + 183 pp. See pp. 33, 53, 126, 128, 130.

Mentions that the "common belief outside of Japan that the new religions, particularly the Sōka-gakkai, also exert a powerful influence in university campuses . . . is not accurate"; of students interviewed, only 1.21% belonged to the New Religions.

19. BEARDSLEY, RICHARD K. "Religion and Philosophy." In *Twelve Doors to Japan*. Edited by John Whitney Hall and Richard K. Beardsley. New York: McGraw-Hill Book Co., 1965, pp. 310-47. See pp. 329-30, 339-43.

General comments on the formation and nature of Japanese New Religions.

20. ____; HALL, JOHN W.; and WARD, ROBERT E. *Village Japan*. Chicago: University of Chicago Press, 1959, 498 pp. See pp. 446, 468.

Notes the almost insignificant presence of Sect Shinto and "indigenous evangelistic sects" in a rice-growing community that is exhaustively studied.

20A. BENNER, PATTERSON D. "The Universality of 'Tongues.'" *Japan Christian Quarterly* 39, no. 2 (Spring 1973): 101-7. See pp. 104-5.

Brief references to the Japanese New Religions as Japanese examples of the universality of "tongues" (glossolalia). Compares Christian and other phenomena of "speaking in tongues."

21. BENZ, ERNST. *Neue Religionen.* Stuttgart: Ernst Klett Verlag, 1971, 179 pp. See pp. 17-24.

A general treatment of the development and characteristics of Japanese New Religions.

22. _____. "'Neue Religionen' in Japan." *Antaios* 2, no. 1 (May 1960): 63-74.

Summarizes the common characteristics of the New Religions.

+23. BERNIER, BERNARD. *Breaking the Cosmic Circle: Religion in a Japanese Village.* Cornell University East Asia Papers, no. 5. Ithaca: Cornell University, Cornell China-Japan Program, 1975, iii + 188 pp. See pp. 116-28, 148-64.

A contrast of Tenrikyō and Sōka Gakkai in an anthropology dissertation on religion in a Japanese village: Tenrikyō blends into village practices but Sōka Gakkai breaks sharply with village rituals.

24. _____. "The Popular Religion of a Japanese Village and Its Transformation." Ph.D. dissertation, Cornell University, 1970, 244 pp. Abstracted in *Dissertation Abstracts International* 31, no. 3 (September 1970): 1027B. University Microfilms International order no. 70-17,073.

Basis for entry 23.

25. BLACKER, CARMEN. "Millenarian Aspects of the New Religions in Japan." In *Tradition and Modernization in Japanese Culture.* Edited by Donald H. Shively. Princeton: Princeton University Press, 1971, pp. 563-600.

Analysis of the founding of Japanese New Religions from the viewpoint of the concept of millenarian movements used for European and non-Western movements.

+26. _____. "New Religious Cults in Japan." *Hibbert Journal* 60 (July 1962): 305-13.

A discussion of the origins of the New Religions in folk religion and popular religion, along with interviews of founders and accounts of visits to New Religions's headquarters.

27. BOBILIN, ROBERT T. "Japanese Peace Movements." In *The Religious Situation: 1968.* Edited by Donald R. Cutler. Boston: Beacon Press, 1968, pp. 461-97.

Describes the involvement of New Religions (especially Oomoto) and related groups (such as Ittōen) in Japanese peace movements.

28. BRADEN, CHARLES S. "Religion in Post-War Japan." *Journal of Bible and Religion* 21, no. 3 (July 1953): 147-53.

Observations of the flourishing New Religions after a visit to several headquarters.

*29. BRAND, J.A., S.J. "Shinkōshūkyō—As religiões novas do Japão" [Shinkōshūkyō—The New Religions of Japan]. *Estudos* 21 (1961): 23-35.

In Portuguese. Cited in *Novas religiões japonêsas no Brasil* (entry 172), p. 38.

30. BRANLEY, BRENDAN R. *Christianity and the Japanese.* Maryknoll, NY: Maryknoll Publications, 1966, x + 271 pp. See pp. vii, 111-21.

Brief comments on "New Religions and Social Mission."

31. BRAUN, NEIL. *Laity Mobilized: Reflections on Church Growth in Japan.* Grand Rapids, MI: William B. Eerdmans Publishing Co., 1971, 224 pp.

Refers to Japanese New Religions as illustrations of how Christian missions should be understood.

32. BROWN, DELMER M. "Japan's Century of Change: The Religious Factor." *Japan Christian Quarterly* 35, no. 1 (Winter 1968): 24-33.

Uses frequent references to the New Religions to reject two "overworked generalizations: one, the Japanese people are not really a religious people; and two, modernization always makes people less religious."

33. BUNCE, WILLIAM K. *Religions in Japan: Buddhism, Shinto, Christianity.* Tokyo and Rutland, VT: Charles E. Tuttle Co., 1955, xi + 194 pp. See pp. 160-65.

Based on a 1948 report entitled "Religions in Japan" (ix + 204 pp.) prepared by the Religions and Cultural Resources Division, Civil Information and Education Section of the Supreme Command for the Allied Powers, this book mentions briefly five classes of New Religions.

34. BUREAU OF RELIGIONS, DEPARTMENT OF EDUCATION. *A General View of the Present Religious Situation in Japan.* Tokyo: Bureau of Religions, Department of Education, 1920, 68 pp.

Useful information on the supervision of the national cult of Shinto and its distinction from "religion" such as Sect Shinto and Buddhism: "While there are yet no special regulations concerning cases of secession or incorporation in the Shinto or Buddhist Sects, such are practically made impossible without the approval of the Minister of Education."

35. BURROWS, EDWIN GRANT. *Hawaiian Americans: An Account of the Mingling of Japanese, Chinese, Polynesian, and American Cultures.* New Haven: Yale University Press, 1947, 288 pp. See pp. 160–63.

Briefly describes several Japanese New Religions in the Hawaiian context of "religious reversion."

36. CALLAWAY, TUCKER N. "Christianity and the Religions of Japan." *Review and Expositor* 58, no. 1 (January 1961): 50–66.

Emphasizes Christian influence on the New Religions, especially Ittōen and Seichō-no-Ie.

*37. CERMENO, ANTONIO. "Las religiones novismas del Japon." *Siglo Mision* 42 (1955): 423–26.

38. CLEMEN, CARL. *Die nichtchristlichen Kulturreligionen in ihrem gegenwärtigen Zustand.* Vol. 1. Leipzig and Berlin: B.O. Teubner, 1921, 123 pp. See pp. 27–33.

Brief remarks on several New Religions that appeared prior to 1920.

39. COLE, ALLAN B. *Political Tendencies of Japanese in Small Enterprises, with Special Reference to the Social Democratic Party.* New York: Institute of Pacific Relations, 1959, ii + 155 pp. See pp. 48–49, 60–61.

Irrationalism leads the otherwise politically conservative men of small enterprise to espouse "mystical and kindred sects" and their political candidates.

40. "The Constitution Investigation Council." *Contemporary Religions in Japan* 8, no. 2 (June 1967): 145–76.

New Religions mentioned from a legal viewpoint.

41. CREEMERS, WILHELMUS H.M. *Shrine Shinto After World War II.*
     Leiden: E.J. Brill, 1968, xviii + 261 pp. See pp. 8-9, 214-16.

     Brief remarks on Sect Shinto in relationship to Shrine Shinto.

42. CURTIS, GERALD L. *Election Campaigning Japanese Style.* New
     York: Columbia University Press, 1971, xiii + 275 pp. See pp. 198-200.

     A brief but valuable comparison of Sōka Gakkai and Kōmeitō campaign
     activities with those of other New Religions.

[+]43. DAVIS, WINSTON BRADLEY. *Toward Modernity: A Developmental
     Typology of Popular Religious Affiliations in Japan.* Cornell East Asia
     Papers, no. 12. Ithaca: Cornell University, Cornell China-Japan
     Program, 1977, 108 pp. See pp. 75-78.

     Brief comparative remarks on the New Religions in the context of a
     historical and sociological overview of the social organization of
     Japanese religions.

44. DeFRANCIS, JOHN, and LINCOLN, V.R. *Things Japanese in Hawaii.*
     Honolulu: University Press of Hawaii, 1973, xiv + 210 pp. See esp. pp.
     69-91.

     Popular impressions of the grounds and activities of some Japanese
     New Religions in Hawaii.

45. DEVARANNE, THEODOR. "Religiöse Inflation in Japan." *Zeitschrift
     für Missionskunde und Religionswissenschaft* 50 (1935): 189-90.

     Comments on the remarkable rise of New Religions (religious inflation)
     in the 1920s and 1930s, interpreted as partly the quest for "a Japanese
     religion for the Japanese people."

[+]46. DORE, RONALD P. *City Life in Japan: A Study of a Tokyo Ward.*
     Berkeley: University of California Press, 1963, viii + 472 pp. See pp.
     291-373.

     A valuable description of the apparent lack of interest in established
     religions and increasing interest in New Religions in urban Tokyo in the
     1950s.

47. DRUMMOND, RICHARD H. "Japan's 'New Religions' and the Christian
     Community." *Christian Century* 81, no. 50 (9 December 1964): 1521-
     23.

Argues that the New Religions are "authentically religious" and examines the implications for Christianity.

48. DUMOULIN, HEINRICH. "Buddhismus im modernen Japan." *Saeculum* 20 (1969): 291-351. See pp. 317-51. Reprinted in Heinrich Dumoulin, ed., *Buddhismus der Gegenwart* (Freiburg: Herder, 1970), pp. 127-87.

A general description of the historical development of Buddhism in Japan, followed by brief treatment of Buddhist-derived New Religions.

49. DUTERMUTH, FRITZ. "Religion in Sociological Perspective." *Contemporary Religions in Japan*, nos. 1-2 (March-June 1968): 1-29.

Analysis of the emergence and function of Japanese New Religions from the viewpoint of the sociology of religion, seeking universal factors to explain not only Japanese but also Western religious phenomena.

+50. EARHART, H[ARRY] BYRON. "Gedatsu-kai: One Life History and Its Significance for Interpreting Japanese New Religions." *Japanese Journal of Religious Studies* 7, nos. 2-3 (June-September 1980): 227-57.

An interview with a man who was a Christian until middle age, and then entered the New Religion Gedatsu-kai; includes analysis of this life history in terms of the personal dynamics of joining this New Religion.

+51. _____. "The Interpretation of the 'New Religions' of Japan as Historical Phenomena." *Journal of the American Academy of Religion* 37, no. 3 (September 1969): 237-48.

An analysis of the factors that contribute to the rise of the New Religions, balancing the socioeconomic factors over against the prior history of religious forms in Japan.

+52. _____. "The Interpretation of the 'New Religions' of Japan as New Religious Movements." In *Religious Ferment in Asia*. Edited by Robert J. Miller. Lawrence: University of Kansas Press, 1974, pp. 169-88.

An interpretation of Japanese New Religions in terms of new religious movements, focusing on four basic characteristics.

+53. _____. *Japanese Religion: Unity and Diversity*. Belmont, CA: Dickenson Publishing Co., 1969, xi + 115 pp. See pp. 87-95. 2d ed., 1974, viii + 148 pp. See pp. 106-18, 122-24. 3d ed., Belmont, CA: Wadsworth, 1982, xii + 272 pp. Illus. See pp. 168-83, 188-90.

The New Religions treated as a distinctive feature of Japanese religion in the historical period of "formalization and renewal" (1600-present), with brief descriptions of Tenrikyō and Sōka Gakkai.

54.   _____. "New Religions." In *Encyclopedia of Japan*. Edited by Gen Itasaka and Maurits Dekker. Tokyo: Kodansha International, forthcoming.

A general treatment of the formation and nature of Japanese New Religions.

55.   _____, ed. "The New Religions." In *Religion in the Japanese Experience: Sources and Interpretations*. Encino and Belmont, CA: Dickenson Publishing Co., 1974, pp. 237-55.

Two brief chapters introducing English publications by Tenrikyō and Sōka Gakkai, and a general article by the same author, in an anthology of readings on Japanese religion.

56.   EARHART, H[ARRY] BYRON. "The New Religions of Korea: A Preliminary Interpretation." *Transactions of the Korea Branch of the Royal Asiatic Society* 49 (1974): 7-25.

Contains comparative remarks on the formation of new religious movements in Korea and Japan.

57.   _____. "Recent Publications on the Japanese New Religions." *History of Religions* 10, no. 4 (May 1971): 375-85.

A review of one book treating a communal movement (entry 1438) related to Tenrikyō, and three books treating Sōka Gakkai (entries 907, 922, and 1015).

58.   _____. "The Significance of the 'New Religions' for Understanding Japanese Religion." *KBS Bulletin on Japanese Culture* 101 (April-May 1970): 1-9. Reprinted in part in Earhart, "The New Religions" (entry 55), pp. 249-54.

A general interpretation of Japanese New Religions within the context of Japanese religious history.

+59.   _____. "Toward a Theory of the Formation of the Japanese New Religions: A Case Study of Gedatsu-kai." *History of Religions* 20, nos. 1-2 (August-November 1980): 175-97.

Criticizes the "crisis" or "anomie" theory of the development of New Religions and argues for a new theory on the basis of three interrelated factors.

60. EDER, MATTHIAS. *Japan mit und unter dem Buddhismus: Geschichte der japanischen Religion.* Vol. 2. Asian Folklore Studies, monograph 7, pt. 1. Nagoya: Asian Folklore Studies, 1978, 248 pp. See pp. 203-30.

A general treatment of Japanese New Religions in the context of a two-volume history of Japanese religion.

+61. ELLWOOD, ROBERT S., Jr. *The Eagle and the Rising Sun: Americans and the New Religions of Japan.* Philadelphia: Westminster Press, 1974, 224 pp.

A general treatment of the activities of five Japanese New Religions in the United States, featuring first-hand observations and interviews at their branches.

62. _____. *Many Peoples, Many Faiths: An Introduction to the Religious Life of Mankind.* Englewood Cliffs, NJ: Prentice-Hall, 1976, xiii + 365 pp. See pp. 204-7.

General comments on Japanese New Religions in the context of Japanese religion.

63. EPP, ROBERT. Review of *Nihon no shinko shukyo* [Japan's New Religions], by Hiroo Takagi. *Japan Christian Quarterly* 37 (Winter 1971): 53-55.

A review of a 1954 book by Hiroo Takagi, an early standard interpretation of Japanese New Religions.

*64. FANTOLI, ANNIBALE. "L'attuale situazione religiosa del Giappone." *Civiltà cattolica* 115 (19 September 1967): 527-41.

Cited in *Cumulative Bibliography of Asian Studies, 1941-1965* 2: 12.

65. FISHER, GALEN M. *Creative Forces in Japan.* New York: Missionary Education Movement of the United States and Canada, 1923, viii + 248 pp. See pp. 126-33.

Notes dissatisfaction with old religions and the appeal of popular sects.

66. FLORENZ, KARL. "Die Japaner." In *Lehrbuch der Religionsgeschichte.* Vol. 1, edited by Chantepie de la Saussaye. 4th rev. ed. Edited by Albert Bertholet and Eduard Lehmann. Tübingen: J.C.B. Mohr (Paul Siebeck), 1925, pp. 262-422. See pp. 344-48.

Notes the extreme gap between Shrine Shinto and folk Shinto; describes briefly the thirteen members of Sect Shinto.

67. FRAGER, ROBERT, and ROHLEN, THOMAS P. "The Future of a
     Tradition: Japanese Spirit in the 1980s." In *Japan: The Paradox of
     Progress*. Edited by Lewis Austin. New Haven and London: Yale
     University Press, 1976, pp. 255-78.

     Compares and contrasts New Religions with other religious groups and
     other social movements in terms of Japanese "spirit" (or *seishin*).

*68. GAY, J. LÓPEZ. "Las nuevas religiones en Japán." *Misiones
     Extranjeras* 45 (1965): 41-63.

     Cited in Fernando M. Basabe et al., *Religious Attitudes of Japanese
     Men* (entry 17), p. 5.

69. GERLITZ, PETER. *Gott erwacht in Japan: Neue fernöstliche
     Religione und ihre Botschaft vom Glück*. Freiburg: Verlag Herder,
     1977, 173 pp.

     Views the Japanese New Religions in the light of Christian missions,
     interpreting them through categories such as secularization and
     syncretism. Features separate chapters on five New Religions.

70. GONÇALVES, RICARDO MARIO. "A religião no Japão na época da
     emigração para o Brasil e suas repercussões em nosso pais" [Religion in
     Japan in the period of emigration to Brazil and its repercussions in our
     country]. In *O Japonês em São Paulo e no Brasil*. São Paulo: Centro
     de Estudos Nipo-Brasileiros, 1971, pp. 58-73.

     In Portuguese. A brief analysis of the historical background of Sect
     Shinto and the New Religions, their major groups, and their activities
     in Brazil.

71. GUARIGLIA, GUGLIELMO. "Prophetismus und Heilserwartungs-
     Bewegungen   als   völkerkundliches   und   religionsgeschichtliches
     Problem." *Wiener Beiträge für Kultur und Linguistik* 13. Horn and
     Vienna: Verlag Ferdinand Berger, 1959, pp. 1-322. See pp. 249-53.

     An attempt to treat Tenshō-Kōtai-Jingū-Kyō (or Odoru-shūkyō) and
     Tenrikyō in a worldwide comparative typology.

72. GUNDERT, WILHELM. *Japanische Religionsgeschichte: Die
     Religionen der Japaner und Koreaner in geschichtlichem Abriss
     dargestellt*. Tokyo: Taiheiyosha, 1935.   Photomechanical
     reproduction. Stuttgart: D. Gundert Verlag, 1943, xvii + 267 pp. See
     pp. 128-39, 158-61, 181-82, 204.

A prewar treatment of several New Religions, considered as sect developments of Shinto and extensions of Buddhism.

73. HAMBRICK, CHARLES H. "Tradition and Modernity in the New Religious Movements of Japan." *Japanese Journal of Religious Studies* 1, nos. 2-3 (June–September 1974): 217-52.

Concludes that "it is the traditional religious symbols that create and maintain the world of the new religious movements."

74. HAMMER, RAYMOND JACK. "The Idea of God in Japan's New Religions—with Special Reference to Tenrikyo, Konkokyo, Sekaikyuseikyo, Omotokyo, Reiyukai, Risshokoseikai, P.L. Kyodan, Seicho no Ie and Ananaikyo." Ph.D. dissertation, University of London, 1961, 334 pp.

Analysis of the idea of god (*kami*) in the New Religions as understood through their historical emergence from Shinto, Buddhism, Confucianism, and Taoism.

75. _____. "Japan." In *Religions of the World: From Primitive Beliefs to Modern Faiths*. Edited by Geoffrey Parrinder. New York: Grosset & Dunlap, 1971, pp. 307-31. See pp. 321-31.

In a general chapter on Japanese religion, briefly describes the major New Religions and their characteristics.

*76. _____. "Japan's New Religions." *Frontier* 5, no. 1 (1962): 356-61.

Cited in *Index to Religious Periodical Literature* 5: 167.

77. _____. *Japan's Religious Ferment*. New York: Oxford University Press, 1962, 207 pp. See pp. 135-45, 188-92.

A survey of the New Religions in the light of the history of Japanese religion, viewing them as a reaction to cultural crisis.

78. _____. "Popular Religion and the New Religions of Japan." *Japanese Religions* 3, no. 2 (Summer 1963): 1-9.

The importance of understanding the New Religions in terms of "popular religion."

79. _____. "The Retreat from Eschatology in Some of Japan's New Religions." In *X. International Kongress für Religionsgeschichte*. Marburg: Kommissionsverlag N.G. Ehvert, 1961, pp. 125-27 (abstract of the full paper, which is included in his "The Idea of God . . . ," entry 74).

"Retreat from eschatology" refers to the fact "that thought about the future does not loom largely in those religions under consideration."

80. HAMMITZSCH, HORST. "Die Religionen als gesellschafts und staatsbildende Faktoren im neuen Japan." *Saeculum* (1968): 74-82.

Brief reference to the New Religions as an example of religious change in postwar Japan.

81. HERBERT, JEAN. *Bibliographie du shintô et des sectes shintôïstes.* Leiden: E.J. Brill, 1968, 72 pp.

Lists 1,182 publications in Japanese and Western languages, but does not cover Sect Shinto either systematically or exhaustively.

82. _____. *Dieux et sectes populaires du Japon.* Paris: Éditions Albin Michel, 1967, 287 pp. See pp. 123-213, 215-19.

A treatment of the thirteen bodies of Sect Shinto with brief comments on New Religions of Buddhist origin.

83. _____. *Shintô: At the Fountain-Head of Japan.* New York: Stein & Day, 1967, 622 pp. See pp. 515-24.

Brief treatment of "Sectarian Shinto"; also quotes Shinto authorities on the distinction between "Shrine Shinto" and "Sectarian Shinto."

84. HODOUS, LEWIS. "Religious Ferment in Japan." *Chinese Recorder* 52, no. 6 (June 1921): 375-85.

Mentions Tenrikyō, Remmon-kyō, and Oomoto as part of the widespread religious ferment in Japan.

[+]85. HOLTOM, DANIEL C. *The National Faith of Japan: A Study in Modern Shinto.* London: Kegan Paul, Trench, Trubner & Co., 1938. Reprint. New York: Paragon Book Reprint Corp., 1965, xiii + 329 pp. Illus. See pp. 189-286.

The first major study of Sect Shinto in a Western language. Still an important work on the thirteen members of Sect Shinto in prewar times.

86. _____, and HONAGA, M. "The Religious and Ethical Teachings of the Modern Shintō Sects." In *Christian Movement in Japan, Korea, and Formosa.* Twenty-second Annual Issue. Kobe: Federation of Christian Missions, 1924, pp. 249-68.

See Daniel C. Holtom, *The National Faith* (entry 85), for similar material.

87. HOPKINS, E[DWARD] WASHBURN. *The History of Religions*. New York: Macmillan Co., 1918, 624 pp. See p. 287.

Mentions Tenrikyō and Remmon-kyō as examples of "superstitious and licentious practices" in modern Shinto.

+88. HORI, ICHIRŌ. "Penetration of Shamanic Elements into the History of Japanese Folk Religion." In *Festschrift für Ad. E. Jensen.* Vol. 1. Edited by Eike Haberland, Meinhard Schuster, and Helmut Straube. Munich: Klaus Renner Verlag, 1964, pp. 245-65. Also included in Ichirō Hori, *Folk Religion in Japan: Continuity and Change*, ed. Joseph M. Kitagawa and Alan L. Miller (Chicago: University of Chicago Press, 1968), pp. 181-251.

Treats generally the origin and characteristics of the New Religions, including an analysis of lives of some founders of New Religions to show the shamanic elements found therein.

+89. _____, and TODA, YOSHIO. "Shinto." In *Japanese Religion in the Meiji Era.* Edited by Hideo Kishimoto. Translated by John F. Howes. Tokyo: Ōbunsha, 1956, pp. 35-98.

Traces the history and activities of "nationalistic Shinto," and how, in spite of the relative lack of religious freedom from 1868 to 1912, independent sects (Sect Shinto) arose.

+89A. _____, et al., eds. *Japanese Religion: A Survey by the Agency for Cultural Affairs.* Tokyo and Palo Alto: Kodansha International, 1972, 272 pp.

In addition to the article by Ken Arai, "New Religious Movements" (entry 9A), and other articles on Japanese religions, Part 2 "Specific Religious Organizations," pp. 161-232, and Part 3 "Statistics," pp. 233-63 contain concise information (including addresses, numbers of clergy, and numbers of members) about individual New Religions.

90. HSU, FRANCIS L.K. *Iemoto: The Heart of Japan*. Cambridge, MA: Schenkman Publishing Co., 1975, xiv + 260 pp. See pp. 173-79.

Chapter 11, "The *Iemoto* Pattern in Religion," written "with the assistance of Professor Esyun Hamaguchi," contains a section that offers an interpretation of the Japanese New Religions as "Old Wines in New Bottles," variations of Japanese family and social patterns.

91.   HUNTER, LOUISE H. *Buddhism in Hawaii: Its Impact on a Yankee Community.* Honolulu: University of Hawaii Press, 1971, x + 266 pp. See pp. 193-97.

Brief comments on New Religions as means of maintaining Japanese identity and sense of direction, especially during and after World War II.

[+]92.   IKADO, FUJIO. "Trend and Problems of New Religions: Religion in Urban Society." In *The Sociology of Japanese Religion.* Edited by Kiyomi Morioka and William H. Newell. Leiden: E.J. Brill, 1968, pp. 101-17. Printed simultaneously in *Journal of Asian and African Studies* 3, nos. 1-2: 101-17.

Analysis of statistical and sociological information about the membership of the New Religions that shows there is widespread exaggeration concerning the extent of the religious revival and its supposed "threat" to modern Japan.

93.   INTERNATIONAL INSTITUTE FOR THE STUDY OF RELIGIONS. *Directory of the Sectarian Shinto Federation and the Principal Shinto Shrines of Japan.* Directory no. 5. Tokyo: International Institute for the Study of Religions, 1957, 40 pp.

See pp. 1-6 for addresses and information about sectarian Shinto. For more current information, addresses, and statistics, see Ichiro Hori, et al., eds., *Japanese Religion* (entry 89A); and "Statistics on Religious Organizations in Japan, 1947-1972" (entry 216A).

94.   _____. *New Religions, Bahai, Islam and the Japan Free Religious Association.* Directory no. 4. Tokyo: International Institute for the Study of Religions, 1958, 75 pp.

Lists the "present" (1958) leader, address, and official bulletins of many New Religions, in both English and Japanese. For more current information, addresses, and statistics, see Ichirō Hori, et al., eds., *Japanese Religion* (entry 89A), and "Statistics on Religious Organizations in Japan, 1947-1972" (entry 216A).

95.   _____. "What Is a 'New Religion'?" *Contemporary Religions in Japan* 1, no. 2 (June 1960): 70-71.

A note clarifying the ambiguity of the term "New Religion."

96.　IWAMOTO, TOKUICHI.　"Present State of Sectarian Shintō."　In *Research Tour Papers, Tokyo.* Mimeographed, pp. 21-25.

Traces the development of Sect Shinto out of conditions of the Tokugawa period (especially Confucian influence) and its interaction with New Religions.

*97.　IWATA, SUMIE.　*New Religions in Japan through the Eyes of a Christian.* Tokyo, 1960.

Cited in Werner Kohler, *Die Lotus-Lehre und die modernen Religionen in Japan* (entry 118), p. 288.

98.　JAECKEL, THEODOR.　"Psychological and Sociological Approaches to Japan's New Religions." *Japanese Religions* 2, no. 1 (1960): 6-13.

The Japanese New Religions are indigenous movements that provide social cohesion in a dissolving society, spiritual certainty in time of psychic crisis.

99.　*Japan-Manchoukuo Year Book, 1934.* Tokyo: Japan-Manchoukuo Year Book Co., 1934, 1094 pp. See pp. 157-58.

An official statement of the distinction between "sectarian" and "non-sectarian" Shinto.　(Similar information in yearbooks for 1935 and 1936.)

100.　JAPAN, MINISTRY OF EDUCATION.　*Religions in Japan.* Tokyo: Religious Affairs Section, Research Bureau, Ministry of Education, Government of Japan, 1959. 2d ed., 1963, 136 pp.

Includes information and statistics on Sect Shinto and the New Religions.

101.　*The Japanese Immigrant in Brazil.* 2 vols. Tokyo: University of Tokyo Press, 1964-69.　Vol. 1, *Statistical Tables,* edited by Comissão de Recenseamento da Colônia Japonêsa (Burajiru Nikkeijin Jihai Chōsa Iinkai), 1964, 76 pp. See pp. 279-95. Vol. 2, *Narrative Part,* edited by Teiiti Suzuki, 1969, 321 pp. See pp. 121-31, 273-74.

Volume 1 includes statistical tables and figures on New Religions and Shintoists (and a sample questionnaire); volume 2 is an interpretation of the statistics.　Generally, New Religions are grouped under "Japanese religions" (as opposed to "Brazilian religions"); religion is also treated as a factor in other categories, as indicated in the index.

102.   JAPANESE NATIONAL COMMISSION FOR UNESCO, comp. *Japan: Its Land, People, and Culture.* Tokyo: Printing Bureau, Ministry of Finance, 1958. 2d ed., 1964, 885 pp. See pp. 399, 406-7. 3d ed., 1973, xlviii + 702 pp. See pp. 188-89, 195-96.

Brief description of Sect Shinto and several New Religions.

103.   JOHNSON, PAUL E. "The Counselor in Modern Society." In *Rissho Kōsei-kai.* Tokyo: Kōsei Publishing Co., 1966, pp. 167-72.

Describes the need for counseling in modern countries like Japan and mentions the counseling techniques found in Konkōkyō and Risshō Kōsei-kai.

104.   _____. "New Religions and Mental Health." *Journal of Religion and Health* 3, no. 4 (July 1964): 327-34.

Social and personal stress in modern Japan is alleviated by the New Religions, especially through their forms of religious counseling.

105.   JOHNSON, THOMAS W. "Japan's New Religions: A Search for Uniformities." *Kroeber Anthropological Society Papers,* no. 42 (Spring 1970): 99-118.

A general treatment of the common features found in many New Religions.

106.   KAGAWA, TOYOHIKO. *Christ and Japan.* Translated by William Axling. New York: Friendship Press, 1934, vi + 150 pp. See pp. 84-85, 91-97.

A famous (Protestant) Christian's comments on various New Religions: their borrowing from Christianity as well as their down-to-earth evangelistic techniques.

107.   KERNER, KAREN. "Japan's New Religions." *Japan Interpreter* 6, no. 2 (Summer 1970): 135-50.

A general discussion of Japanese New Religions from an anthropological viewpoint (comparing them with African and other movements), with special attention paid to Tenshō-Kōtai-Jingū-Kyō as an example of messianism.

108.   KIMBALL, BRUCE A. "The Problem of Epistemology in Japanese New Religions." *Tenri Journal of Religion* 13 (August 1979): 72-93.

A comparison and criticism of epistemology in the theology of various New Religions.

109.   KISHIMOTO, HIDEO. "The Problem of Religion and Modernization in
        Japan." *Contemporary Religions in Japan* 1, no. 3 (September 1960):
        1-19.

        A critical evaluation of Japanese religions from the viewpoint of
        "modernization," with remarks on the New Religions.

+110.   _____, and WAKIMOTO, TSUNEYA. "Introduction: Religion During
        Tokugawa." In *Japanese Religion in the Meiji Era*. Edited by Hideo
        Kishimoto. Translated by John F. Howes. Tokyo: Ōbunsha, 1956, pp.
        3-33.

        Analysis of the historical and religious context out of which the New
        Religions arose, especially revealing the strict governmental control
        over religion from about 1600 to 1945 and pointing out "Buddhist
        spiritual stagnation."

111.   KITAGAWA, JOSEPH M. "New Religions in Japan: A Historical
        Perspective." In *Religion and Change in Contemporary Asia*. Edited by
        Robert F. Spencer. Minneapolis: University of Minnesota Press, 1971,
        pp. 27-43.

        Analyzes the historical background out of which the New Religions
        developed and comments on their significance in the postwar period.

+112.   _____. *Religion in Japanese History*. New York: Columbia University
        Press, 1966, x + 475 pp. See pp. 214-25, 233-36, 278-84, 306-36.

        Treatment of the New Religions in terms of Japanese religious history,
        showing how they developed out of earlier religious traditions and meet
        particular needs of modern Japanese.

113.   KIYOTA, MINORU. "Buddhism in Japan Today: The Agony of the New
        Generation." In *Studies in Asia, 1966*. Vol. 7, edited by Robert K.
        Sakai. Lincoln: University of Nebraska Press, 1966, pp. 77-88.

        The New Religions are more directly concerned with the people's
        immediate problems than are established religions like Buddhism.

+114.   _____. "Buddhism in Postwar Japan: A Critical Survey." *Monumenta
        Nipponica* 24, nos. 1-2 (1969): 113-36.

        Analyzes the shortcomings of postwar Buddhism by reference to the
        success of New Religions such as Sōka Gakkai.

[+]115.   KOBAYASHI, SAKAE. "Changes in the Japanese Religions after World
          War II." S.T.M. thesis, Union Theological Seminary in the City of New
          York, 1957, 153 pp. See pp. 48-107, 134-35.

          Notes that the New Religions tended to be nationalistic supporters of
          the war effort but in postwar times have emphasized "the international
          nature of religion."

116.   _____. "Changes in Japanese Religions After World War II (Part I)."
          Kwansei Gakuin University Annual Studies 8 (October 1959): 1-53. See
          esp. pp. 46-53.

          A general account of the changes within Japanese religion for the
          period 1945-1951, with specific remarks on Tenrikyō and Konkōkyō.
          (Part II was never published; this appears to be a published version of
          some of the preceding entry.)

117.   _____. "The Peaceful Co-Existence of Intellectual and Magical
          Elements in Japan's New Religions." *Japanese Religions* 1, no. 4
          (December 1959): 28-35.

[+]118.   KOHLER, WERNER. *Die Lotus-Lehre und die modernen Religionen in
          Japan.* Zurich: Atlantis Verlag, 1962, 300 pp.

          A general treatment of New Religions ("modern religions") dependent
          on Nichiren and the Lotus Sutra: Sōka Gakkai, Reiyū-kai, and Risshō
          Kōsei-kai.   Questions the relationship of shamanism and ancestor
          worship to the New Religions.

*119.   _____. "Die modernen Religionen in Japan und ihr Verständnis der
          Mission." In *Lutherisches Missionsjahrbuch 1965*.   Nuremberg:
          Nürnberg Bayer, Missionskonferenz, 1965, pp. 41-60.

*120.   _____. "Neue Religionen." *Ostasien* 2, nos. 5-6 (1959).

          Cited in Werner Kohler, *Die Lotus-Lehre und die modernen Religionen
          in Japan* (entry 118), p. 289.

          KOMAROVSKII, GEORGII EVGEN'EVICH.   *See* Arutiunov, Sergei
          Aleksandrovich and Svetlov, Georgii Evgen'evich (entry 12A).

121.   No entry.

122.   KÖPPING (KOEPPING), KLAUS-PETER. *Religiöse Bewegungen im
          modernen Japan als Problem des Kulturwandels.* Inaugural dissertation,
          Universität zu Köln.   Published under the same title.   Cologne:
          Wienand Verlag, 1974, 159 pp. Illus.

General chapters on theories about cultural change, followed by analysis of three Japanese New Religions.

123. ____. "Sekai Mahikari Bunmei Kyōdan—A Preliminary Discussion of a Recent Religious Movement in Japan." *Contemporary Religions in Japan* 8, no. 2 (June 1967): 101-34.

In analyzing this religious movement from the viewpoint of cultural anthropology, discusses methodological considerations for studying the New Religions, their character as nativistic innovations, and the general significance of Japanese New Religions.

124. KOTÁNSKI, WIESLAW. *Zarys dziejów w Japonii* [Outline history of Japan]. Warsaw: Ksiqzka i Wiedza, 1963, 214 pp. Illus. See pp. 120-29, 152-67.

In Polish. An overview of Shinto sects and some "Buddhist" new movements.

125. KUBOTA, SHOBUN. "Belief in Hokkekyō and Its Development in Japan." In *Research Tour Papers, Tokyo*. Mimeographed, pp. 11-14.

Traces the history of belief in the Lotus Sutra and its contribution to new religious movements.

126. LANCZKOWSKI, GÜNTER. *Die neuen Religionen*. Frankfort: Fischer Taschenbuch Verlag, 1974, 201 pp. See pp. 10-54.

Includes brief overviews of nine Japanese New Religions, as well as treating new religious movements from other areas.

127. LANTERNARI, VITTORIO. *The Religions of the Oppressed: A Study of Modern Messianic Cults*. Translated by Lisa Sergio. New York: Knopf; London: MacGibbon & Kee, 1963, xix + 343 pp. New York: New American Library, 1965, xvi + 286 pp. See pp. 223-27. First published as *Movimenti religiosi di libertà e di salvezza dei popoli oppressi* (Milan: Feltrinelli, 1960), 365 pp. Also published as *Religiöse Freiheits- und Heilsbewegungen unterdrückten Völker*, trans. Friedrich Kollmann (Neuwied: Luchterhand, 1960), 538 pp.

A worldwide comparative study of messianic and prophetic movements, discussed by region, including mention of some Japanese New Religions.

128. LEE, ROBERT. *Stranger in the Land: A Study of the Church in Japan*. London: Lutterworth Press, 1967, xvi + 216 pp. See pp. 135-54.

General remarks on "Appeal of New Religious Groups."

129. LOFTIN, MARION T. "Japanese in Brazil: A Study in Immigration and Acculturation." Ph.D. thesis, Vanderbilt University, 1951, 348 pp. Abstracted in *Dissertation Abstracts* 12 (1952): 759. University Microfilms International order no. 3974. See pp. 86-89, 160-63, 230-38, 256e-256i.

First-hand description of a "Tenri-Kyō Temple" and a "healing ceremony" therein (pp. 256e-256i); Tenrikyō is treated as a Shinto sect, and the earlier references give some information on "Shinto."

130. LOKOWANDT, ERNST. *Die rechtliche Entwicklung des Staats-Shinto in der ersten Hälfte der Meiji-Zeit (1868-1890).* Inaugural dissertation, Rheinische Friedrich-Wilhelms-Universität, 1976, 509 pp. See pp. 304-11. Published under the same title. Studies in Oriental Religions, no. 3. Wiesbaden: Harrassowitz, 1978, ix + 383 pp.

A brief treatment of Sect Shinto in the context of the development of state Shinto.

131. LOUIS-FRÉDÉRIC [pseud.]. *Le shintô, esprit et religion du Japon.* Paris: Bordas, 1972, 159 pp. See pp. 63-69.

A brief treatment of Sect Shinto.

132. LOWELL, PERCIVAL. *Occult Japan or the Way of the Gods: An Esoteric Study of Japanese Personality and Possession.* Boston: Houghton Mifflin Co., 1895, 379 pp. Appeared originally in *Transactions of the Asiatic Society of Japan* 21-22.

Description of various forms of possession that have been very important for the foundation of the "mountain sects" of Shinto and the New Religions in general.

133. McFARLAND, H[ORACE] NEILL. "The New Religions of Japan." *Contemporary Religions in Japan* 1, no. 2 (June 1960): 35-47; no. 3 (September 1960): 30-39; no. 4 (December 1960): 47-69.

Except for the description of Tenrikyō and Ittōen, materials later included in his book *The Rush Hour of the Gods* (entry 136).

134. _____. "The New Religions of Japan." *Perkins School of Theology Journal* 12, no. 1 (Fall 1958): 3-21.

135. _____. "The Present Status of the Religions of Japan." *Journal of Bible and Religion* 26, no. 3 (July 1958): 222-31.

Argues that "functionally the New Religions are crisis religions."

[+]136. _____. *The Rush Hour of the Gods: A Study of New Religious Movements in Japan.* New York: Macmillan Co., 1967, xvii + 267 pp.

Analyzes the "social crisis and the rise of the new religions" and identifies their recurrent characteristics. Treats Konkōkyō, PL Kyōdan, Seichō-no-Ie, Risshō Kōsei-kai, and Sōka Gakkai.

137. MAEYAMA, TAKASHI. "Ancestor, Emperor, and Immigrant: Religion and Group Identification of the Japanese in Rural Brazil (1908-1950)." *Journal of Interamerican Studies and World Affairs* 14, no. 2 (May 1972): 151-82.

Analyzes the rather late success of the Japanese New Religions among Japanese in Brazil, arguing that initially rather low family identity and later rise to middle-class status (and growing family consciousness) are the major factors in this process.

138. MANIKAM, RAJAH B., ed. *Christianity and the Asian Revolution.* Madras: Diocesan Press; New York: Friendship Press, 1954, iv + 293 pp. See pp. 175-84.

Comment on the New Religions in the context of resurgent Asian religions as a challenge to Christianity.

[+]139. MARUKAWA, HITOO. "Religious Circumstances in the Late Tokugawa and the Early Meiji Periods: Religious Backgrounds in the Cradle Years of Tenrikyo." *Tenri Journal of Religion* 11 (1970): 43-78.

A good summary of the sociopolitical conditions, religious beliefs, and customs out of which the first New Religions arose.

140. MASAMUNE, HAKUCHŌ. "Thoughts on the New Religions." *Japan Quarterly* 4, no. 1 (January-March 1957): 65-69.

The New Religions are actually no more naïve than faith in science; they appeal to the inevitable human nostalgia for religious certainty in an age when Buddhism and Christianity have lost their vitality.

141. MATSUMURA, AKIKO. "Psychological Approaches of the New Religions." *Japan Christian Quarterly* 41, no. 2 (Spring 1975): 111-13.

142.   MELTON, J. GORDON. "The Eastern and Middle Eastern Family (Buddhism, Shintoism, and Zoroastrianism)." In *The Encyclopedia of American Religions.* Vol. 2. Wilmington, NC: McGrath Publishing Co., 1978, pp. 393-444.

Includes brief descriptions of Japanese movements, their founders, history, and activities in Hawaii and continental U.S.

142A.   _____, and GEISENDORFER, JAMES V. *A Directory of Religious Bodies in the United States. Compiled from the files of the Institute for the Study of American Religion.* New York: Garland, 1977, xiv + 305 pp.

A comprehensive directory of addresses of religious groups in America, arranged alphabetically; the bulk are Christian and Jewish groups, but for the lists of Japanese religious groups that include New Religions, see p. 275, "Buddhist Bodies," p. 276, "Shinto," and p. 278, "Miscellaneous."

*143.   MIURA, YOSHIKAZU. *Neue Religionen in Japan.* Christus und die Welt, vol. 19. Bad Salzuflen: MBK-Verlag, 1963, 39 pp.

Cited in *Cumulative Bibliography of Asian Studies, 1941-1965* 3: 306.

144.   MIYAKE, TADASHI. "Who Gets the Religious Vote?" *Japanese Christian Quarterly* 44, no. 2 (Spring 1978): 118.

Provides membership figures for politically active religious organizations and analyzes the strategy of the Liberal Democratic Party to mobilize the religious vote.

*145.   MOLINA, GONZALEZ ANTONIO. "'Shinkooshuukyoo,' las nuevas religiones en el Japón." *Razón y fe* 161, no. 745 (February 1960): 153-64.

Cited in *Bibliography of Asian Studies,* 1961-62, p. 650.

146.   MORIOKA, KIYOMI. "Contemporary Changes in Japanese Religion." In *Sociology and Religion: A Book of Readings.* Edited by Norman Birnbaum and Gertrud Lenzer. Englewood Cliffs, NJ: Prentice-Hall, 1969, pp. 382-86.

Brief comments on Japanese New Religions.

+147.   _____. "The Institutionalization of a New Religious Movement." In *Proceedings of Tokyo Meeting of the International Conference on Sociology of Religion.* Edited by Organizing Committee for Tokyo

Meeting of CISR 1978. Tokyo: Organizing Committee for Tokyo Meeting of CISR 1978, 1978, pp. 217-45. Reprinted in *Japanese Journal of Religious Studies* 6, nos. 1-2 (March-June 1979): 239-80.

An incisive analysis of institutionalization procedures in any new religious movement, with major focus on Risshō Kōsei-kai and comparative remarks on other Japanese New Religions.

+148.   _____. *Religion in Changing Japanese Society*. Tokyo: University of Tokyo Press, 1975, xvi + 231 pp.

A collection of essays on changing social and religious patterns in postwar Japan by a leading Japanese sociologist of religion; the essays describe the general context of the New Religions and provide incisive comments on the New Religions in relationship to other religious developments.

149.   _____. "Les religions contemporaines du Japon: Coexistence et conflit." *Revue française de sociologie* 8 (July-September 1967): 348-54.

150.   _____, and SHIMPO, MITSURU. "The Impact of the Physical Movement of Population on Japanese Religions after World War II." In *Actes de la lle Conférence Opatija* (Conférence internationale de sociologie religieuse). Lille, France: Édition CISR, n.d., pp. 189-211. Reprinted in Kiyomi Morioka, *Religion in Changing Japanese Society* (Tokyo: University of Tokyo Press, 1975), pp. 155-67.

Analyzes the impact of population movement on the decline of organized religions and the growth of New Religions.

151.   MUCCIOLI, MARCELLO. *Lo shintoismo, religione nazionale del Giappone*. Milan: Instituto Editorale Galileo, 1948, 143 pp. See pp. 124-31.

A brief treatment of Sect Shinto.

152.   MULHOLLAND, JOHN F. *Hawaii's Religions*. Rutland, VT and Tokyo: Charles E. Tuttle Company, 1970, 344 pp. See esp. pp. 270-90.

Brief comments on the history and activities of Japanese New Religions in Hawaii, including their addresses.

+153.   MURAKAMI, SHIGEYOSHI. *Japanese Religion in the Modern Century.* Translated by H[arry] Byron Earhart. Tokyo: University of Tokyo Press, 1980, xvii + 186 pp. Illus.

A critical analysis of the development of Japanese New Religions out of grassroots religious movements, in spite of governmental suppression; treats all the major New Religions and many lesser known New Religions (all of which are included in the book's index). For Murakami's original book (in Japanese), see Appendix C in the present work.

154. _____. "New Religions of Japan." In *The Symposium on Family and Religion in East Asian Countries.* Edited by Chie Nakane and Akira Goto. Tokyo: Center for East Asian Cultural Studies, 1972, pp. 17-27. Reprinted from *East Asian Cultural Studies* 11, nos. 1-4 (March 1972).

A convenient overview of the development and activities of Japanese New Religions.

155. _____. "Les religions nouvelles au Japon." *Social Compass* 17, no. 1 (1970): 137-51.

An analysis of the New Religions in terms of their historical background, their relationship to social and economic factors, and their expression of conservative values.

+156. NAKAJIMA, HIDEO. "On Some Problem in the Classification of Shinto." *Tenri Journal of Religion* 11 (December 1970): 36-42.

A critical discussion of the notion of Kyōha Shintō (Sect Shinto) in the light of New Religions.

157. NAKAMURA, HAJIME. *Ways of Thinking of Eastern Peoples: India-China-Tibet-Japan.* Revised English translation. Edited by Philip P. Wiener. Honolulu: East-West Center Press, 1964, xx + 712 pp. See pp. 449-67.

Remarks on the Japanese tendency towards "Absolute Devotion to a Specific Individual Symbolic of the Human Nexus," helpful for understanding the phenomenon of founders in modern religious movements.

158. NEBREDA, ALFONSO M. "L'étudiant japonais en face du problème religieux: Ombres et lumières." *Études* 307 (December 1960): 361-70.

The New Religions are part of the religious confusion that students face.

159. _____. "The Legacy of the West: The Japanese University Student Confronts Religion (Part I)." *Monumenta Nipponica* 20 (1965): 15-40. See pp. 34-40.

Concludes that "when confronted with the New Religions, the students are strongly and unanimously opposed to them." (The other part of this article, in the subsequent issue of *Monumenta Nipponica*, does not deal with religion.)

160. "New Religions of Japan." *Hibbert Journal* 62, no. 244 (October 1963): 10-15.

A general treatment, mainly a summary of Harry Thomsen, *The New Religions of Japan* (entry 233).

161. "New Religions of Japan." *Herder Correspondence* (October 1963), pp. 22-26.

161A. NEWNAN, EDNA S. "Female Leadership Roles in Japan's New Religions: Their Relation to Shamanism and Max Weber's Charisma Theory." M.A. thesis, University of Michigan, 1956, ii + 151 pp.

Available at the Asia Library of the University of Michigan.

161B. NICHOLSON, SAMUEL O. "New Religious Movements in Japan." M.A. thesis, University of Michigan, 1956, ii + 151 pp.

Available at the Asia Library of the University of Michigan.

162. NIELSEN, NIELS C., Jr. "Japan's 'New Religions.'" *Christian Century* 74 (October 1957): 1196-98.

In spite of certain deficiencies, "positively, these new faiths serve as a barrier to communism."

163. _____. *Religion and Philosophy in Contemporary Japan*. Rice Institute Pamphlets (Houston) 43, no. 4 (1957): 1-132. See pp. 82-109.

A survey of Japanese religion in its different aspects, briefly treating New Religions.

*164. _____. "As novas religiões do Japão" [The New Religions of Japan]. *Unitas* 20 (1958): 25-32.

In Portuguese.

165. NISHITANI, KEIJI. "The Religious Situation in Present-Day Japan." *Contemporary Religions in Japan* 1, no. 1 (March 1960): 7-24.

A famous philosopher's analysis of contemporary Japanese religion, especially religious indifference and nihilism.

+166.   NISHIYAMA, SHIGERU; SHIMAZONO, SUSUMU; SHIRAMIZU, HIROKO; and TSUSHIMA, MICHITO. "The Vitalistic Conception of Salvation in Japanese New Religions: An Aspect of Modern Religious Consciousness." In *Proceedings of Tokyo Meeting of the International Conference on Sociology of Religion.* Edited by Organizing Committee for Tokyo Meeting of CISR 1978. Tokyo: Organizing Committee for Tokyo Meeting of CISR 1978, 1978, vi + 284 pp. See pp. 74–91. Reprinted in *Japanese Journal of Religious Studies* 6, nos. 1–2 (March-June 1979): 139–61.

A valuable synthetic overview of "the common underlying structure to the teachings of the various New Religions."

+167.   NIWANO, NIKKYO.   *Lifetime   Beginner: An   Autobiography.* Translated by Richard L. Gage. Tokyo: Kōsei Publishing Co., 1978, 300 pp. Illus. See esp. pp. 227–30.

This autobiography by the cofounder of Risshō Kōsei-kai provides valuable insight into the process whereby New Religions develop; a number of New Religions other than Risshō Kōsei-kai are mentioned in the work.

168.   NIYEDA (NIEDA), ROKUSABURŌ. "New Religion in Japan—Japanese People's Religion." *Religions in Japan at Present* (1958), pp. 23–26.

Treats the New Religions as the attempt to break through the traditional political control over religion and to relate religion directly to daily life.

168A.   NORBECK, EDWARD.   *Religion and Society in Modern Japan: Continuity and Change.* Houston: Tourmaline Press, 1970, vii + 232 pp. Also printed as *Rice University Studies* 56, no. 1 (Winter 1970). See pp. 10–43, 161–217.

An introductory chapter on general features of the New Religions (origin, founders, doctrine, organization, and membership) followed by appendixes describing Sōka Gakkai, Risshō Kōsei-kai, PL Kyōdan, and Seichō-no-Ie.

169.   NORDSTOKKE, KJELL.   "Seitas e orientalismo: Sua infiltracão no Brasil" [Sects and orientalism: Their infiltration in Brazil]. In *Anuário Evangélico 1980, 9º ano.* Edited by Editora Sinodal. São Leopoldo: Editora Sinodal, 1980, pp. 83–91.

In Portuguese. A general treatment of New Religions, especially the Japanese New Religions present in Brazil.

170. _____. *Utfordringen fra Brasil* [The challenge from Brazil]. Oslo: Luther forlag, 1975, 111 pp. See pp. 86-98.

In Norwegian. A general treatment of Seichō-no-Ie, Sekai Kyūsei-kyō, and PL Kyōdan in Brazil.

171. *Nouveaux Mélanges Japonais*. Mimeographed, no. 1 (March 1953)-no. 22 (April 1961).

Occasional articles on the New Religions translated from Japanese into French.

172. *Novas religiões japonêsas no Brasil, por uma equipe de Franciscanos de Petrópolis* [Japanese New Religions in Brazil, by a team of Franciscans from Petropolis]. Vozes em Defesa da Fe, Serie 2, Caderno 60. Petropolis, Brazil: Editora Vozes Limitada, 1964, 36 pp.

In Portuguese. Treats especially Sōka Gakkai, Tenrikyō, and Seichō-no-Ie.

+173. OFFNER, CLARK B. "Individual Values in the New Religious Movements of Japan." *Japan Christian Quarterly* 39, no. 1 (Winter 1973): 31-38.

States that "the contemporaneous manifestation of new religious vigor can be related to [the] search for relevant individual values and personal happiness."

174. _____. "Resurgence of Non-Christian Religions." In *The Japan Christian Yearbook 1966*. Edited by Gordon K. Chapman. Tokyo: Kyo Bun Kwan (The Christian Literature Society of Japan), 1966, pp. 32-42.

Analysis of dissatisfaction with *"obsolete, but rigid forms"* in established religions, and charismatic leadership in the New Religions as an explanation of this "resurgence."

+175. _____, and STRAELEN, HENRY (HENRICUS J.J.M.) van. *Modern Japanese Religions, with Special Emphasis upon Their Doctrines of Healing*. Tokyo: Rupert Enderle, 1963, 296 pp.

A Protestant and Roman Catholic missionary jointly describe the New Religions in terms of faith healing and the concept of deity; Straelen treats Tenrikyō while Offner treats "Omoto-related" and "Nichiren-related" religions. See the reviews by Shūten Ōishi et al. (entry 182) and Joseph J. Spae (entry 215).

176. OGUCHI, IICHI. "Common People and Religion." Translated by Angelus Aschoff. *Missionary Bulletin* 10, no. 8 (October 1956): 633-34; no. 9 (November 1956): 695-99; no. 10 (December 1956): 780-83; 11, no. 1 (January 1957): 79-82.

Mentions the New Religions in the context of magic, shamanism, and healing.

177. _____. "Foundation and Characteristics of the 'New Religions.'" In *Research Tour Papers, Tokyo*. Mimeographed, pp. 7-10.

Interesting overview of the New Religions as socioreligious phenomena.

178. _____. "Founder and Organizer of Religious Group—A Problem of Religious Authority in Japan." In *Proceedings of the IXth International Congress for the History of Religions, 1958*. Tokyo: Maruzen, 1960, pp. 382-83.

Notes that many of the founders of the New Religions both possessed charisma and became objects of worship.

[+]179. _____, and TAKAGI, HIROO. "Religion and Social Development." In *Japanese Religion in the Meiji Era*. Edited by Hideo Kishimoto. Translated by John F. Howes. Tokyo: Ōbunsha, 1956, pp. 313-51.

Examines the roots of religious phenomena such as the New Religions in social developments of the Tokugawa (1600-1867) and Meiji (1868-1912) periods.

180. ŌISHI, SHŪTEN. Review of *Nihon ni okeru Kirisuto-kyō to sho-shūkyō* [The religious encounter between Christianity and other religions in Japan], by Masatoshi Doi, Yasuo Mizoguchi, and Sakae Kobayashi. *Contemporary Religions in Japan* 3, no. 2 (June 1962): 165-75.

Includes remarks on the New Religions from the viewpoint of Japanese Christians.

181. _____. Review of *Nihon no shinkō shūkyō* [The newly established religions in Japan], by Hiroo Takagi. *Contemporary Religions in Japan* 1, no. 2 (June 1960): 59-63.

A review of several valuable Japanese scholarly publications on the New Religions.

[+]182. _____, et al. "A Review Article. The New Religious Sects of Japan." *Contemporary Religions in Japan* 5, no. 1 (March 1964): 45-80; no. 3 (September 1964): 221-31.

Review of *The New Religions of Japan*, by Harry Thomsen (entry 233), and *Modern Japanese Religions*, by Clark B. Offner and Henry (Henricus J.J.M.) van Straelen (entry 175). Response by representatives of the New Religions to their depiction in two English-language treatments of the New Religions, alleging many factual errors and misunderstandings.

183. OOMS, HERMAN. "The Religion of the Household (A Case Study of Ancestor Worship in Japan)." *Contemporary Religions in Japan* 8, nos. 3-4 (September-December 1967): 201-333.

Comments on the interaction of New Religions and "ancestor worship" found in field research.

184. OSAKI, NORIO. "A Study of Interdenominational Cooperation within Each of Three Japanese Religions in Los Angeles: Shinto, Buddhism, and Christianity." M.A. thesis, University of Southern California, 1941, 131 pp. See pp. 1-4, 14-26.

Included in the treatment of "Shinto" are Shindō Honkyoku (Daijingū-kyō), Taisha-kyō, Konkō-kyō, and Tenrikyō.

*185. OYA, SOICHI. "Dic Inflation der Religionen in Japan." *Die Auslese* (1934), 3 pp.

Cited in Jean Herbert, *Bibliographie du shintô et des sectes shintôïstes* (entry 81), p. 42.

186. PLATH, DAVID W. *The After Hours: Modern Japan and the Search for Enjoyment*. Berkeley and Los Angeles: University of California Press, 1964, xi + 222 pp. See pp. 60, 164, 174, 179.

Brief remarks on several New Religions in the context of postwar use of leisure time.

[+]187. _____. "The Fate of Utopia: Adaptive Tactics in Four Japanese Groups." *American Anthropologist* 68, pt. 2 (1966): 1152-62.

A brief analysis of four Japanese examples of utopian varieties of "revitalization."

[+]188. _____. "Modernization and Its Discontents: Japan's Little Utopias." *Journal of Asian and African Studies* 4, no. 1 (January 1969): 1-17. Reprinted in Joseph R. Gusfield, ed., *Protest, Reform, and Revolt: A Reader in Social Movements* (New York: John Wiley & Sons, 1970), pp. 90-107.

Describes the variety of utopian movements found in Japan and compares them with Western counterparts.

[+]189.   RAJANA, EIMI WATANABE. "New Religions in Japan: An Appraisal of Two Theories." In *Modern Japan: Aspects of History, Literature and Society*. Edited by W.G. Beasley. Berkeley: University of California Press, 1975, p. 187-97.

Criticism of the theory that the New Religions are substitutes for the loss of the emperor after World War II; criticism of the theory that the New Religions arose as substitutes for social institutions (as "antidotes of anomie").

190.   _____. "A Sociological Study of New Religious Movements: Chilean Pentecostalism and Japanese New Religions." Ph.D. dissertation, University of London, 1974, 228 pp.

Briefly treats five Japanese New Religions, discusses the general characteristics of these movements in sociological categories, and compares them with Chilean pentecostalism.

191.   RAMMING, MARTIN, ed. *Japan-Handbuch: Nachschlagewerk der Japankunde*. Berlin: Steiniger, 1941, 740 pp. See pp. 535-37.

Brief remarks on Sect Shinto.

192.   RAMSMEYER, ROBERT L. "Finances in the New Religions and the Christian Church." *Japan Christian Quarterly* 37 (Spring 1972): 84-89.

A comparison of finances and religious organizations for branches of Risshō Kōsei-kai, Konkōkyō, Tenrikyō, and Sōka Gakkai, with several Protestant churches in a Kyushu city.

193.   RAPER, ARTHUR F., et al. *The Japanese Village in Transition*. Report no. 136. Tokyo: General Headquarters, Supreme Commander for the Allied Powers, Natural Resources Section, 1950, 272 pp. See pp. 221-28.

Except for the presence of sectarian Shinto, "the wave of new Shinto and Buddhist sects which has been sweeping the whole country since the Surrender has hardly brought a ripple to the 13 villages. . . ."

194.   REISCHAUER, AUGUST KARL. "Religion in the Japan of To-day." *International Review of Missions* 26 (July 1937): 322-33.

A prewar recognition of the changing religious situation, one result of which was "new religious cults."

195.   RICCO, MARIO. *Religione della violenza e religione del piacere nel nuovo Giappone.* Florence: Saggi, 1967, 139 pp.

Includes separate chapters on Sōka Gakkai, Tenrikyō, and Seichō-no-Ie.

*196.   RIGMARK, W. "Nya religioner i Japan" [New Religions in Japan]. *Svensk Missionstidskrift* 40, no. 1 (1972): 4-11.

In Swedish. Cited in *Index to Religious Periodical Literature* 10 (January 1971-December 1972): 264.

197.   ROCHEDIEU, EDMOND. *Le shintoïsme et les nouvelles religions du Japan.* Paris: Garnier Frères; Geneva: Edito-Service, 1968, 255 pp. Illus. See pp. 199-230.

General characteristics of the New Religions.

198.   ROSENKRANZ, GERHARD. *Fernost—wohin? Begegnungen mit den Religionen Japans und Chinas im Umbruch der Gegenwart.* Heilbronn: Eugen Salzer Verlag, 1940, 304 pp. See pp. 119-27.

Brief treatment of Sect Shinto and its largest member, Tenrikyō; mentions nationalistic tendency of Sect Shinto.

199.   ____. *Der Weg der Götter (Shinto): Gehalt und Gestalt der Japanischen Nationalreligion.* Munich: Arbeitsgemeinschaft für Zeitgeschichte, 1944, 223 pp. See pp. 11-12, 121-31.

Brief remarks on Sect Shinto.

200.   ROTERMUND, HARTMUT O. "Les nouvelles religions du Japon." In *Encyclopédie de la Pléiade; Histoire des religions.* Vol. 3, pp. 520-41.

Brief treatment of the historical background of the New Religions and the characteristics of individual New Religions.

*201.   SACON, Y.H. "A Study of the Religious Organizations in Japanese Communities in America." Research Report, University of Southern California, 1932, vi + 231 pp. Illus. See pp. 154-91.

Source: card catalog, University of Southern California library.

202.   SAUNDERS, KENNETH. "Glimpses of the Religious Life in New Japan." *Japanese Religions* 2, no. 1 (January 1922): 70-80.

A criticism of the New Religions, especially Oomoto, as nationalistic and vulgar.

[+]203.   SCHIFFER, WILHELM. "New Religions in Postwar Japan." *Monumenta Nipponica* 11 (April 1955): 1-14.

A general introduction to the New Religions, which follows Reihō Masunaga in limiting the New Religions to "those religions . . . which originated shortly before, during, or after World War II."

*204.   _____. "New Religions of Japan." *Today's Japan*, no. 4 (1956).

Cited in Harry Thomsen, *The New Religions of Japan* (entry 233), p. 259.

205.   *Sectarian Shinto (The Way of the Gods).* Edited by Shinto Shogakukai (The Society for Promoting Shinto). Tokyo: Japan Times & Mail, 1937, 62 pp.

A brief description of each of the thirteen members of Sect Shinto by this prewar society, specially prepared for delegates to the World Education Conference.

206.   SHIBATA, C. "New Religions and the Christian Church." *Japan Christian Quarterly* 37, no. 3 (Summer 1971): 173-80. Reprinted in *Lutheran World* 19, no. 1 (1972): 59-64.

An analysis of the origin, growth, and practices of the New Religions, leading to the conclusion that the New Religions provide lessons on how to indigenize the Christian church in Japan.

[+]207.   SHIMAZONO, SUSUMU. "The Living Kami Idea in the New Religions of Japan." *Japanese Journal of Religious Studies* 6, no. 3 (September 1979): 389-412.

The best synthetic interpretation of the nature of founders (and foundresses) as living *kami* in the rise and institutionalization of New Religions.

208.   SIEFFERT, RENÉ. *Les religions du Japon.* Paris: Presses Universitaires de France, 1968, 132 pp. See pp. 112-17, 128-31.

Brief treatment of popular Shinto and New Religions in the context of the history of Japanese religions.

209.   SMITH, ROBERT J. *Ancestor Worship in Contemporary Japan.* Stanford: Stanford University Press, 1974, xix + 266 pp. See pp. 34-38, 60-63, 73, 148.

Traces the continuity of traditional ancestor worship within the New Religions: "the syncretic sects that the Japanese call the New

Religions have continued to foster the household ideal and concepts of filial piety."

+210.   _____. "The Ethnic Japanese in Brazil." *Journal of Japanese Studies* 5, no. 1 (Winter 1979): 53-70. See pp. 62-63.

Brief but succinct comments on the contrasting situations in Brazil and U.S.-Canada for Japanese religions generally and the New Religions specifically.

211.   SOLOMON, TED J.   "The Response of Three New Religions to the Crisis in the Japanese Value System." *Journal for the Scientific Study of Religion* 16, no. 1 (March 1977): 1-14.

Analyzing PL Kyōdan, Risshō Kōsei-kai and Sōka Gakkai, concludes that "The three religions are trying to alleviate social anomie not only through a reaffirmation of traditional values . . . but also through a reformulation of the value system that incorporates many modern values of an industrial society."

*212.   SPAE, JOSEPH J.   "Faith Healing and the New Religions." *Missionary Bulletin* 10 (1956): 518-23.

Cited in personal communication from Joseph J. Spae to H[arry] Byron Earhart, 14 December 1969.

213.   _____. *Japanese Religiosity*.   Tokyo: Oriens Institute for Religious Research, 1971, 313 pp.

Many interesting comments on the New Religions are included in this general interpretation of aspects of "Japanese religiosity."

214.   _____. "The New Religions." *Missionary Bulletin* 9, no. 10 (October 1955):   583-87; no. 11 (November 1955):   670-73; 10, no. 2 (March 1956):   125-29; no. 4 (May 1956):   277-80; no. 9 (November 1956): 668-73; no. 10 (December 1956):   746-50; 12, no. 6 (July 1958): 440-44; no. 8 (October 1958):   586-90; no. 10 (December 1958):   748-51; *Japan Missionary Bulletin* [title of journal changed from *Missionary Bulletin* to *Japan Missionary Bulletin*] 13, no. 4 (May 1959):   238-44; no. 8 (October 1959):   514-17; 14, no. 1 (January-February 1960):   26-29; no. 5 (June 1960):   321-25; no. 7 (August-September 1960):   454-57; no. 10 (December 1960):   654-56.

Brief introductions to various New Religions.

215. _____. "The New Religions: A Review Article." *Contemporary Religions in Japan* 4, no. 2 (June 1963): 169-77.

Critical review of *Modern Japanese Religions*, by Clark B. Offner and Henry (Henricus J.J.M.) van Straelen (entry 175), "the first sizeable book in English on the New Religions of Japan."

216. _____. "The Religions of Japan." *Missionary Bulletin* 9, no. 7 (July 1955): 410-14; nos. 8-9 (August-September 1955): 501-4.

A survey of members of Sect Shinto and Konkōkyō.

216A. "Statistics on Religious Organizations in Japan, 1947-1972." *Japanese Journal of Religious Studies* 2, no. 1 (March 1975):   45-64; nos. 2-3 (June-September 1975): 175-206; no. 4 (December 1975): 289-316; 3, no. 1 (March 1976): 63-87; nos. 2-3 (June-September 1976): 223-46; no. 4 (December 1976):   307-30; 4, no. 1 (March 1977):   75-97; nos. 2-3 (June-September 1977): 213-39; no. 4 (December 1977): 293-314.

Convenient lists of the information religious groups must submit to the national government in order to gain corporate status as a "religious juridical person":   number of religious buildings, clergy, and adherents. Because religious organizations can designate the category under which they wish to be listed, the "New Religions" in this bibliography may be found in this set of articles under various headings.

[+]217. STRAELEN, HENRY (HENRICUS J.J.M.) van.   "The Japanese New Religions." *Numen* 9 (1962): 228-40.

A brief definition of the New Religions and their main characteristics.

218. _____. "The Japanese New Religions Are Not New." *Neue Zeitschrift für Missionswissenschaft* 20 (1964): 263-70.

Analyzes the "different kinds of worship" found in the New Religions to prove "that the Japanese New Religions relentlessly continue the traditional religious mentality of the Japanese people."

219. _____. *Modern Japan, het land der felle contrasten* [Modern Japan, land of many contrasts]. Voorhout: Uitgeverij Foreholte, 1940, 210 pp. See pp. 101-2. 2d ed., 1945, 223 pp. See pp. 101-2.

In Dutch. A pre-World War II comment on the "at least 800 new sects" that had arisen in previous decades "notwithstanding a strict police surveillance."

220. _____. *Religions nouvelles du Japon.* N.P., n.d., 30 pp. Reprinted from *Église Vivante* 3, nos. 5–6 (1961): 344–56, 441–55.

221. SUGAI, TAIKA. "The Soteriology of New Religions." *Japanese Religions* 6, no. 2 (1969): 23–46.

An attempt to define "New Religions" and identify their special characteristics, using the founders of Tenrikyō and Oomoto to illustrate the notion of salvation in Japanese New Religions.

222. _____, comp. "Statistics of Japanese Religions." *Japanese Christian Quarterly* 37, no. 1 (Winter 1971): 20–22.

Brief list of statistics of membership, etc. for most religious groups, including New Religions.

223. SUGIYAMA, HEISUKE. "Religious Racketeering." *Contemporary Japan* 5, no. 4 (March 1937): 612–17.

Referring to Tenrikyō, Hito no Michi, and Oomoto, he claims that "what is common to all these cults is the fact that either their founder or their successors have amassed great fortunes and live in luxury through contributions offered them by their followers."

+224. TAKAGI, HIROO. "The Rise of the New Religions." *Japan Quarterly* 11, no. 2 (April–June 1964): 283–92.

By analyzing Japanese history he shows that "Sōka Gakkai is a typical manifestation in present-day terms of the religious outlook of the Japanese."

225. TAKAHASHI, KYOJIRO. "A Social Study of the Japanese Shinto and Buddhism in Los Angeles." M.A. thesis, University of Southern California, 1937, 134 pp. See pp. 61–74, 85–89, 119–21.

Includes history, organization, and statistics for four groups of Sect Shinto.

225A. TAKEUCHI, AIJI; KOBAYASHI, SAKAE; and MIZOGUCHI, YASUO. "The New Religions of Japan: A Panel Discussion." In *Glimpses of Social Work in Japan.* Edited by Dorothy Dessau. Rev. ed. Tokyo: Social Workers' International Club of Japan, 1968, pp. 20–27.

A general assessment of the characteristics and activities of the New Religions; one claim is that "the new religions function as social welfare organizations."

226.   TANAKA, JIRŌ. "The Meiji and Present Constitutions Compared." In *Religion and State in Japan*. International Institute for the Study of Religions, Bulletin no. 7 (September 1959), pp. 59–95.

Describes constitutional treatment of religion and political control of religion (including mention of the dispute concerning the "Kagoshima Branch of Tokumitsu Kai of Hitonomichi").

*227.   THELLE, NOTTO NORMANN. "De 'nye religioner' i Japan: En fornyelse av de tradisjonelle religioner pa legmannsbasis?" [The "New Religions" in Japan: A renewal of the traditional religions on a lay basis?]. *Norsk Tidsskrift for Misjon* 16, no. 3 (1962): 129–41.

In Norwegian. Citation provided by Harold Turner.

228.   THOMPSON, STEPHEN I. "Religious Conversion and Religious Zeal in an Overseas Enclave: The Case of the Japanese in Bolivia." *Anthropological Quarterly* 41, no. 4 (October 1968): 201–8.

General comments on New Religions, especially Sōka Gakkai, in the context of religious activities of Japanese immigrants in Bolivia.

229.   THOMSEN, HARRY, ed. *Bibliography of the New Religions*. Kyoto: Christian Center for the Study of Japanese Religions, 1959, 37 pp.

Contains mainly English and Japanese materials for sixteen New Religions.

230.   _____. "Japan's New Religions." *International Review of Missions* 48 (July 1959): 283–93. Reprinted in *Japan Christian Quarterly* 25, no. 4 (October 1959): 292–300.

Emphasizes Christian influence in the growth of the New Religions and points out six main characteristics.

231.   _____. "'Neue Religionen.'" In *Christus Kommt nach Japan*. Edited by Gerhard Rosenkranz. Bad Salzuflen: Verlag für Missions- und Bibel-Kunde, 1959, pp. 39–53.

General description of the New Religions and their major characteristics.

232.   _____. "New Religions of Japan." In *Readings in Eastern Religious Thought*. Vol. 3, *Chinese and Japanese Religions* edited by Allie M. Frazier. Philadelphia: Westminster Press, 1969, pp. 218–66.

Materials reprinted from his *The New Religions of Japan* (entry 233).

+233.   _____. *The New Religions of Japan*. Rutland, VT: Charles E. Tuttle
          Co., 1963, 269 pp. Illus. Reprint. Westport, CT: Greenwood Press,
          1978.

          One of the first English books surveying the New Religions and their
          characteristics. See the reviews by Shūten Ōishi, et al. (entry 182) and
          R.J. Zwi Werblowsky (entry 244).

234.   _____. "Numerical Strength of the New Religions." *Japanese Religions*
          1, no. 4 (January 1960): 3-4.

          A note on membership figures of eleven New Religions for 1958 and
          1959.

235.   _____, ed. *A Religious Map of Japan*. Kyoto: Christian Center for the
          Study of Japanese Religions, 1959, 51 pp.

          "The present map gives the location and address of the headquarters of
          all Buddhist sects in Japan, the *principal Shinto shrines*, the
          headquarters of *all the New Religions*, and the *main Buddhist training
          centers*." See International Institute for the Study of Religions, *New
          Religions* . . . (entry 94) for the Sino-Japanese rendering of these
          addresses; some of the organizations have moved since 1959, and many
          of the addresses have been changed. For more current information,
          addresses, and statistics, see Ichirō Hori, et al., ed., *Japanese Religion*
          (entry 89A), or "Statistics on Religious Organizations in Japan, 1947-
          1972" (entry 216A).

236.   UMEDA, YOSHIHIKO. "Concept of *Kami* in Shintoistic Sects." In
          *Proceedings, The Second International Conference for Shinto Studies.
          Theme: Continuity & Change*. Edited by Organizing Committee of the
          Second International Conference for Shinto. Tokyo: Nihon Bunka
          Kenkyūsho (Institute for Japanese Culture and Classics), Kokugakuin
          University, 1968, pp. 15-21.

          Includes remarks on *kami* in some New Religions.

237.   UNDERWOOD, A[LFRED] C. *Shintoism: The Indigenous Religion of
          Japan*. London: Epworth Press, 1934, 126 pp. See pp. 104-9.

          A popular summary of the thirteen members of Sect Shinto.

+238.   UNION OF THE NEW RELIGIOUS ORGANIZATIONS IN JAPAN,
          RESEARCH OFFICE, ed. "Reminiscences of Religion in Postwar
          Japan." *Contemporary Religions in Japan* 6, no. 2 (June 1965): 111-
          203; no. 3 (September 1965): 295-314; no. 4 (December 1965): 382-402;

7, no. 1 (March 1966): 51-79; no. 2 (June 1966): 154-87; no. 3 (September 1966): 217-73.

Interesting commentary on postwar religious developments from the viewpoint of the New Religions.

239.   UYTTENDAELE, FRANCIS F. "Les religions nouvelles au Japon." In *Devant les Sectes non-chrétiennes: Rapports et compte rendu de la XXXIe semaine de missiologie.* Museum Lessianum, Section Missiologique, no. 42. Paris: Desclée De Brouwer, 1961, pp. 196-209.

A general treatment of the New Religions in terms of founders, organization, doctrine, and major characteristics.

240.   WALDENFELS, HANS. "Moderne religiöse Bewegungen in Japan als Impulse fur eine christliche Theologie?" *Verbum* (Rome) 13, nos. 1-2 (1972): 155-72.

241.   "War of the Sects." *Newsweek* 67 (7 March 1966): 86.

Notes competition between Sōka Gakkai and other New Religions.

+242.   WATANABE, BAIYŪ. "Modern Japanese Religions: Their Success Explained." *Monumenta Nipponica* 13 (1957): 153-62.

Offers statistical information and suggests "nine causes to which [the New Religions] owe their existence and their great influence on the masses."

243.   WENDT, INGEBORG Y. "Buddhistische und shamanistische Elements im Säkularisierungsprozess des modernen Japan." *Zeitschrift für Religions- und Geistesgeschichte* 33 (1971): 319-38.

Includes brief references to the founders of New Religions.

244.   WERBLOWSKY, R.J. ZWI. Review of *The New Religions of Japan*, by Harry Thomsen (entry 233). *Journal for the Scientific Study of Religion* 5, no. 2 (Spring 1966): 299-304.

By criticizing this work he indicates generally the deficiencies in most Western treatments of the New Religions.

245.   WILSON, BRYAN R. "The New Religions: Some Preliminary Considerations." In *Proceedings of Tokyo Meeting of the International Conference on Sociology of Religion 1978*, edited by Organizing Committee for Tokyo Meeting of CISR 1978. Tokyo: Organizing Committee for Tokyo Meeting of CISR 1978, 1978, pp. 112-30.

Reprinted in *Japanese Journal of Religious Studies* 6, nos. 1-2 (March–June 1979): 193-216.

A sociological analysis of generic aspects of Japanese and Western New Religions, such as newness and attack on spiritual elitism.

246. _____. *Religious Sects: A Sociological Study.* New York: McGraw-Hill Book Co., 1970, 256 pp. Illus. See pp. 10-11, 218-25.

Brief discussion of Japanese New Religions in the light of an elaborate typology for interpreting "religious sects" in cross-cultural perspective.

247. WITTE, JOHANNES. *Japan zwischen zwei Kulturen.* Leipzig: J.C. Hinrichs, 1928, xii + 505 pp. See pp. 256-62.

Brief treatment of Sect Shinto (especially Tenrikyō) and Oomoto.

248. _____. "Neue Religionen in Japan." *Zeitschrift für Missionskunde und Religionswissenschaft* 32 (1917): 97-100.

Describes the growth of Oomoto (called Daihonkyo) as an illustration of the new religious movements.

*249. WOODARD, WILLIAM P. "Japan's New Religions." *Japan Harvest* 5 (Winter 1957): 18.

Cited in H[orace] Neill McFarland, "The New Religions of Japan" (entry 133, 1, no. 2), p. 38.

250. _____. "Religion in Japan in 1961: New Religions." *Contemporary Religions in Japan* 3, no. 1 (March 1962): 39-41.

Cites the continued growth of New Religions in 1961.

251. _____. "A Statistical Survey of Religions in Japan." *Contemporary Religions in Japan* 2, no. 4 (December 1961): 25-106; 3, no. 1 (March 1962): 67-99; no. 2 (June 1962): 193-204; no. 3 (September 1962): 280-90; no. 4 (December 1962): 279-88.

Includes figures on the New Religions.

252. _____. "Study on Religious Juridical Persons Law, Text of the Law No. 126 of 1951." *Contemporary Religions in Japan* 25, no. 3 (1958): 418-70; no. 4 (1959): 635-57; 26, no. 1 (1959): 96-115; no. 2 (1959): 293-312.

Text and discussion of the new law governing religious bodies in postwar Japan.

253. YANAGAWA, KEIICHI, and MORIOKA, KIYOMI, eds. *Hawaii Nikkei Shūkyō no Tenkai to Genkyō.* Tokyo: Tōkyō Daigaku Shūkyōgaku Kenkyūshitsu, 1959, 277 pp.

In Japanese. Includes English-language materials such as addresses of New Religions and the by-laws of Sekai Kyūsei-kyō.

254. YINGER, J[OHN] MILTON. *The Scientific Study of Religion.* New York: Macmillan Co., 1970, x + 593 pp. See pp. 169-71, 265, 272-73.

A sociological interpretation of Japanese New Religions as "antidotes to anomie."

255. YOSHIMURA, TADAAKI. *Commentary on Documents Regarding Establishment of Sectarian Shintoism.* Tokyo: Shinshūkyō Daikyōchō Shuppanbu (also Kokusai Shuppan Insatsusha, International Publishing & Printing Co.), 1935, 26 pp. plus 55 pp. In Japanese.

Attempts to "explain in detail . . . the cause and consequence of the emanation of public documents regarding each Shinto sect, judging from historical facts," treating the thirteen groups of Sect Shinto.

256. _____. *Shinto (The Way of the Gods).* Tokyo: Japan Time & Mail, 1935, 65 pp. Illus.

Brief treatments of fifteen Shinto sects.

257. YOSHIMURA, TADACHI. "What Is Sectarian Shinto?" *Religions in Japan at Present* 2 (1961): 20-28.

258. YOUNG, ARTHUR MORGAN. *The Rise of Pagan States: Japan's Religious Background.* New York: W. Morrow & Co.; London: George Allen & Unwin, 1939, 224 pp. See pp. 180-94.

Brief remarks on Sect Shinto.

259. ZIMMERMANN, WERNER. *Licht im Osten. Geistiges Nippon.* Munich: Drei Eichen Verlag, 1954, 112 pp. Illus.

Observations of several New Religions as part of "spiritual Japan," by the leader of a religious organization in Europe.

PART II

BIBLIOGRAPHY OF INDIVIDUAL NEW RELIGIONS

Ananaikyō

Denominational

(Unless otherwise specified, published at Shimizu by International General Headquarters of Ananaikyō.)

260. *The Ananai: A Journal for Truth Seekers.* Spring Special, 1959, 111 pp.

261. *Brief Biography of Rev. Yonosuke Nakano, President of the International Organization for Cultivating Human Spirit.* Tokyo: Publication Bureau, IOCHS World Headquarters, n.d., 56 pp. Illus.

262. *A guide to Ananai-kyō.* [195?], 26 pp. Illus.

263. *The Report on the First World Religion Congress.* 1954, 328 pp.

264. *The Report on the Second World Religion Congress.* 1954, 388 pp.

265. *The Report on the Third World Religion Congress.* 1955, 367 pp.

266. *The Report on the Fourth World Religion Congress.* 1953, 188 pp.

267. *Report on the Fifth World Religion Conference.* 1955, 224 pp.

268. *The Report of the Sixth World Religion Correspondence Congress.* 1955, 278 pp.

269. *The Report of the Seventh World Religion Correspondence Congress.* 1956, 266 pp.

270. *Report of the Eighth World Religions Congress.* 1956, 309 pp.

271.   *What Is Ananaikyo?* 1960, 32 pp.

272.   NAKANO, YONOSUKE. *A Guide to Ananaikyo.* 1955, 26 pp.

273.   _____. *Information of the International Religious Federation.*

274.   _____. *The Universe Has the Spirit.* 1954, 230 pp.

275.   _____. *The Universe Viewed from the World of the Spirit.* Compiled by
       Shin Negami. 1956, 182 pp.

       Periodicals

276.   *The Ananai.*

277.   *OISCA Bulletin Board* [Organization for Industrial Spiritual and
       Cultural Advancement-International] (Tokyo). June 1977-. Bimonthly.

       Secondary

278.   HAMMER, RAYMOND JACK.   "The Idea of God in Japan's New
       Religions" (entry 74), pp. 116-24.

279.   HERBERT, JEAN. *Dieux et sectes populaires du Japon* (entry 82), pp.
       179-82.

280.   KOBAYASHI, SAKAE. "Changes in the Japanese Religions after World
       War II (entry 115), pp. 78-82.

281.   SPAE, JOSEPH J.   "Ananaikyō, The Universal Religion."   *Japan
       Missionary Bulletin* 14, no. 1 (January-February 1960): 26-29.

282.   THOMSEN, HARRY. *The New Religions of Japan* (entry 233), pp. 143-
       52.

283.   ZIMMERMANN, WERNER. *Licht im Osten* (entry 259), pp. 16-24.

Bodaiji Mission

Denominational

No publications known.

Secondary

284. MULHOLLAND, JOHN F. *Hawaii's Religions* (entry 152), p. 274.

Bussho–Gonen Kai

Denominational

285. *Guide to Bussho-Gonen Kai.* Tokyo: Headquarters of Bussho–Gonen Kai, 1967, 24 pp. Illus.

Secondary

No publications known.

Byakkō Shinkō–kai

Denominational

(Unless otherwise specified, published at Ichikawa-shi, Chiba-ken by Brotherhood of Prayers for Peace of the World.)

*286. GOI, MASAHISA. *Evil, Good, and the Cosmic Mind.* Cited in other publications by Byakkō Shinkō–kai.

287. _____. *God and Man.* Translated by Shunsuke Takago. Ichikawa, Chiba: White Light Association, 1977, v + 144 pp.

288. _____. *Japan and World Peace Movement.* Translated by Shosaku Hara and Susumu Takahashi. Ichikawa-shi, Chiba-ken: World Peace Prayer's Society, n.d., 14 pp.

289.   _____. *Man and His Karma*. Translated by Mrs. Akama. Ichikawa, Chiba: White Light Association, n.d., 10 pp.

290.   _____. *Man and the True Way of His Life*. Translated by T. Minakami. N.d., 16 pp.

291.   _____. *May Peace Prevail on Earth!* Translated by K. Azuma. N.d., 2 pp. (Also German and Portuguese versions.)

292.   _____. *The Prayer for Peace of the World*. Translated by T. Minakami. N.d., 10 pp.

Periodicals

293.   *Heywa* (Japan). Spring 1979-. Published quarterly by the Society of Prayer for World Peace Japan.

Secondary

No publications known.

Chōwadō Henjōkyō Mission of Hawaii

Denominational

294.   FUJITA, YUKEI. *The Law of Harmony in Health and Physical Culture*. Tokyo: Chowa Shuppansha, 1929.

Secondary

295.   MULHOLLAND, JOHN F. *Hawaii's Religions* (entry 152), p. 288.

296.   YAMA, EVELYN K., and NIYEKAWA, AGNES M. "Chowado." *Social Process in Hawaii* 16 (1952), pp. 48-58.

Dōtoku Kagaku

Denominational

297. *Towards Supreme Morality.* Kashiwa: Institute of Moralogy, 1969, 65 pp. Rev. ed., 1970, 64 pp.

298. HIROIKE, CHIBUSA, and HIROIKE, CHIKURO. *An Introduction to Moral Science.* Translated by the Institute of Moralogy. Kogane: Institute of Moralogy, 1942, 274 pp.

299. HIROIKE, CHIKURŌ. *The Characteristics of Moralogy and Supreme Morality.* Translated and edited by The Institute of Moralogy. New rev. ed. Tokyo: Institute of Morality, 1966, x + 274 pp. (First English Ed., 1942.)

300. _____. *Father of Moralogy: a Pictorial Autobiography.* Chiba Ken, Japan: Dōtoku Kagaku Kenkyūjo, 1970, 59 pp. Illus.

Secondary

301. SPAE, JOSEPH J. "Dotoku Kagaku, Moralogy." *Japan Missionary Bulletin* 12, no. 10 (December 1958): 748-51.

Fusō-kyō

Denominational

302. *Sectarian Shinto (The Way of the Gods)* (entry 205), pp. 4-8.

Secondary

303. GUNDERT, WILHELM. *Japanische Religionsgeschichte* (entry 72), pp. 129-30.

+304. HOLTOM, DANIEL C. *The National Faith of Japan* (entry 85), pp. 223-27.

Gedatsu-kai

Denominational

(Unless otherwise specified, published at San Francisco by Gedatsu Church of America.)

305.   *English Prayer Book.* N.p.: Gedatsu Church of America, n.d., 17 pp.

306.   *Gedatsu Ajikan Kongozen Meditation.* Preface by G. Shiroishi. Los Angeles: n.p. ["Printed by the George Ohsawa Macrobiotic Foundation, San Francisco"], 1974, ii + 18 pp.

307.   *The Goreichi.* Kitamotojuku, Kitamoto-shi, Saitamaken: Gedatsu-kai, 1973, 23 pp. Illus. In English and Japanese; Japanese title *Goreichi Annai.*

308.   *Manual for Implementation of Gedatsu Practice.* N.p., 1965, v + 35 pp.

+309.   KISHIDA, EIZAN. *The Character and Doctrine of Gedatsu Kongo.* Translated by Louis K. Ito. 1969, 160 pp. Illus.

310.   _____. *Dynamic Analysis of Illness Through Gedatsu.* Translated by Louis K. Ito. N.p., June 1962, 153 pp.

311.   _____. *Gateway to Gedatsu.* N.d., 30 pp. Expanded ed. Tokyo: Gedatsu Kai, 1976, 33 pp.

312.   _____. *Health and Spiritual Cultivation.* Translated by Louis K. Ito. Japan: n.d., 42 pp.

Periodicals

313.   *Gedatsu Companion* (Los Angeles).

Secondary

+314.   EARHART, H[ARRY] BYRON. "Gedatsu-kai: One Life History and Its Significance for Interpreting Japanese New Religions" (entry 50).

[+]315. ____. "Toward a Theory of the Formation of the Japanese New Religions: A Case Study of Gedatsu-kai" (entry 59).

[+]316. LEBRA, TAKIE SUGIYAMA. "Ancestral Influence on the Suffering of Descendants in a Japanese Cult." In *Ancestors*. Edited by William H. Newell. The Hague: Mouton Publishers, 1976. See pp. 219-30.

317. ____. "The Interactional Perspective of Suffering and Curing in a Japanese Cult." *International Journal of Social Psychiatry* 20, nos. 3-4 (Autumn-Winter 1974): 281-86.

[+]318. ____. "Taking the Role of Supernatural 'Other': Spirit Possession in a Japanese Healing Cult." In *Culture-Bound Syndromes, Ethnopsychiatry, and Alternate Therapies*. Edited by William P. Lebra. Mental Health Research in Asia and the Pacific, vol. 4. Honolulu: University Press of Hawaii, 1976, pp. 88-100. Reprinted as "Spirit Possession: The 'Salvation Cult,'" in Takie Sugiyama Lebra, *Japanese Patterns of Behavior* (Honolulu: University Press of Hawaii, 1976), pp. 232-47.

319. OPLER, MARVIN K. "Japanese Folk Beliefs and Practices, Tule Lake, California." *Journal of American Folklore* 63 (October-December 1950): 383-97.

[+]320. ____. "Two Japanese Sects." *Southwestern Journal of Anthropology* 6 (1950): 69-78.

Genshi Fukuin Undō

Denominational

321. TESHIMA, IKURO. *Introduction to the Original Gospel Faith*. Tokyo: Light of Life Press, 1970.

Periodicals

322. *Light of Life*. Special English edition of *Seimei no Hikari*; see issues such as October and November 1973.

Secondary

+323.   CALDAROLA, CARLO. *Christianity: The Japanese Way.* Leiden:
        E.J. Brill, 1979, viii + 234 pp. See pp. 192-208.

324.   _____. "The Makuya Movement in Japan." *Japanese Religions* 7, no. 4
        (1972): 18-34.

324A.   KREIDER, ROY. "Christian Sect from Japan Makes Eighth Pilgrimage
        to Israel." *Christian News From Israel,* n.s. 23, no. 4 (Spring 1973):
        262.

                                    Hommichi

Denominational

(Unless otherwise specified, published at Osaka by Hommichi.)

325.   *The Advent of the Savior.* Guide of the Road, special issue, no. 10.
        [1950?].

326.   *Cleansing of the World.* Osaka: Tenri Hommichi, 1950, 16 pp.

327.   *The Difference Between Honmichi and Tenrikyo.* N.d., 13 pp.

328.   *Divine Words Concerning Cleansing Mind.* 1951, 64 pp.

329.   *Doctrines and Divine Miracles of Honmiti.* [Takaisi-tyō], 1956, viii +
        352 pp.

330.   *The Doro-umi-koki. (Tenrikyo's Creation Story).* 1950, 28 pp.

331.   *Faith and Superstition.* Guide of the Road, no. 4. 1947, 8 pp.

332.   *The Great Way of the World.* 1950, 17 pp.

333.   *Guide-Posts: An Introduction to "Honmiti" (A Religion in Japan).*
        1952, 96 pp.

334.   *The History of Tenri Hommichi.* 1950, 35 pp.

335. *How to Put an End to War*. Osaka: Tenri Hommichi, 1950, 10 pp.

336. *How to see the Tenri-Hommichi?* Guide of the Road, no. 9. [1950?], 10 pp.

337. *Japanese Mythology and Emperor System*. *Origin of the World*. Guide of the Road, nos. 13 and 7. [1949-1950?], 43 pp. [Two works bound as one: *Japanese Mythology and Emperor System*, pp. 1-29; *Origin of the World*, pp. 32-43.]

338. *The Origin of Sickness*. Guide of the Road, no. 16. 1949, 12 pp.

339. *The Outline of the Doctrine*. 1950, 49 pp.

340. *The View of Life and the World*. 1950, 20 pp.

341. *The World of Gods*. Guide of the Road, no. 12. 1950, 16 pp.

Secondary

341A. MURAKAMI, SHIGEYOSHI. *Japanese Religion in the Modern Century* (entry 153). See pp. 75-79, 99-100.

Hommon Butsuryū-shū

Denominational

No publications known.

Secondary

342. MURAKAMI, SHIGEYOSHI. *Japanese Religion in the Modern Century* (entry 153). See pp. 17-18, 87-88.

Ichigen no Miya

Denominational

No publications known.

Secondary

+343.   SANADA, TAKAAKI. "After a Prophecy Failed: A Reappraisal of a
Japanese Case." In *Proceedings of Tokyo Meeting of the International
Conference on Sociology of Religion.* Edited by Organizing Committee
for Tokyo Meeting of CISR 1978. Tokyo: Organizing Committee for
Tokyo Meeting of CISR 1978, 1978, 284 pp. See pp. 131-46. Reprinted
in *Japanese Journal of Religious Studies* 6, nos. 1-2 (March–June
1979): 217-37.

+344.   ____, and NORBECK, E[DWARD]. "Prophecy Continues to Fail: A
Japanese Sect." *Journal of Cross-Cultural Psychiatry* 6, no. 3
(September 1975): 331-45.

Iesu no Mitama Kyōkai Kyōdan

Denominational

No publications known.

Secondary

345.   ANZAI, SHIN. "Newly-adopted Religions and Social Change on the
Ryukyu Islands (Japan) (With Special Reference to Catholicism)" (entry
8).

346.   BRAUN, NEIL. *Laity Mobilized: Reflections on Church Growth in
Japan* (entry 31), pp. 37, 161, 171-73.

+347.   YAMADA, HIROSHI, and BETHEL, DAYLE M. "The Spirit of Jesus
Church." *Japanese Christian Quarterly* 30, no. 3 (July 1964): 220-24.

Izumo Taisha-kyō

Denominational

348. *Izumo-Oyashiro-kyo. The Wost* [*sic*; Most?] *Natural Form of Jinja-Shinto.* Taisha-machi, Shimane Prefecture, Japan: Izumo-Oyashiro-Kyo, [197?], 155 pp. Illus.

349. *Sectarian Shinto (The Way of the Gods)* (entry 205), pp. 53-57.

Secondary

350. HERBERT, JEAN. *Dieux et sectes populaires du Japon* (entry 82), pp. 128-29.

⁺351. HOLTOM, DANIEL C. *The National Faith of Japan* (entry 85), pp. 199-204.

⁺352. SCHWARTZ, M.L. "The Great Shrines of Idzumo: Some Notes on Shintō, Ancient and Modern." *Transactions of the Asiatic Society of Japan* 41, pt. 4 (1913): 493-681.

Jikkō-kyō

Denominational

353. *Sectarian Shinto (The Way of the Gods)* (entry 205), pp. 9-12.

354. SHIBATA, REIICHI (REUCHI). "Shintoism." In *The World's Parliament of Religions.* Vol. 1, edited by John Henry Barrows. Chicago: Parliament Publishing Co., 1893, pp. 451-55. (Also printed in other works recording this parliament.)

355. Untitled address. In *Congress of Japanese Religionists.* Tokyo: Kinkodo Publishing Co., [1905?]. See pp. 42-45.

Secondary

356.   GUNDERT, WILHELM. *Japanische Religionsgeschichte* (entry 72), pp. 129-30.

+357. HOLTOM, DANIEL C.   *The National Faith of Japan* (entry 85), pp. 216-23.

Kagami no Hongi

Denominational

No publications known.

Secondary

358.   SPAE, JOSEPH J.   "Mirrorism (Kagami no hongi) or Lightianity (Hikari-kyō)." *Missionary Bulletin* 9, no. 10 (October 1955): 583-87.

Kami Ichijō-kyō

Denominational

359.   YONETANI, GYOKUSUISEN.   "The History of Kamiichijoism." Typescript, personal files of H[arry] Byron Earhart, 6 pp.

Secondary

No publications known.

Kōdō-chi-kyō

Denominational

No publications known.

Secondary

+360. "Kōdō-chi-kyō, a Strange Religion." In *Reminiscences of Religion in Postwar Japan.* Edited by Union of the New Religious Organizations in Japan, Research Office (entry 238), pp. 243-48.

Kōdō Kyōdan

Denominational

(Unless otherwise specified, published at Yokohama by Kōdō Kyōdan.)

361. *Hieisan and Kodosan Buddhist Services for celebrating the Completion of the Main Auditorium of Enryakuji Temple and commemorating the Latest Anniversary of the Passing Away of Saint Jikaku.* 1964, pages not numbered. Illus.

362. *Kodo-kyodan: Layman Buddhism in Japan.* N.d., 40 pp.

363. *Pictorial Kodo-san Hanamatsuri.* N.d., 50 pp. Illus.

364. OKANO, KIMIKO. *The Heart of Bodhisattva.* 1970.

365. OKANO, SHODO. *An Introduction to Kodo Kyodan Buddhism.* Translated by Taitetsu Unno. Postscript by Ken Shiiya. 1967, 252 pp. Illus.

Periodicals

366. *Kodo News.*

Secondary

No publications known.

Kokuchūkai

Denominational

(Unless otherwise specified, published at Tokyo by The Kokuchūkai.)

367. *Graphic Biography of Chigaku Tanaka.* Translated by Alfred Bloom. [1965], 30 pp.

368. *What Is Nichirenism? Buddhist Reformation in Japan. (Advocacy of the Kokuchukai).* 1954, 12 pp.

369. KUWABARA (KINVABARA), T.J., trans.   "The Nichiren Sect of Buddhism" and "Nichiren Tradition in Pictures" [translated from the work of Chigaku Tanaka].   In *The Open Court* 27, no. 5 (May 1913): 289-301; no. 6 (June 1913): 334-50.

370. TANAKA, CHIGAKU.   *What is Nippon Kokutai?   Introduction to Nipponese National Principles.* Translated by Kishio Satomi. Tokyo: Shishio Bunko, 1935-36.   Nos. 1-12 (continuous pagination), 335 pp. Appendix 1, "Translator's General Explanation," Kishio Satomi, 7 pp. Appendix 2, "The Emperor Jimmu (The Founder of Nippon)," trans. W.G. Aston, 27 pp.

Secondary

+371. LEE, EDWIN B. "Nichiren and Nationalism: The Religious Patriotism of Tanaka Chigaku." *Monumenta Nipponica* 30, no. 1 (Spring 1975): 19-36.

372. MORRIS, IVAN I. *Nationalism and the Right Wing in Japan: A Study of Post-War Trends.* London: Oxford University Press, 1960, 476 pp. See p. 185 for Tanaka Chigaku, founder of Kokuchūkai.

373. SATOMI, KISHIO.   *Japanese Civilization, Its Significance and Realization.   Nichirenism and the Japanese National Principles.* London: Kegan Paul, Trench, Trubner & Co., 1923; New York: E.P. Dutton, 1924. Reprint. 1929, xiv + 238 pp. See pp. 228-30. (See also Tanaka in Denominational materials.)

374.   VALISINHA, DEVAPRIYA (General Secretary of Maha Bodhi Society of India). "Congratulations to the 50th Anniversary of the Kokuchukai." In *Kokuchūkai Gojūnen no Ayumi*. 1964, p. 37.

Konkōkyō

Denominational

(Unless otherwise specified, published at the city of Konkō by Konkō Hombu Kyōchō.)

375.   *The Founder of Konko Religion*. 1966, 108 pp.

376.   *Konko-kyo: A New Religion of Japan*. 1945, 8 pp. Reprint. 1958.

377.   *Outline of the History and Present Situation since World War II*. 1956.

378.   *The Sacred Scriptures of Konkokyo*.   Konko-cho, Okayama-ken: Headquarters of Konkokyo, 1973, 71 pp.

379.   *The Sacred Scriptures of Konkokyo. With an Introduction*. Translated by Konkokyo Hombu. 1933, xxxiii + 48 pp.

380.   ANDO, ICHIMARU, trans. "The Scriptures." Unpublished paper, 1963, 92 pp. In the files of Konkō-kyo headquarters. In Russian.

381.   FUKUDA, YOSHIAKI. *Hand Book of the Konko Mission*.   San Francisco: Konko Mission, n.d., 43 pp.

382.   FUKUSHIMA, YOSHITSUGU. "On the Faith of Konko Daijin—An Introductory Outline of the Faith of the Founder of Konkokyo." Unpublished paper, 1961, 28 pp.   In the files of Konkō-kyo headquarters.

383.   HATA, YASUSHI. "A Konko-kyo Minister's comments on 'Konkō-kyō' by Dr. Delwin Schneider." *Contemporary Religions in Japan* 4, no. 4 (December 1963): 358-59. See entry 412.

384.   No entry.

385.   MIYAKE, TOSHIO. "The Obligation of Religion in our Era." In *The World Religions Speak on "The Relevance of Religion in the Modern World".* Edited by Finley P. Dunne, Jr. The Hague: Dr. W. Junk N.V. Publishers, 1970, pp. 182-86.

386.   NISHIMURA, SHOZEN. *Manual of Konkokyo.* 1956.

387.   OFUCHI, CHIHIRO.   *The Faith of Konko Daijin.*   Konkokyo Headquarters, 1972.

388.   OKAMOTO, MASAYUKI. *The Life of the Founder.* Translated by Yutaka Yokoyama. Konkō Kyōtosha Foundation, 1962, 133 pp. Illus. (Japanese and English text.)

389.   SATO, KAZUO. *Konkōkyō.* International Institute for the Study of Religions, 1962.

390.   _____. *Sacred Scriptures.* 1933, 81 pp.

391.   *Sectarian Shinto (The Way of the Gods)* (entry 205), pp. 13-17.

392.   TAKAHASHI, ICHIRO. "The Essence of Konko-kyo." Translated by Yoshitsugu Fukushima. Unpublished paper, 1961, 66 pp. In the files of Konkō-kyō headquarters.

Periodicals

393.   *The Journal of the Konkokyo Theological Research Institute.*

Secondary

394.   ANESAKI, MASAHARU. *History of Japanese Religion* (entry 3), p. 372.

395.   BACH, MARCUS. *Strangers at the Door* (entry 13), pp. 125-28.

396.   CLARK, EDWARD M. "Konko Kyo." *Japan Evangelist* 32 (April 1925): 125-29; (May 1925): 164-68.

397.   _____. "Kon-Kō-Kyō (A Modern Sect of Shintoism)." Ph.D. dissertation, Edinburgh University, 1924, iv + 145 pp. Copy in the personal files of H[arry] Byron Earhart.

398. DUTHU, J.B. "La secte Konkō." *Mélanges japonais* 6, no. 21 (January 1909): 1-22.

399. EMBREE, JOHN F. *Acculturation Among the Japanese of Kona, Hawaii.* Memoirs of the American Anthropological Association, no. 59. Menasha, WI: American Anthropological Association, 1941, 162 pp. See p. 119.

400. GUNDERT, WILHELM. *Japanische Religionsgeschichte* (entry 72), pp. 136-37.

401. HAMMER, RAYMOND JACK. "The Idea of God in Japan's New Religions" (entry 74), pp. 94-105, 186-243.

402. HOLTOM, DANIEL C. "Konkō Kyō—A Modern Japanese Monotheism." *Journal of Religion* 13, no. 3 (July 1933): 279-300.

+403. _____. *The National Faith of Japan* (entry 85), pp. 257-66.

404. KOBAYASHI, SAKAE. "Changes in the Japanese Religions after World War II" (entry 115), pp. 53-58.

405. LANCZKOWSKI, GÜNTHER. *Die neuen Religionen* (entry 126), pp. 23-27.

406. LIPP, FREDRICK. "The Religious Dimension and Practical Function of the Kekkai in the Church of the Konko-kyo Religion." Unpublished paper, 1961, 14 pp. In the files of Konkō-kyō headquarters.

+407. McFARLAND, H[ORACE] NEILL. *The Rush Hour of the Gods* (entry 136), pp. 97-122.

408. MURAKAMI, SHIGEYOSHI. *Japanese Religion in the Modern Century* (entry 153), pp. 15-17, 44-46.

409. OPLER, MARVIN K. "Two Japanese Sects." *Southwestern Journal of Anthropology* 6 (1950): 69-78.

+410. PETTAZZONI, RAFFAELE. "Sur un prétendu monothéisme Japonais." In *Proceedings of the IXth International Congress for the History of Religions, 1958.* Tokyo: Maruzen, 1960, pp. 393-97.

+411. ROTH, WILHELM, with KONDŌ, RYŌSUKE. "Konkōkyō: Die Lehre von Konko." *Mitteilungen der Deutschen Gesellschaft für Natur- und Völkerkunde Ostasiens* 26, pt. A (1932): 1-35.

+412. SCHNEIDER, DELWIN B. *Konkokyo, A Japanese Religion: A Study in the Continuities of Native Faiths.* Tokyo: International Institute for the Study of Religions, 1962, xv + 166 pp.

413. _____. "Konkokyo: A Religion of Meditation." *Contemporary Religions in Japan* 2, no. 1 (March 1961): 39-54.

414. SPAE, JOSEPH J. "Konkōkyō." *Missionary Bulletin* 9, nos. 8-9 (August-September 1955): 501-4.

415. THOMSEN, HARRY. *The New Religions of Japan* (entry 233), pp. 69-78.

Kurozumi-kyō

Denominational

*416. KIYAMA, K. *The Life of a Great Man, Kurozumi-Munetada.* Cited in Harry Thomsen, *Bibliography of the New Religions* (entry 229), p. 13.

417. KURADA, T. *The Truth of Kami (The Founder of the Kurozumi Sect).* Tokyo, 1893.

418. KUROZUMI, TADAAKI. *Kurozumi Munetada and His Religion.* N.p., 1979, 17 pp.

419. *Sectarian Shinto (The Way of the Gods)* (entry 205), pp. 18-21.

420. TANAKA, GORO. *The Brief Outline of the Kurozumi-kyo, the most Genuine Japanese Religious Faith.* Omoto, Okayama: Nisshinsha, 1956, 10 pp. (Japanese and English text.)

Secondary

421. ANESAKI, MASAHARU. *History of Japanese Religion* (entry 3), p. 315.

422. CARY, O. "The Kurozumi Sect of Shinto." *Andover Review* 11, no. 46 (June 1889): 640-49.

423. DUTHU, J.B. "Kurozumi-Kyō: La secte shintoiste Kurozumi." *Mélanges japonais* 5 (1908): 131-51, 284-307, 420-42.

424. GUNDERT, WILHELM. *Japanische Religionsgeschichte* (entry 72), pp. 130-31.

425. HAMMER, RAYMOND JACK. "The Idea of God in Japan's New Religions" (entry 74), pp. 75-79.

426. HEPNER, CHARLES WILLIAM. "The Fundamental Ideas of Kurozumi Munetada and their Sources." *Transactions of Meiji Japan Society* 45 (1936): 1-5.

426A. _____. *The Kurozumi Sect of Shintō*. Ph.D. dissertation, Yale University, 1933, 298 pp.

+427. _____. *The Kurozumi Sect of Shintō*. Tokyo: Meiji Japan Society, 1935, xviii + 263 pp.

+428. HOLTOM, DANIEL C. *The National Faith of Japan* (entry 85), pp. 245-56.

429. LANCZKOWSKI, GÜNTER. *Die neuen Religionen* (entry 126), pp. 11-15.

430. LAUBE, JOHANNES. "Zur Bedeutungsgeschichte des Konfuzianistischen Begriffs 'Makoto' ('Wahrhaftigkeit')." In *Fernöstliche Kultur.* Edited by Helga Wormit. Marburg: N.G. Elwert Verlag, 1975, pp. 100-57. See pp. 139-47.

431. MURAKAMI, SHIGEYOSHI. *Japanese Religion in the Modern Century* (entry 153), pp. 12-13.

432. THOMSEN, HARRY. *The New Religions of Japan* (entry 233), pp. 61-67.

Maruyama-kyō

Denominational

No publications known.

Secondary

433. MURAKAMI, SHIGEYOSHI. *Japanese Religion in the Modern Century* (entry 153), pp. 49-50, 134-35.

Miizu-kai

Denominational

434. KAWAZURA (KAWATSURA), BONJI. *Manifesto*. Translated by Shunji Inoue. Tokyo: Miizu-kai, 1965, 16 pp. Illus. (Plus Japanese text.)

435. SHIRADO, NAKAKO. *An Introduction to Shinto of Rev. Bonji Kawazura*. Tokyo: Miizu-Kai, n.d., 8 pp.

Secondary

No publications known.

Misogi-kyō

Denominational

436. *Sectarian Shinto (The Way of the Gods)* (entry 205), pp. 22-26.

Secondary

437. GUNDERT, WILHELM. *Japanische Religionsgeschichte* (entry 72), pp. 131-32.

+438.   HOLTOM, DANIEL C. *The National Faith of Japan* (entry 85), pp. 240-44.

Nyorai-kyō

Denominational

No publications known.

Secondary

439.   ANESAKI, MASAHARU. *History of Japanese Religion* (entry 3), pp. 310-13.

+440.   DUMOULIN, HEINRICH, and ISHIBASHI, TOMONOBU. "Aus dem Kanon der Nyoraikyo." *Monumenta Nipponica* 1, no. 1 (1938): 222-41.

441.   GUNDERT, WILHELM. *Japanische Religionsgeschichte* (entry 72), pp. 137-39.

+442.   ISHIBASHI, TOMONOBU. "Eine unbekannte Volksreligion in Japan." *Proceedings of the Imperial Academy of Japan* 4 (1928): 4-7, 89-91. See also *Commemoration Volume of the Science of Religion in Tokyo Imperial University* (Tokyo: Herald Press, 1934), pp. 229-42.

443.   WALEY, ARTHUR. "Kono Tabi: A Little-known Japanese Religion." *Bulletin of the School of Oriental Studies* 7 (1933-35): 105-9. Reprinted in Arthur Waley, *The Secret History of the Mongols and Other Pieces* (New York: Barnes & Noble, 1963), pp. 141-46.

Ontake-kyō

Denominational

444.   *Sectarian Shinto (The Way of the Gods)* (entry 205), pp. 27-30.

Secondary

⁺445.   HOLTOM, DANIEL C.   *The National Faith of Japan* (entry 85), pp. 227-31.

⁺446.   LOWELL, PERCIVAL.   *Occult Japan or the Way of the Gods* (entry 132), esp. pp. 1-192.

447.   WALTON, W[ILLIAM] H. MURRAY.   *Scrambles in Japan and Formosa.* London: Edward Arnold Co., 1934, 304 pp. Illus. See pp. 99-141.

Oomoto

Denominational

(Unless otherwise specified, published at Kameoka by the Oomoto Headquarters or the Oomoto Central Office.)

448.   *A alegria de viver* [The joy of living]. Translated by J. de C. Bretas. 1974, 198 pp. In Portuguese.

449.   *Brief Sketch of Oomoto.* N.d., 15 pp.

450.   *Dek gvidprincipoj de la Oomoto-movado, kan la komentoj de Jasuo Sakurai* [Ten guiding principles of the Oomoto movement, with comments by Yasuo Sakurai]. 1960, 24 pp. In Esperanto.

451.   *Diálogos elucidativos para a Juventude* [Enlightening dialogues for youth]. Translated by J. de C. Bretas. 1966, 98 pp. In Portuguese.

452.   *The Foundation of Japanese Culture and the Oomoto Religion: Relation between the Culture in Tamba Region and the Oomoto Religion.* Translated by Yoshi Suzumori. 1957, 11 pp. (Also French edition, translated H. Kato.)

453.   *Giganto Onisabro Degûĉi reviviĝas en Parizo* [The giant Onisaburo Deguchi comes to life again in Paris]. 1975, 23 pp. In Esperanto.

454.   No entry.

455.   *Guide de la voie.* 1957, 14 pp.

456.   *La hombildo de diversaj religioj* [The human picture of various religions]. 1970, 34 pp. In Esperanto.

457.   *Kio estas Oomoto?* [What is Oomoto?]. 1933, 93 pp. In Esperanto.

458.   *Kiss of Peace.* 1978, 96 pp. (Pages numbered right to left.) Illus.

459.   *La konfliktoj en Manĉurio kaj Ŝanhajo: Pri la agado de Universale Homama Asocio en Ĉinujo* [The conflicts in Manchuria and Shanghai: On the action of the Universal Love and Brotherhood Movement in China]. 1932. In Esperanto.

460.   *Kvinteto: Ekstraktoj el verkoj de Nao, Onisabro, Sumiko, Hidemaru kaj Naohi Deguĉi* [Quintet: Extracts from works by Nao, Onisaburo, Sumiko, Hidemaru, and Naohi Deguchi]. Translated by T. Nakamura. 1965, 63 pp. In Esperanto.

461.   *Memorlibro de Oomoto—internacia festivalo* [Memory-book of Oomoto—international festival]. 1965, 73 pp. In Esperanto.

462.   *Noo (Japana klasika dancdrama)* [Noh (Japanese classical dance drama)]. Translated by T. Mikami. 1963, 15 pp. In Esperanto.

463.   *Ofudesaki, The Holy Scriptures of Oomoto: Excerpts.* Translated by Iwao P. Hino. 1974.

464.   *The Oomoto Art Exhibition in Europe and America.*   1976, 92 pp. (Pages numbered right to left.) Illus.

465.   *Oomoto: Ever Living Up to Peace Doctrine.* 1962, 29 pp.

465A. *Oomoto Incidents and Oomoto Under World Scrutiny.* Translated by Yoshi Suzumori. 1957, 15 pp.

466.   *Oomoto: La nova spirita movado* [Oomoto: The new spiritual movement]. Ayabe, 1924, 8 + 40 pp. In Esperanto.

467.   *The Oomoto Movement: Its Origin, Aims and Objects and the Universal Love and Brotherhood Association.* 1950. 2d ed., 1952, 33 pp. 3d ed., 1955, 48 pp.

468. *Oomoto—sepdekjara* [Oomoto—seventy years old]. 1967, 20 pp. In Esperanto.

469. *Oomoto's View of Art.* 1957, 8 pp.

470. *Oomoto, the New Spiritual Movement.* Pamphlet. Ayabe: Oomoto Overseas Office, 1925.

471. *The Outline of Oomoto.* 1958, 34 pp. 2d ed., enlarged and revised, 1968, 92 pp., with Errata slip. 3d ed., ed. Iwao Hino, 1970.

472. *Partial Portraits of Master Onisaburo Deguchi.* Translated by Yoshi Suzumori. 1957, 22 pp.

473. *El plan general de Oomoto.* 1961, 27 pp.

474. *Putevodnoe slovo* [Word of guidance]. Translated by M. Kobayashi. 1962, 14 pp. In Russian.

475. *Q's and A's on Oomoto for Young Adults.* 1975, 66 pp.

476. *Universal Love and Brotherhood Movement.* ULBA Headquarters, 1977, 16 pp.

477. *Utafesta poemaro* [Poetry collection of Uta-celebration]. 1966, 104 pp. In Esperanto.

478. *What is Oomoto?* Paris: European Oomoto Office. 1926, 56 pp. 2d ed, [Kameoka]: n.p., 1935, 136 pp. Illus.

479. DEGUCHI, E. *Comments on the Oomoto Ofudesaki.* Translated by I. Hino. 1976, 38 pp.

480. DEGUCHI, ISAO. "Oomoto (Great Foundation)." *Contemporary Religions in Japan* 4, no. 3 (September 1963): 230-39.

481. DEGUCHI, KYŌTARŌ (DEGUTI, KIOTARO). *My Travels in Esperanto-land.* Translated by Michael A.L. Lamb. 1968, 189 pp. Illus.

482. _____. *Onisaburo Deguchi: Un grand homme.* 1972, 233 pp.

483. DEGUCHI, NAO. *Scripture of Oomoto.* Translated by Teruo Nakamura, 1957, 11 pp.

484. DEGUCHI, ONISABURO. *Didactic Poems by O. Deguchi (A Selection from "Aizen no Miti")*. Translated by Hikosaku Yanagijima. 1957, 30 pp.

485. _____ (DEGUĈI, ONISABRO). *Fundamento de animo* [Basis of spirit]. 1931. In Esperanto.

486. _____. *A Guide to God's Way: Extracts from the Scripture, "Miti no Siori" Written in 1925.* Translated by Teruo Nakamura. 1957, 23 pp. (Also French edition, trans. H. Kato.)

487. _____ (DEGUTSHI). "Mitshi-no shiori—Blumen auf dem Wege. . . . (Aus der Bruderbewegung, Oomoto)." *Die Weisse Fahne* 12 (1931): 568-69.

488. _____. *Perpoema vortaro Esperanto-Japana* [Esperanto-Japanese dictionary in poetry]. 2d ed., 1971, 450 pp. In Esperanto.

489. HINO, IWAO P. "The Grand Festival of the Omoto Foundress." *Contemporary Religions in Japan* 4, no. 3 (September 1963): 239-43.

490. _____. *A Little Glossary of Religious Terms.* 1975, 31 pp.

491. _____, trans. *Memoirs by O. Deguchi.* 1957, 21 pp.

492. _____, ed. *The Outline of Oomoto.* 1958. 2d ed., enlarged and revised, 1968. 3d ed., 1970, 92 pp.

493. INOUE, TOMEGORŌ. *Klarigo de Kamigakari, laŭ la verkoj de Sinjoro Onisabro Deguĉi* [Explanation of *Kamigakari*, according to the works of Mr. Onisaburo Deguchi]. Translated by Nishimura Kōgetsu. Paris, 1926. In Esperanto.

494. ITOO, EIZOO; ESUMI, NORIYA; and NAKAMURA, TAZUO. *Kvindek jaroj de Esperanto en Oomoto* [Fifty years of Esperanto in Oomoto]. 1973. In Esperanto.

495. MURAI, TŌJŪRŌ. *What Is "Oomoto"? Why Do We Believe in Oomoto?* 1957, 14 pp.

496. NAKAMURA, T. *Enciklopedieto Japana* [A little Japanese encyclopedia]. N.p.: KOSMO, 1964, 217 pp. In Esperanto.

497. NISHIMURA, KŌGETSU. *Origino de Oomoto: Sankta vivo de Nao Deguĉi, kreintino de Oomoto-movado* [Origin of Oomoto: Holy life of Nao Deguchi, foundress of the Oomoto movement]. Ayabe, 1925. In Esperanto.

498. _____, ed. *Sambishû, sinjoro laŭdata: Dediĉaĵoj al S-ro Onisabro Deguĉi okaze de lia reliberiĝo* [Sambishû, a highly praised gentleman: Dedications to Mr. Onisaburo Deguchi on the occasion of his regaining freedom]. 1928. In Esperanto.

499. _____ (NISHIMURA, KOOGECU), and SCHMIDT, K.O.   *Oomoto. Neugeist in Japan. Lehre und Praxis. Alltagsbemeisterung durch japanische Geistesschulung.*   Bücher der "Weissen Fahne" 42. Pfullingen in Wurtemberg: Johannes Baum Verlag, 1927, 30 pp.

500. OKAKURA, K[AKUZŌ]. *La libro de teo* [The book of tea]. Translated by T. Nakamura. N.p.: KOSMO, 1965, 132 pp. In Esperanto.

501. ONO, EIICHI.   "Personal Testimony: Recovery from Cancer." *Contemporary Religions in Japan* 4, no. 3 (September 1963): 244-47.

502. SAKURAI, YASUO, ed. *The Basic Teachings of Oomoto*. Translated by Teruo Nakamura. 1955. 2d ed., 1961, 36 pp.

503. _____. *Guiding Principles of Oomoto: Movement*. 1960, 26 pp. (Also Esperanto edition, trans. T. Nakamura; Portuguese edition, trans. Mozart Varella; Spanish edition, trans. Shigenori Kakui.)

504. STEINER, R. *The New Outline of Oomoto*. 1977, 30 pp.

505. No entry.

      Periodicals

506. *Oomoto*. 1925-32, 1950-. Esperanto bimonthly.

507. *Oomoto*. 1956-. English quarterly. Official organ of Oomoto and Universal Love and Brotherhood Association.

508. *Oomoto Internacia* [Oomoto International].   Monata organo de Universala Homama Associo. (Paris), 1925-32. Kameoka, 1933-35. In Esperanto.

509. *Oomoto, oficiala organa de Oomoto kaj U.H.A.* [Oomoto, Official Organ of Oomoto and U.H.A.]. 1950-. In Esperanto.

510. *Verda Mondo.*

Secondary

511. ANESAKI, MASAHARU. *History of Japanese Religion* (entry 3), pp. 397-98.

512. *L'art d'Onisaburō (1871-1948) et de son école.* Paris: Musée Cernuschi, 1972, 83 pp. Illus.

513. BENZ, ERNST. *Asiatische Begegnungen: Stationen einer Reise nach Japan und Indien.* Düsseldorf and Cologne: Eugen Diederichs Verlag, 1963, 300 pp. See pp. 178-201.

514. BRADEN, CHARLES S. *Modern Tendencies in World Religions.* London: Allen & Unwin; New York: Macmillan Co., 1933, xi + 343 pp. See pp. 147-49.

515. BURKERT, RUDOLF. "Ōmoto oder von der Hütte Gottes auf Erden." *Die Glocke* 9, no. 1 (1929): 10-11.

516. DEVARANNE, THEODOR. "Fortgang der Omotokyo-Bewegung." *Zeitschrift für Missionskunde und Religionswissenschaft* 40 (1925): 24-25.

517. FERNANDES, GONÇALVES. "Uma seita nipo-brasileria: A Associação Universal Humanitária" [A Japanese-Brazilian sect: The Universal Love and Brotherhood Association]. In *O sincretismo religioso no Brasil.* Curitiba, Brazil: Editora Guira, 1941, pp. 77-94. Illus. In Portuguese.

518. FRANCK, FREDERICK. *An Encounter with Oomoto. "The Great Origin": A Faith Rooted in the Ancient Mysticism and the Traditional Arts of Japan.* West Nyack, NY: Cross Currents, n.d. [© 1975], 63 pp.

519. GERLITZ, PETER. *Gott erwacht in Japan: Neue fernöstliche Religionen und ihre Botschaft vom Glück* (entry 69), pp. 75-102.

520.   GRAY, WALLACE. "Oomoto and Teilhard de Chardin: Two Case Studies in Revitalization." *Japanese Religions* 8, no. 1 (March 1974): 19-46.

521.   HAMMER, RAYMOND JACK. "The Idea of God in Japan's New Religions" (entry 74), pp. 106-15.

522.   HERBERT, JEAN. *Aux sources du Japon. Le Shinto.* Paris: Éditions Albin Michel, 1964, 374 pp. See pp. 304-5.

523.   _____. *Dieux et sectes populaires du Japon* (entry 82), pp. 166-79.

523A.   HIBBARD, E.L. "Interview with Leaders of Oomoto-Kyo." *Japan Christian Quarterly* 28 (October 1962): 228-32.

524.   HÜCKEL. "Die Rolle der Oomoto ('Religion')." *Zeitschrift für Missionskunde und Religionswissenschaft* 43 (1928): 117-19.

525.   KITAMURA, R. "Oomoto: Nova spirita movado en Japanujo" [Oomoto: A new spiritual movement in Japan]. *Esperanto* (Geneva) 20 (1924): 40-41. In Esperanto.

526.   KOBAYASHI, SAKAE. "Changes in the Japanese Religions after World War II" (entry 115), pp. 65-71.

+527.   _____. "Ōmoto, A Religion of Salvation." *Japanese Religions* 1, no. 2 (April 1960): 38-50.

528.   KOHLER, WERNER. *Die Lotus-Lehre und die modernen Religionen in Japan* (entry 118), pp. 58-68.

529.   KUNZE, R. "Eine neue Religion in Japan." *Ostasiatische Rundschau* 2 (1921): 104-7.

530.   LANCZKOWSKI, GÜNTER. *Die neuen Religionen* (entry 126), pp. 27-32.

531.   "Leaders of Outlawed Sect Placed on Trial." *China Weekly Review* 89 (22 July 1939): 247.

+532.   LINS, ULRICH. *Die Ōmoto-Bewegung und der radikale Nationalismus in Japan.* Inaugural dissertation, Universität zu Köln, 1976. Published under the same title. Studien zur Geschichte des neunzehnten Jahrhunderts, no. 8. Munich: R. Oldenbourg Verlag, 1976, 300 pp.

533. LJUNGDAHL, VILMAR. "Oomoto-kyo, en ny religion? Japanese bolsjevism" [Ōmoto-kyō, a New Religion? Japanese Bolshevism]. *Svensk Tidskrift* 2 (1921): 167-78. In Swedish.

+534. MURAKAMI, SHIGEYOSHI. *Japanese Religion in the Modern Century* (entry 153), pp. 70-75, 85-86, 95-99, 133-35.

535. NADOLSKI, THOMAS PETER. "Ōmoto and the Japanese Imperial Government." In *Nihon bunka kenkyū ronshū/Studies in Japanese Culture.* Vol. 2. Tokyo, 1973, pp. 26-32.

536. _____. "The Socio-political Background of the 1921 and 1935 Ōmoto Suppressions in Japan." Ph.D. dissertation, University of Pennsylvania, 1975, 286 pp. Abstracted in *Dissertation Abstracts International* 36, no. 5 (November 1975): 3048A. University Microfilms International order no. 75-24,107.

537. NIETO, C. "Die Prophetin von Ayabe und der Omoto Kyo." *Die katholischen Missionen* (1921): 131.

538. OFFNER, CLARK B., and STRAELEN, HENRY (HENRICUS J.J.M.) van. *Modern Japanese Religions* (entry 175), pp. 61-70.

539. "Ōmoto-Kyō, an Account of One of Japan's Popular Faiths, By a Japanese Scholar." *Chronicle Reprints*, no. 1. Kobe: Japan Chronicle, 1920.

RAZUMOV, S.P. See Tanin, O., and Yohan, E. (entry 544A).

540. SAUNDERS, KENNETH. "Glimpses of the Religious Life in New Japan" (entry 202).

541. SCHILLER, EMIL. "Ōmotokyō, die neueste Religion Japans." *Zeitschrift für Missionskunde und Religionswissenschaft* 38 (1923): 97-116, 129-42. Reprinted in *Das Junge Japan* 2, no. 1 (1925): 9-27; no. 7: 1-15.

*541A. SIBIRYAKOV, P. "Kamioka" [Kameoka]. *Gunbao*, 7 and 12 February 1932. In Russian. Cited in O. Tanin and E. Yohan, *Militarism and Fascism in Japan* (entry 544A), pp. 252-53.

542. SOUHART, ODETTE. "Ōmoto-kyō. Polythéisme moderne." *Bulletin de la Société franco-japonaise de Paris* 48 (April-June 1921): 89-92.

543.   SPAE, JOSEPH J.   "Ōmotokyō."   *Missionary Bulletin* 10, no. 9
       (November 1956): 668-73.

544.   SUGAI, TAIKA.   "The Soteriology of New Religions" (entry 221), pp.
       38-44.

544A. TANIN, O., and YOHAN, E. (pseud.).   *Militarism and Fascism in
       Japan*.   Introduction by Karl Radek.   London: M. Lawrence; New
       York: International Publishers, 1934, vi + 320 pp. See pp. 81, 252-53.
       Note: apparently the author of this work, who usually wrote under the
       pen name of O.S. Tarkhanov, is S.P. Razumov; see E. Stuart Kirby,
       Russian Studies of Japan: An Exploratory Survey (New York: St.
       Martin's Press), 1981, xvi + 226. See esp. pp. 31-32, 208.

545.   THOMSEN, HARRY.   *The New Religions of Japan* (entry 233), pp. 127-
       41.

546.   TUCKER, BEVERLEY D.   "Christian Worship with Omoto-kyo."
       Japanese Religions 9, no. 4 (July 1977): 60-63.

547.   WITTE, JOHANNES.   "Missionsarbeit der japanischen Omotokyo
       Religion in Europa."   *Zeitschrift für Missionskunde und
       Religionswissenschaft* 41 (1926): 144-46.

548.   _____.   "Neue Religion in Japan" (entry 248).

549.   _____.   "Neues von der Daihonkyō (Ōmotokyō)–Sekte." *Zeitschrift für
       Missionskunde und Religionswissenschaft* 35 (1921): 150-55.

550.   _____.   "Eine Propagandaschrift der neuen Religion Japans, der
       Omotokyo."   *Zeitschrift für Missionskunde und Religionswissenschaft*
       40 (1925): 225-42.

551.   _____.   "Verfolgung der Omotokyo-Bewegung in Japan." *Zeitschrift für
       Missionskunde und Religionswissenschaft* 37 (1923): 60-61.

552.   _____.   "Zwei Abschnitte aus der Reikai-Monogatari der Omotokyo."
       Zeitschrift für Missionskunde und Religionswissenschaft 40 (1925):
       257-69.

553.   "Worshippers of God."   *Hibbert Journal* 64, no. 252 (Autumn 1965): 16-
       18.

554.   ZIMMERMANN, WERNER. *Licht im Osten* (entry 259), pp. 42–50.

PL Kyōdan

Denominational

(Unless otherwise specified, published at Tondabayashi by The Perfect Liberty Order.)

555.   *Calendário PL (Anual)* [The PL calendar]. Editora Vida Artistica E.V.A. Rio de Janeiro: Publiçacões da Instituição Religiosa Perfect Liberty no Brasil. In Portuguese.

556.   *An Essay on the Way of Life.* N.d., 13 pp. N.d., 36 pp. (Text in English and French.)

557.   *A Guide to a Happy Life.* N.d., 8 pp.

558.   *How to Live a Happy Life: Introduction to Church of Perfect Liberty.* Glendale, CA: North American Headquarters, 1978.

559.   *PL.* 1958, 24 pp. 1959, 32 pp. (Text in English and French.) 1964, 20 pp. (Also Portuguese edition.)

560.   *PL: A Modern Religion for Modern Man.* [1968], 23 pp. Illus.

561.   *The PL Handbook.* 1964, 16 pp. (Later reissued, without songs, as *The PL Kyōten.*) (Also Spanish edition.)

562.   *The PL Kyōten.* N.d., 12 pp. (Foldout). (Taken from *The PL Handbook.*)

563.   *Perfect Liberty: Guide to Perfect Liberty.* Glendale, CA: North American Headquarters, 1975.

564.   *Perfect Liberty—How to Lead a Happy Life.* 1951, 82 pp. 1958.

565.   MIKI, TOKUCHIKA. *A arte de educar os filhos* [The art of educating children]. Editora Vida Artistica E.V.A. Rio de Janeiro: Publicações da Instituição Religiosa Perfect Liberty no Brasil, 246 pp.   In Portuguese.

566.   _____. *A arte do amor* [The art of love]. Editora Vida Artistica E.V.A. Rio de Janeiro: Publicações da Instituição Religiosa Perfect Liberty no Brasil. In Portuguese.

*567.   _____. *Sayings of the Master.* Typescript. Cited in Jean Herbert, *Bibliographie du shintô* (entry 81), item no. 518.

*568.   _____. "The True Way of Life." Typescript. Cited in H. Neill McFarland, *The Rush Hour of the Gods* (entry 136), p. 246.

569.   _____. *Vida e arte* [Life and art]. Editora Vida Artistica E.V.A. Rio de Janeiro: Publicações da Instituição Religiosa Perfect Liberty no Brasil. In Portuguese.

570.   YASHIMA, JIRŌ. *An Essay on the Way of Life.* 1950, 113 pp.

*571.   YUASA, TATSUKI. "An Introduction to an Artistic Life." Typescript. Cited in Werner Kohler, *Die Lotus-Lehre und die modernen Religionen in Japan* (entry 118), p. 291.

572.   _____. "PL (Perfect Liberty)." *Contemporary Religions in Japan* 1, no. 3 (September 1960): 20-29.

Periodicals

573.   *Jornal Perfeita Liberdade—Quinzenal* [Journal of Perfect Liberty]. Rio de Janeiro: Publicações de Instituição Religiosa Perfect Liberty no Brasil. Biweekly journal. In Portuguese.

574.   *PL—Revista P/A Paz Universal--Trimestral* [PL—Magazine for universal peace]. Rio de Janeiro: Publicações de Instituição Religiosa Perfect Liberty no Brasil. Quarterly journal. In Portuguese.

575.   *Perfect Liberty.*   Glendale, CA: North American Headquarters. Monthly.

Secondary

576. ABE, YOSHIYA. "Religious Freedom under the Meiji Constitution" (entry 1). See 11, nos. 3-4 (September-December 1970): 227-46.

577. BACH, MARCUS. *The Power of Perfect Liberty. Out of Japan: A Creative Breakthrough in Humanity's Quest for a New Man in a New Age.* Englewood Cliffs, NJ: Prentice-Hall, 1971, 163 pp. (Portuguese translation, *A força da Perfeita Liberdade* [Rio de Janeiro: Edições Bloch], 1972.)

578. _____. *Strangers at the Door* (entry 13), pp. 105-9.

+579. BAIRY, MAURICE A. *Japans neue Religionen* (entry 14), pp. 70-111.

580. ELLWOOD, ROBERT S., Jr. *The Eagle and the Rising Sun: Americans and the New Religions of Japan* (entry 61), pp. 178-205.

581. HAMMER, RAYMOND JACK. "The Idea of God in Japan's New Religions" (entry 74), pp. 161-65, 244-59.

582. _____. "The Scriptures of Perfect Liberty Kyodan: A Translation with a Brief Commentary." *Japanese Religions* 3, no. 1 (Spring 1963): 18-26.

583. HERBERT, JEAN. *Dieux et sectes populaires du Japon* (entry 82), pp. 189-96.

+584. KOHLER, WERNER. *Die Lotus-Lehre und die modernen Religionen in Japan* (entry 118), pp. 68-87.

585. _____. "Der PL-Kyōdan." *Ostasien* 6 (1961-62).

586. LANCZKOWSKI, GÜNTER. *Die neuen Religionen* (entry 126), pp. 43-48.

+587. McFARLAND, H[ORACE] NEILL. *The Rush Hour of the Gods* (entry 136), pp. 123-44.

588. MURAKAMI, SHIGEYOSHI. *Japanese Religion in the Modern Century* (entry 153), pp. 86-88, 98-99, 141-42, 158-59.

588A. NORBECK, EDWARD. *Religion and Society in Modern Japan: Continuity and Change* (entry 168A), pp. 197-209.

589. OFFNER, CLARK B., and STRAELEN, HENRY (HENRICUS J.J.M.) van. *Modern Japanese Religions* (entry 175), pp. 82-88.

590. RAJANA, EIMI WATANABE. "A Sociological Study of New Religious Movements: Chilean Pentecostalism and Japanese New Religions" (entry 190), pp. 68-74.

591. SCHILLER, EMIL. "Eine neue religiöse Sekte in Japan." *Zeitschrift für Missionskunde und Religionswissenschaft* 51 (1936): 112-13.

592. SOLOMON, TED J. "The Response of Three New Religions to the Crisis in the Japanese Value System" (entry 211).

593. SPAE, JOSEPH J.   "PL Kyōdan, The Perfect Liberty Order." *Missionary Bulletin* 12, no. 8 (October 1958): 586-90.

594. THOMSEN, HARRY. *The New Religions of Japan* (entry 233), pp. 183-98.

Reiyū-kai

Denominational

595. *The Reiyukai Shakaden Completion Ceremony, November 9, 1975.* N.p.: Reiyukai, 1975. Pages not numbered. (Editions in Japanese, English, French, Portuguese, and Spanish.)

596. KOTANI, KIMI, ed. *A Guide to Reiyū-kai.* Tokyo: Reiyūkai Kyōdan, 1958, 25 pp. (Also issued in November 1958 under the title *Reiyu-kai and Social Services.*)

Periodicals

597. *Circle* (The International Reiyukai Magazine). Tokyo: International Extension Bureau.

598. *Inner Trip Friends.* Los Angeles, 1978-.

599. *The Reiyu Kaiho*. In English, 1968-.

Secondary

600. HAMMER, RAYMOND JACK. "The Idea of God in Japan's New Religions" (entry 74), pp. 142-46.

+601. HARDACRE, HELEN. "Sex-Role Norms and Values in Reiyukai." *Japanese Journal of Religious Studies* 6, no. 3 (September 1979): 445-60.

602. KOBAYASHI, SAKAE. "Changes in the Japanese Religions after World War II" (entry 115), pp. 83-87.

+603. KOHLER, WERNER. *Die Lotus-Lehre und die modernen Religionen in Japan* (entry 118), pp. 235-53.

604. LANCZKOWSKI, GÜNTER. *Die neuen Religionen* (entry 126), pp. 32-36.

605. MURAKAMI, SHIGEYOSHI. *Japanese Religion in the Modern Century* (entry 153), pp. 88-91, 105-6, 142-43.

606. NIWANO, NIKKYO. *Lifetime Beginner: An Autobiography* (entry 167), pp. 75-78, 82-86, 99.

+607. OFFNER, CLARK B., and STRAELEN, HENRY (HENRICUS J.J.M.) van. *Modern Japanese Religions* (entry 175), pp. 91-95.

608. SPAE, JOSEPH J. "Reiyūkai." *Japan Missionary Bulletin* 14, no. 10 (December 1960): 654-56.

609. THOMSEN, HARRY. *The New Religions of Japan* (entry 233), pp. 109-16.

Remmon-kyō

Denominational

No publications known.

Secondary

609A.   ASTON, WILLIAM GEORGE. *Shinto: The Way of the Gods.* London:
        Longmans, Green & Co., 1906, ii + 490 pp. See p. 376.

⁺610.   GREENE, DANIEL CROSBY. "Remmon Kyō Kwai." *Transactions of
        the Asiatic Society of Japan* 29 (1901): 17-33.

611.   HAAS, HANS. "Remmon Kyō, die Lotustorsekte." *Zeitschrift für
        Missionskunde und Religionswissenschaft* 18 (1903): 73-81.

⁺612.   LLOYD, ARTHUR. "The Remmon Kyō." *Transactions of the Asiatic
        Society of Japan* 29 (1901): 1-16.

613.   MURAKAMI, SHIGEYOSHI. *Japanese Religion in the Modern Century*
        (entry 153), pp. 50-51.

Risshō Kōsei-kai

Denominational

(Unless otherwise specified, published at Tokyo by Kōsei Publishing
Co., or Risshō Kōsei-kai.)

614.   *Fundamental Buddhism Based on the Teachings of Rissho-Koseikai.*
        [1964].

615.   *A Guide to Rissho Kosei Kai.* 48 pp. (English and Japanese text.)

616.   No entry.

617.   *Kyoden, Extracts from the Threefold Lotus Sutra.* 1968.

618.   *Myoho-Renge-Kyo Narabi Ni Kai-Ketsu.* Edited by Rissho Kosei-kai.
        1970. (A romanized prayer book.)

619.   *Myōhō-Renge Kyō: The Sutra of the Lotus Flower of the Wonderful
        Law.* Translated by Bunnō Katō. Revised by W.E. Soothill and Wilhelm
        Schiffer. 1971, xii + 440 pp.

+620. *Risshō Kōsei-kai.* 1966, 172 pp. Illus.

621. *Risshō Kōsei-kai.* 1966, 110 pp. ("Offprint from the book with the same title.")

622. *Risshō Kōsei-kai, A New Buddhist Laymen's Movement in Japan: An Introduction.* [1968], pages not numbered. (Taken from *Risshō Kōsei-kai* [entry 620].)

623. *Rissho Kosei-kai: An Organization of Buddhist Laymen.* [Tokyo: Kosei Publishing Co., 197?], 24 pp. (Also French and German editions.)

624. *Rissho Kosei-kai—For Our New Members.* 1972, iv + 108 pp. Illus.

*625. "A Summary of the Rissho Kosei Society." Typescript. Cited in H[orace] Neill McFarland, "The New Religions of Japan." *Contemporary Religions in Japan* 1, no. 3 (September 1960): 37.

625A. *The Threefold Lotus Sutra: Innumerable Meanings, the Lotus Flower of the Wonderful Law, and Meditation on the Bodhisattva Universal Virtue.* Translated by Bunnō Katō, Yoshirō Tamura, and Kōjirō Miyasaka with revisions by W.E. Soothill, Wilhelm Schiffer, and Pier P. Del Campana. New York: Weatherhill; Tokyo: Kosei, 1974 [hardcover and paper], xviii + 383 pp. Previously published in part as *Muryōgi-kyō, the Sutra of Innumerable Meanings, and Kanfugengyō, the Sutra of Meditation on the Bodhisattva Universal-Virtue* (Tokyo: Kosei Publishing Company, 1974), xi + 78 pp.

626. INTERNATIONAL INSTITUTE FOR THE STUDY OF RELIGIONS. *Rissho Kosei Kai: A New Buddhist Laymen's Movement in Japan.* Tokyo: Risshō Kōsei-kai and International Institute for the Study of Religions, 1963, 17 pp.

627. KAMOMIYA, JŌKAI. "Rissho Kosei Kai." *Contemporary Religions in Japan* 2, no. 1 (March 1961): 30–38.

628. NIWANO, NIKKYŌ. *Buddhism for Today: A Modern Interpretation of the Threefold Lotus Sutra.* 1976 [hardcover and paper], xxvii + 472 pp.

629. _____. *A Buddhist Approach to Peace.* Translated by Masuo Nezu. 1977, 162 pp. Illus.

630. _____. *Honzon: The Object of Worship of Rissho Kosei-kai.* Translated by Chido Takeda and Wilhelm Schiffer. 1969, 95 pp.

+631. _____. *Lifetime Beginner: An Autobiography* (entry 167).

632. _____. *The Lotus Sutra, Life and Soul of Buddhism: A Modern Introduction to the Lotus Sutra Giving a Better Understanding of the Buddha's Teachings.* Translated by Kōjirō Miyasaka, Wilhelm Schiffer, and Howard B. Gilman. 1971, 264 pp.

633. _____. "My View of Christianity: A Leader of One of the 'New Religions' Looks at Christianity." In *The Japan Christian Yearbook.* Edited by Hallam C. Shorrock, Jr. and Joseph J. Spae. Tokyo: Kyo Bun Kwan (The Christian Literature Society of Japan), 1968, pp. 112-15.

634. _____. *The Richer Life.* Translated by Richard L. Gage. 1975, 138 pp. First paperback ed., 1979, 169 pp.

635. _____. *Travel to Infinity: An Autobiography of the President of an Organization of Buddhist Laymen in Japan.* Translated by Chido Takeda and Wilhelm Schiffer. 1968, 192 pp. Illus.

636. TAMURA, YOSHIRŌ, trans. *Muryōgi-kyō: The Sutra of Innumerable Meanings. Kanfugen-gyō: The Sutra of Meditation on the Bodhisattva Universal-Virtue.* Revised by Pier P. Del Campana. 1974, xi + 78 pp.

Periodicals

637. *Dharma World.* Tokyo: Kosei Publishing Co. May 1974-. Monthly.

Secondary

638. BACH, MARCUS. *Strangers at the Door* (entry 13), pp. 116-18.

639. DALE, KENNETH J. "Authority in Rissho Koseikai." *Japan Missionary Bulletin* 23, no. 8 (September 1969): 457-66. Reprinted from Ninth Hayama Missionary Seminar, 1968, *By What Authority?*

+640. _____, and AKAHOSHI, SUSUMU. *Circle of Harmony: A Case Study in Popular Japanese Buddhism with Implications for Christian Mission.* South Pasadena, CA: William Carey Library, 1975, xviii + 211 pp.

641. _____. "An Investigation of the Factors Responsible for the Impact of *Hoza* of Rissho Koseikai as a Means of Religious Propagation and Education in Contemporary Japan." Th.D. dissertation, Union Theological Seminary in the City of New York, 1970, 511 pp. Abstracted in *Dissertation Abstracts International* 31, no. 6 (December 1970): 2752A. University Microfilms International order no. 70-24,140.

642. DUMOULIN, HEINRICH. "Buddhismus im modernen Japan" (entry 48), pp. 324-30.

643. GERLITZ, PETER. *Gott erwacht in Japan: Neue fornöstliche Religionen und ihre Botschaft vom Glück* (entry 69), pp. 103-28.

644. _____. "Kathartische und therapeutische Elements in der Seelsorge der Risshō Kōsei-kai." *Zeitschrift für Religions- und Geistesgeschichte* 27, no. 4 (1975): 346-56.

+645. GUTHRIE, STEWART ELLIOTT. "A Japanese 'New Religion': Risshō Kōsei Kai in a Japanese Farming Village." Ph.D. dissertation, Yale University, 1976, 402 pp. Abstracted in *Dissertation Abstract International* 40, no. 8 (February 1980): 4652A-53A. University Microfilms International order no. 8002718.

646. HAMMER, RAYMOND JACK. "The Idea of God in Japan's New Religions" (entry 74), pp. 147-56.

647. ITALIAANDER, ROLF. *Harmonie mit dem Universum. Zwiegespräch zwischen Europa und Japan.* Forewords by Werner Kohler, Nikkyo Niwano, and Pater Hamasaki Masao. Freiburg: Aurum Verlag, 1978, 190 pp. Illus.

648. _____, ed. *Eine Religion für den Frieden. Die Rissho Kosei-kai. Japanische Buddhisten für die Ökumene der Religionen.* Foreword by Werner Kohler. Erlanger Raschenbücher, no. 23. Erlangen: Verlag der Evangelisch-Lutherischen Mission, 1973, 170 pp. Illus.

649. _____. *Wer seinen Bruder nicht liebt. . . . : Begegnungen und Erfahrungen in Asien.* Erlangen: Verlag der Evangelisch-Lutherischen Mission, 1978, 185 pp. See pp. 120-53.

650. KOBAYASHI, SAKAE. "Changes in the Japanese Religions after World War II" (entry 115), pp. 88-91.

+651.   KOHLER, WERNER. *Die Lotus-Lehre und die modernen Religionen in Japan* (entry 118), pp. 253-64.

652.   LANCZKOWSKI, GÜNTER. *Die neuen Religionen* (entry 126), pp. 36-38.

+653.   McFARLAND, H[ORACE] NEILL. *The Rush Hour of the Gods* (entry 133), pp. 173-93.

654.   MASIÁ, JUAN. "Risshokoseikai: Un budismo popular moderno." *Razón y fe* 177, no. 844 (May 1968): 527-34.

+655.   MORIOKA, KIYOMI. "The Institutionalization of a New Religious Movement" (entry 147).

656.   MULLINS, GEORGE AUSTIN. "Conversion: Rissho Kosei-kai and Christian." *Japan Christian Quarterly* 35, no. 2 (Spring 1969): 112-18.

656A.   _____. "New Religions? An Examination of Criteria for Determining the States of a Religious Movement, Based upon a Detailed Study of the Origins of the Church of Jesus Christ of Later-Day Saints, Christian Science and Rissho Kosei-kai." Ph.D. dissertation, University of Melbourne [Australia], 1973, 293 pp.

657.   MURAKAMI, SHIGEYOSHI. *Japanese Religion in the Modern Century* (entry 153), pp. 106-7, 143-44, 158-59, 162-63.

658.   NISHIO, HARRY K. "Comparative Analysis of the Risshō Kōseikai and the Sōka Gakkai." *Asian Survey* 7, no. 11 (November 1967): 776-90.

658A.   NORBECK, EDWARD. *Religion and Society in Modern Japan: Continuity and Change* (entry 168A), pp. 185-96.

659.   OFFNER, CLARK B., and STRAELEN, HENRY (HENRICUS J.J.M.) van. *Modern Japanese Religions* (entry 175), pp. 95-98.

660.   PHILIPS, JAMES M. "An Interview on Rissho Koseikai and Christianity." *Japan Christian Quarterly* 29, no. 4 (October 1962): 222-27.

661.   RAJANA, EIMI WATANABE. "A Sociological Study of New Religious
        Movements: Chilean Pentecostalism and Japanese New Religions"
        (entry 190), pp. 74-79. See also Eimi Watanabe (entry 666).

662.   SOLOMON, TED J. "The Response of Three New Religions to the
        Crisis in the Japanese Value System" (entry 211).

663.   SPAE, JOSEPH J. "Popular Buddhist Ethics: Risshōkōseikai." *Japan
        Missionary Bulletin* 20 (1966): 101-9, 232-41. Reprinted in Joseph J.
        Spae, *Japanese Religiosity* (Tokyo: Oriens Institute for Religious
        Research), 1971, pp. 231-48.

664.   _____. "Risshōkōseikai," *Japan Missionary Bulletin* 14, no. 5 (June
        1960): 321-25.

665.   THOMSEN, HARRY. *The New Religions of Japan* (entry 233), pp. 117-
        26.

+666.   WATANABE, EIMI. "Rissho Kosei-kai: A Sociological Observation of
        Its Members, Their Conversion and Their Activities." *Contemporary
        Religions in Japan* 9, nos. 1-2 (March-June 1968): 75-151. See also
        Eimi Watanabe Rajana (entry 661).

667.   WEEKS, J. STAFFORD. "Rissho Kosei-kai: A Cooperative Buddhist
        Sect." In *Religious Ferment in Asia*. Edited by Robert J. Miller.
        Lawrence: University of Kansas Press, 1974, pp. 156-68.

Seichō-no-Ie

Denominational

(Unless otherwise specified, published at Tokyo by the Seicho-no-Ie
Foundation   or   the   Seicho-no-Ie-Foundation   Divine   Publication
Department.)

668.   DAVIS, ROY EUGENE. *Miracle Man of Japan: The Life and Work of
        Masaharu Taniguchi, One of the Most Influential Spiritual Leaders of
        our Times*. Lakemont, GA: CSA Press, 1970, 159 pp. Illus.

        HOLMES, FENWICKE L.   See Taniguchi, Masaharu, and Holmes,
        Fenwicke L. (entry 679).

669. INTERNATIONAL INSTITUTE FOR THE STUDY OF RELIGIONS. "Seicho-no-Ie. Taken from Seicho-no-Ie Publications." *Contemporary Religions in Japan* 4, no. 3 (September 1963): 212-29.

670. TANIGUCHI, MASAHARU. *Divine Education and Spiritual Training of Mankind.* 1956, 249 pp.

671. _____. *The Holy Sutra of Seicho-No-Ie.* 1966, 44 pp. (Taken from Masaharu Taniguchi, *Truth of Life* [entry 677].)

672. _____. *The Human Mind and Cancer.* 1972, 350 pp.

673. _____. *The Nectarean Shower of Holy Doctrines.* 94th printing. 1959, pages not numbered. (Taken from Masaharu Taniguchi, *Truth of Life* [entry 677]).

674. _____. *Recovery from All Diseases: Seicho-No-Ie's Method of Psychoanalysis.* 1963, v + 260 pp.

675. No entry.

676. _____. *365 Golden Keys to the Summit of Fulfillment.* 1974, 323 pp.

677. _____. *Truth of Life.* 7 vols. 1961-1977. Vol. 1, *Truth of Life* (Tokyo: Seicho-no-Ie Foundation, 1961), 320 pp. (Also in an earlier edition, *Seimei no Jisso* [Truth of life], trans. Kakuwo Ohata, revised by the author [Tokyo: Komyoshiso-Fukyukai, 1937], 148 pp., Japanese text, 61 pp.) Vol. 2, *The Spiritual Essence of Man* (Playa Del Rey, CA: Seicho-no-Ie Truth of Life Publishing Department, 1979), 200 pp. Vol. 3, *Spiritual Key to Abundant Life* (Tokyo: Seicho-no-Ie Foundation Divine Publication Department, 1971), 237 pp. Vol. 5, *The Mystical Power Within* (Playa Del Rey, CA: Seicho-no-Ie Los Angeles & No. American Missionary Hq., 1975), 191 pp. Vol. 7, *Wondrous Way to Infinite Life and Power* (Playa Del Rey, CA: Seicho-no-Ie Truth of Life Movement, 1977), 232 pp.

678. _____. *You Can Heal Yourself.* 1961, 248 pp.

679. _____, and HOLMES, FENWICKE L. *The Science of Faith: How to Make Yourself Believe.* Tokyo: Nippon Kyobun-sha Co., 1962, viii + 272 pp. Original publication New York: Dodd, Mead & Co., 1953.

Periodicals

680.   *Gekkan*. Published in six languages.

681.   *Seicho-No-Ie*. English, Portuguese, and Spanish editions.

682.   *Seicho-No-Ie Truth of Life Movement*. Playa Del Rey, CA: Seicho-no-Ie Truth of Life Publishing Department. Monthly.

Secondary

683.   CURTIS, GERALD L. *Election Campaigning Japanese Style* (entry 42), pp. 199-200.

684.   ELLWOOD, ROBERT S., Jr. *The Eagle and the Rising Sun: Americans and the New Religions of Japan* (entry 61), pp. 147-77.

685.   HAMMER, RAYMOND JACK. "The Idea of God in Japan's New Religions" (entry 74), pp. 132-41.

686.   IIERBERT, JEAN. *Dieux et sectes populaires du Japon* (entry 82), pp. 182-88.

687.   HUNTER, LOUISE H. *Buddhism in Hawaii: Its Impact on a Yankee Community* (entry 91), pp. 194-95.

688.   KOBAYASHI, SAKAE. "Changes in the Japanese Religions after World War II" (entry 115), pp. 96-103.

689.   KOHLER, WERNER. *Die Lotus-Lehre und die modernen Religionen in Japan* (entry 118), 88-89.

690.   LIND, ANDREW W. *Hawaii's Japanese: An Experiment in Democracy*. Princeton, NJ: Princeton University Press, 1946, vii + 264 pp. See pp. 208-10.

+691.   McFARLAND, H[ORACE] NEILL. *The Rush Hour of the Gods* (entry 136), pp. 145-72.

692. MAEYAMA, TAKASHI. "O imigrante e a religião: Estudo de uma seita religiosa japonêsa no Brasil" [Immigrant and religion: A study of a Japanese religious sect in Brazil]. M.A. thesis, São Paulo, Escola de Sociologia e Politica, 1967, 307 pp. In Portuguese.

693. _____. "Religião, parentesco e as classes medias" [Religion, kinship, and the middle classes]. In *Assimilação e integração dos japoneses no Brasil*. Edited by Hiroshi Saito and Takashi Maeyama. Petropolis, Vozes, and São Paulo: Ed. da Universidade de São Paulo, 1973, 558 pp. See pp. 240-72, esp. pp. 255-57. In Portuguese. Reprinted from Takashi Maeyama, "Religion, Kinship and the Middle Classes of the Japanese in Urban Brazil," mimeographed (Cornell University, Department of Anthropology, 1970).

694. MOREAU, J-PAULIN. "'Seicho no ie, compagnie Limitée,' nouvelle religion japonaise au capital de 5 millions." *Les missions catholiques* 68, no. 3255 (1936): 497-503.

695. MURAKAMI, SHIGEYOSHI. *Japanese Religion in the Modern Century* (entry 153), pp. 85-86, 165-66.

695A. NORBECK, EDWARD. *Religion and Society in Modern Japan: Continuity and Change* (entry 168A), pp. 210-17.

696. NORDSTOKKE, KJELL. "Seicho-no-ie." In *Anuário evangélico 1978 7$^{\underline{Q}}$ ano*. Edited by Editora Sinodal. São Leopoldo, 1978, pp. 139-45.

697. *Novas religiões japonêsas no Brasil, por uma equipe de Franciscanos de Petrópolis* (entry 172), pp. 27-37.

698. OFFNER, CLARK B., and STRAELEN, HENRY (HENRICUS J.J.M.) van. *Modern Japanese Religions* (entry 175), pp. 71-76.

699. RICCO, MARIO. *Religione della violenza e religione del piacere nel nuovo Giappone* (entry 195), pp. 103-39.

700. _____. "Seicho-no-Ie." In *As novas seitas*, by Alain Woodrow. São Paulo: Edições Paulinas, 1979, pp. 217-41. Appendix.

701. SMITH, BRADFORD. *Americans from Japan*. Philadelphia: J.B. Lippincott Co., 1948, xxi + 409 pp. See pp. 100-1, 175, 388-89.

702. SPAE, JOSEPH J. "Seichō no Ie." *Missionary Bulletin* 10, no. 10 (December 1956): 746–50.

703. THOMSEN, HARRY. *The New Religions of Japan* (entry 233), pp. 153–72.

+704. WIMBERLEY, [HICKMAN] HOWARD. "The Knights of the Golden Lotus." *Ethnology* 11, no. 2 (April 1972): 173–86.

+705. _____. "Seicho-no-Ie: A Study of a Japanese Religio-Political Association." Ph.D. dissertation, Cornell University, 1967, 261 pp. Abstracted in *Dissertation Abstracts* 28, no. 6 (December 1967): 2245B. University Microfilms International order no. 67-17,258.

706. _____. "Self-realization and the Ancestors: An Analysis of Two Japanese Ritual Procedures for Achieving Domestic Harmony." *Anthropological Quarterly* 42, no. 1 (January 1969): 37–51.

707. _____. "Some Social Characteristics of a *Seicho-no-Ie* Congregation in Southern Japan." *Journal of Asian and African Studies* 42, no. 3 (July 1969): 186–201.

708. ZIMMERMANN, WERNER. *Licht im Osten* (entry 259), pp. 105–7.

Sekai Kyūsei-kyō

Denominational

(Unless otherwise specified, published at Atami or Los Angeles by Sekai Kyūsei-kyō Headquarters, or Church of World Messianity.)

709. *Church of World Messianity*. N.d., pages not numbered.

710. *The Dedication of the New Hall of Worship in Atami, Japan.* [1972], 118 pp.

711. *Experiences of Members in the Divine Light Program.* 1974, 128 pp.

712. *Fragments from the Teachings of Meishu-sama.* 1965, 72 pp.

713.   *Home Gathering Messages.* Mimeographed. 32 pp. (Translations from *Chijo Tengoku*) [No other publication information except "Church of World Messianity" on cover.]

714.   *Hoshi (Giving Service).* Question and Answer Series, no. 4. 1979, 48 pp.

715.   *An Introduction to World Messianity.*   Color pamphlet.   Atami: Messianic General Company, 1976, pages not numbered.

716.   *Introductory Course of World Messianity and Joining the Church.* Question and Answer Series, no. 2. 1976, 70 pp.

717.   *Johrei.* Mimeographed. [Ca. 1977], 8 pp., pages not numbered.

718.   *"Jōrei": Its Administration.* 1955.

719.   *The Law of Order.*

720.   *The Light from the East, a Biography of Mokichi Okada, Founder of World Messianity.* Mimeographed. N.d., 48 pp.

721.   *Members' Handbook.* N.d., 19 pp.

722.   *Nature Farming.* Booklet Series, no. 1. 1966, 18 pp.

723.   *Ohikari.* Question and Answer Series, no. 1. 1976, 50 pp.

724.   *Prayers.* Rev. ed. [1965], 29 pp.

725.   *Prayers and Gosanka (Poems to Be Chanted).*   106 pp.   [Printed in "large edition" and "pocket edition".]

726.   *Reminiscences About Meishu-sama.* 2 vols. 1969–70. Vol. 1, by Nidai-sama and Kyoshu-sama, 1969, 77 pp. Illus. Vol. 2, *Meishu-sama's Mystic Nature,* by members, 1970, 92 pp. Illus.

727.   *Report on the Pilgrimage to the Mother Church.* 1970, 44 pp.

728.   *Sampai.* Question and Answer Series, no. 3. 1977, 60 pp.

729.   *Sounds of the Dawn.* 2 vols. 1971–73. Vol. 1, "English translation of poems transposed into waka rhythm by Lisa Taylor Melton, Editor,

Translations Division, Los Angeles, California, U.S.A.," 1971, 239 pp. Vol. 2, 1973, 264 pp.

730. *Study Material for Spiritual Growth.* 1964, 40 pp. Reprint. 1969.

731. *Teachings by Nidai-sama.* 2 vols. 1970-72. Vol. 1, *Prayer, Johrei, Faith,* 1970, 155 pp. Vol. 2, *Steps to Spiritual Unfoldment, Fulfilling Our Mission,* 1972, 148 pp.

732. *World Messianity and What It Means.* 1957, 1963, 22 pp. Rev. ed., 1968, 31 pp. 1979, 32 pp.

733. *The World Messianity Graphic.* 1956. (English and Japanese text.)

734. FUJIEDA, MASAKAZU. "The Church of World Messianity (Sekai Kyūsei-kyō)." *Contemporary Religions in Japan* 1, no. 4 (December 1960): 24-34.

735. HIGUCHI, KYOKO. *Introduction to World Messianity.* 1955.

736. KAWAI, TERUAKI. *My Wish for Youth Members.* 1978, 94 pp.

737. MEISHU-SAMA. *Teachings of Meishu-Sama.* 2 vols. Translated by Kiyoko Higuchi. 1960. Vol. 1, v + 58 pp. Rev. ed., 1965, 75 pp. Reprint. 1979. Vol. 2, 1968, 99 pp. [Meishu-Sama is the religious title of Mokichi Okada.]

738. OKADA, MOKICHI. *Excerpts from the Teachings of Meishu-sama.* 1947, 60 pp.

739. YANAGAWA, KEIICHI, and MORIOKA, KIYOMI, eds. *Hawaii Nikkei Shūkyō no Tenkai to Genkyō* (entry 253), pp. 241-48.

Periodicals

740. *Bulletin of World Messianity.* [Title varies slightly: it was superseded by *Dawn of Paradise* and is sometimes titled *World Messianity.*]

741. *Chijo Tengoku Messages.* [See such special issues as October 1975 edition.]

742. *The Glory.* [Other organs published in the U.S.A., such as *Wings of Light.*]

Secondary

743. BACH, MARCUS. *Strangers at the Door* (entry 13), pp. 121-25.

744. ELLWOOD, ROBERT S., Jr. *The Eagle and the Rising Sun: Americans and the New Religions of Japan* (entry 61), pp. 111-46.

744A. HAMBRICK, CHARLES H. "World Messianity: A Study in Liminality and Communitas." *Religious Studies* 15, no. 4 (December 1979): 539-53.

745. HAMMER, RAMOND JACK.   "The Idea of God in Japan's New Religions" (entry 74), pp. 125-31.

746. KOBAYASHI, SAKAE. "Changes in the Japanese Religions after World War II" (entry 115), pp. 72-77.

747. MURAKAMI, SHIGEYOSHI. *Japanese Religion in the Modern Century* (entry 153), pp. 140-42.

+748. OFFNER, CLARK B., and STRAELEN, HENRY (HENRICUS J.J.M.) van. *Modern Japanese Religions* (entry 175), pp. 76-83.

749. SPAE, JOSEPH J.   "Sekai Kyūseikyō or Sekai Meshiya-kyō, World Messianity." *Japan Missionary Bulletin* 13, no. 4 (May 1959): 238-44.

750. SPICKARD JIM. "Shamanistic Renewal in Two Changing Cultures: Sekai Kyuseikyo in Japan and America." Unpublished paper, November 1975; with added notes, October 1977, Center for the Study of New Religious Movements.

751. THOMSEN, HARRY. *The New Religions of Japan* (entry 233), pp. 173-82.

Sekai Mahikari Bunmei Kyōdan

Denominational

*752.   *The Art of Spiritual Purification.* Tokyo, 1973. Cited in Peter Gerlitz, *Gott erwacht in Japan: Neue fernöstliche Religionen und ihre Botschaft vom Glück* (entry 69), p. 173.

Secondary

753.   No entry.

754.   GERLITZ, PETER. *Gott erwacht in Japan: Neue fernöstliche Religionen und ihre Botschaft vom Glück* (entry 69), pp. 139-52.

755.   KÖPPING, KLAUS-PETER. *Religiöse Bewegungen im modernen Japan als Problem des Kulturwandels* (entry 122), pp. 77-88.

+756.   _____. "Sekai Mahikari Bunmei Kyōdan—A Preliminary Discussion of a Recent Religious Movement in Japan" (entry 123).

Shinnyo-en

Denominational

757.   *The Way to Nirvana.* Tokyo: Shinnyo-en, 1967, 39 pp. Illus.

Periodicals

758.   *The Nirvanians.*

Secondary

+759.   SHIRAMIZU, HIROKO. "Organizational Mediums: A Case Study of Shinnyo-en." *Japanese Journal of Religious Studies* 6, no. 3 (September 1979): 414-44.

Shinrei-kyō

Denominational

760.   OTSUKA, KANICHI, et al. *Divination and Power: An Eastern Science and Teachings of Master Kanichi Otsuka.* Tokyo: Metaphysic Scientific Institute, 1962, 82 pp.

761.   YONEKURA, ISAMU. "Shinreikyo: The Fountainhead of Miracles." *The East* (May-June 1979): 70-72.

Secondary

762.   KÖPPING, KLAUS-PETER. *Religiöse Bewegungen im modernen Japan als Problem des Kulturwandels* (entry 122), pp. 89-97.

763.   MULHOLLAND, JOHN F. *Hawaii's Religions* (entry 152), pp. 288-89.

764.   "Shinrei-kyo. Healing Truths. The Thoughts of Master Otsuka." *Info* 4, no. 1 (January 1958): 30-32.

Shinri-kyō

Denominational

765.   *Sectarian Shinto (The Way of the Gods)* (entry 205), pp. 36-39.

Secondary

+766.   HOLTOM, DANIEL C. *The National Faith of Japan* (entry 85), pp. 195-99.

Shinshū-kyō

Denominational

767.   *Sectarian Shinto (The Way of the Gods)* (entry 205), pp. 40-44.

Secondary

+768.   HOLTOM, DANIEL C. *The National Faith of Japan* (entry 85), pp. 233–40.

Shintō Shūsei-ha

Denominational

769.   *Sectarian Shinto (The Way of the Gods)* (entry 205), pp. 45–48.

Secondary

+770.   HOLTOM, DANIEL C. *The National Faith of Japan* (entry 85), pp. 205–10.

Shintō Taikyō

Denominational

771.   *Sectarian Shinto (The Way of the Gods)* (entry 205), pp. 31–35.

Secondary

+772.   HOLTOM, DANIEL C. *The National Faith of Japan* (entry 85), pp. 190–95.

Shintō Taisei-kyō

Denominational

773.   *Sectarian Shinto (The Way of the Gods)* (entry 205), pp. 49–52.

Secondary

[+]774.   HOLTOM, DANIEL C. *The National Faith of Japan* (entry 85), pp. 210-
          14.

Shintō (or Shindō) Tenkōkyo

Denominational

775.   *Kojiki.* Translated and annotated by Shunji Inoue. Fukuoka: Nihon
       Shuji Kyoiku Renmei, 1966, 225 pp. 1st ed., 1958. Reprints. 1959,
       1960, 1961, 1962, 1964, 1965. Mimeographed. Newly revised, 1966.

776.   TOMOKIYO, YOSHISANE. *Shumpu-Henro (Pilgrimage in the Spring
       Breeze).* Mimeographed. Translated and annotated by Shunji Inoue.
       Iwakiyama, Tabuse: Shintō Tenkō-kyo, 1961, 134 pp. (Also a larger
       work with the same title, 1961, 373 pp.)

Secondary

No publications known.

Shūyōdan Hōsei-kai

Denominational

No publications known.

Secondary

777.   HAMMITZSCH, HORST. "Shuyodan: Die Erneuerungsbewegung des
       gegenwärtigen Japans." *Deutsche Gesellschaft für Natur- und
       Völkerkunde Ostasiens* 28, pt. J (1939): 1-16.

Sōka Gakkai (usually known outside Japan as Nichiren Shōshū)

Denominational

(Unless otherwise specified, published at Tokyo by Seikyo Press, or Seikyo Shimbunsha.)

778.   *The Buddhist Democracy.* This is the Sokagakkai Series, no. 7. N.d., 15 pp. (Also published in seven other languages.)

779.   *Culture and Religion.* This is the Sokagakkai Series, no. 9. N.d., 19 pp. (Also published in seven other languages.)

780.   *Doctrines on Nichiren Shoshu.* 1957, 4 pp.

⁺781.   *The 8th National Convention, June 25-27, 1970.* [Tokyo]: Komeito Party, [1970], 163 pp.

782.   *Head Temple Taisekiji.* This is the Sokagakkai Series, no. 5. 19 pp. (Also published in seven other languages.)

783.   *Introduction au bouddhisme.* Sable-sur-Sarthe, France: Nichiren Shoshu Française, 1975, 157 pp.

784.   *The Komeito: Clean Government Party.* Policy Bureau, Komeito, n.d., pages not numbered. Illus.

785.   *The Liturgy of Nichiren Shoshu.* Tokyo: Nichiren Shoshu Fukyokai, 1961, 48 pp. [Tokyo]: Nichiren Shoshu Academy, 1973, 48 pp. [Japanese and romanized prayers.]

786.   *The Lotus Sutra: Its History and Practice Today.* Santa Monica, CA: World Tribune Press, 1977, 78 pp. Illus.

787.   *Min-on Concert Association.* 1967, pages not numbered. (Also German edition.)

788.   *NSA "Blue Hawaii Convention" 1975 Photo Album: "A Salute to the American Bicentennial."* Santa Monica, CA: World Tribune Press, 1975, 96 pp. Illus.

789.   *NSA 1974 Photo Album.* Santa Monica, CA: World Tribune Press, 1974, 160 pp. Illus.

790.   *Nichiren Shoshu: El Budismo Verdadero.*   Tokyo: Editorial Seikyo Press, 1970. 101 pp.

791.   *Nichiren Shoshu Sokagakkai.* N.d., pages not numbered. Illus.

⁺792. *The Nichiren Shoshu Sokagakkai.* 1966, 217 pp. Illus. [This is a "completely revised edition" of *The Sokagakkai*, entry 801.]

793.   *The Nichiren Shoshu Sokagakkai: Annual Graphic Report, 1966.* 235 pp. [Compiler has searched but cannot confirm existence of subsequent editions.]

794.   *Nichiren Shoshu Sokagakkai Photographic, 1968.*   1968, 227 pp. Photographs, with Japanese and English captions.   [Compiler has searched but cannot confirm existence of subsequent editions.]

795.   *Nichiren Shoshu Through Pictures.* 1961, 64 pp. Illus.

796.   *No Boundary in True Religion.* This Is the Sokagakkai Series, no. 2. N.d., 15 pp. (Also published in seven other languages.)

797.   *Practice of Believers.* This Is the Sokagakkai Series, no. 4. N.d., 14 pp. (Also published in seven other languages.)

798.   *The Road to Creation: President Ikeda's Visits to Universities of the World.* 1974, 201 pp. Illus.

       Shakubuku Kyōten. See Noah S. Brannen, trans. (entry 905).

799.   *Sho-Hondo.* 1972, 71 pp.

800.   *Soka University.*   N.p., n.d., pages not numbered.   [A brochure explaining the various divisions of the university curriculum, etc.]

801.   *The Sokagakkai.* 1960, 146 pp. Illus. Revised and enlarged ed., 1962, 172 pp. (See also entry 792 for a "completely revised edition.")

802.   *Sokagakkai and Culture Movement.* This is the Sokagakkai Series, no. 3. N.d., 16 pp. (Also published in seven other languages.)

803.   *Sokagakkai and Komeito.* This Is the Sokagakkai Series, no. 6. N.d., 19 pp. (Also published in seven other languages.)

804. *Sokagakkai and Nichiren Shoshu.* This Is the Sokagakkai Series, no. 1
      (25 October 1964), 19 pp. (Also published in seven other languages.)

805. *Taisekiji.* Pamphlet and map. N.p., n.d., pages not numbered.

806. *The 10th National Convention, June 13-14, 1972.* [Tokyo]: Komeito,
      (1972), 96 pp.

807. *What is Shakubuku?* This Is the Sokagakkai Series, no. 8. N.d., 19 pp.
      (Also published in seven other languages.)

808. *Why Is Religion Necessary?* This Is the Sokagakkai Series, no. 10. N.d.,
      19 pp. (Also published in seven other languages.)

809. AKIYA, EINOSUKE. *Guide to Buddhism.* 1968, 117 pp.

810. IKEDA, DAISAKU. *Be a Leader Who Walks With the People.* [Tokyo:
      International Bureau, Soka Gakkai, 1977], 32 pp.

811. _____. *Buddhism, the First Millennium.* Translated by Burton Watson.
      Tokyo: Kodansha International, 1977, 172 pp.

812. _____. *Buddhism: The Living Philosophy.* Tokyo: The East
      Publications, 1974, 94 pp. 2d ed., 1976, 98 pp.

813. _____. "Can Faith Move Mountains?" *Asia Magazine* (18 October
      1964): 6.

814. _____. *Complete Works of Daisaku Ikeda.* Vol. 1, 1968, 553 pp.

815. _____. *The Creative Family: Life-force of the New Society.*
      [Tokyo]: Nichiren Shoshu International Center, [1977], xv + 158 pp.

816. _____. *Creative Life Force.* [Tokyo: International Bureau, Soka
      Gakkai, 1974], 18 pp.

817. _____. *Dialogue on Life.* 2 vols. Tokyo: Nichiren Shoshu International
      Center, 1976-77. Vol. 1, *Buddhist Perspectives on Life and the
      Universe*, 1976, xxi + 243 pp. Vol. 2, *Buddhist Perspectives on the
      Eternity of Life*, 1977, xiii + 268 pp.

818. _____. *The Future Is Your Responsibility*. Translated by Richard L. Gage. [Tokyo: International Bureau, Soka Gakkai, 1974], 18 pp.

819. _____. *Glass Children and Other Essays*. Translated by Burton Watson. Tokyo: Kodansha International, 1979, 172 pp.

820. _____. *The Global Unity of Mankind*. Translated by Richard L. Gage. [Tokyo: International Bureau, Soka Gakkai, 1974], 28 pp.

821. _____. *Guidance Memo*. 1966, ix + vi + 297 pp.

822. _____. *Guidance Memo*. Translated by George M. Williams. Santa Monica, CA: World Tribune Press, [1975], 288 pp.

823. _____. *A Historical View of Buddhism*. [Tokyo: International Bureau, Soka Gakkai, 1977], 40 pp.

+824. _____. *The Human Revolution*. 4 vols. 1965-68. Vol. 1, 1968, iii + 275 pp. Vol. 2, 1966, iii + 277 pp. Vol. 3, 1966, 277 pp. Vol. 4, 1968, 284 pp. (Also Portuguese edition of Vol. 1 and French edition of Vol. 2.) Also published under the same title, condensed and translated from the original Japanese *Ningen Kakumei* [Human revolution]. 3 vols. New York: Weatherhill, 1972-76. Vol. 1, 1972, xvi + 250 pp., illus., with a foreword by Arnold J. Toynbee, contains Vols. 1 and 2 of the original; Vol. 2, 1974 (2d printing, with corrections, 1977), with a foreword by Arnold J. Toynbee, contains Vols. 3 and 4 of the original; Vol. 3, 1976, ix + 140 pp., illus., contains Vols. 5 and 6 of the original.

825. _____. *Lectures on Buddhism*. 4 vols. 1962-67. Vol. 1, translated by Takeo Kamio. 1962, 292 pp. Vol. 2, translated by Takeo Kamio. 1962, 298 pp. Vol. 3, translated by Translation Division. 1966, 241 pp. Vol. 4, translated by General Overseas Bureau. 1966, 346 pp.

826. _____. *The Living Buddha: An Interpretive Biography*. Translated by Burton Watson. New York: Weatherhill, 1976, x + 148 pp. Illus.

827. _____. *Ma conception de la vie*. N.p., 1972, 146 pp.

828. _____. *A New Road to East-West Cultural Exchanges*. Translated by Richard L. Gage. [Tokyo: International Bureau, Soka Gakkai, 1975], 21 pp.

829. _____. *On Middle-of-the-Road Government.* The Komeito Series, no. 2. Tokyo, 1967, 12 pp.

830. _____, with NEMOTO, MAKOTO. *On the Japanese Classics: Conversations and Appreciations.* Translated by Burton Watson. New York: Weatherhill, 1979, 202 pp.

831. _____. *Paroles offertes à mes juenes amis.* Sceaux: Nichiren Shoshu Française, 1974, pages not numbered.

832. _____. *La philosophie de la vie: Entretien à trois entre Messieurs Daisaku Ikeda, Masahiro Kitagawa, et Yoichi Kawada.* 2 vols. Sceaux: Nichiren Shoshu Française, 1973-75. Vol. 1, 1973, 151 pp. Vol. 2, 1975, 205 pp.

833. _____. *A Proposal for Lasting Peace.* Translated by Richard L. Gage. Tokyo: International Bureau, Soka Gakkai, 1973, 38 pp.

834. _____. *Protecting Human Life.* Translated by Charles S. Terry. [Tokyo: International Bureau, Soka Gakkai, 1973], 32 pp.

835. _____. *Science and Religion.* 2d ed., 1965, xiii + 353 pp.

836. _____. *Seminars for Hope and Growth.* [Tokyo: International Bureau, Soka Gakkai, 1975], 41 pp.

837. _____. *Soka Gakkai.* 1961.

838. _____. *Soka Gakkai: Its Ideals and Tradition.* Tokyo: International Bureau, Soka Gakkai, 1976, 30 pp.

839. _____. *Le Soka Gakkai: son ideal, sa tradition.* [Tokyo: Soka Gakkai, 1977], 28 pp.

840. _____. *Songs from My Heart: Poems and Photographs by Daisaku Ikeda.* Tokyo: Seikyo Press, 1976. New York: Weatherhill, 1978, 111 pp. Illus. ("This book, in both its original Japanese version and English translation, was first published, in deluxe editions, in 1976 by Seikyo Press, Tokyo, on the occasion of the publisher's twenty-fifth anniversary.")

841. _____. *Les sources de la santé et de la jeunesse.* [Tokyo: Soka Gakkai, 1977], 48 pp.

842.   _____. *Sources of Health and Youthfulness*. [Tokyo: International Bureau, Soka Gakkai, 1976], 39 pp.

843.   _____.   *Toward a Third Great Revival*.   Translated by Charles S. Terry. [Tokyo: International Bureau, Soka Gakkai, 1974], 23 pp.

844.   _____. *Toward the Twenty-First Century*. Translated by Richard L. Gage.   Tokyo: International Bureau, Soka Gakkai, 1974, 17 pp. Reprinted in Daisaku Ikeda, Toward the 21st Century: Addresses by Daisaku Ikeda (Tokyo: Soka University Student International Center, 1978), viii + 135 pp. See pp. 49-59.

845.   _____. *La vie de Shakyamuni: Dialogue entre Daisaku Ikeda et Issamu Nosaki*. Sceaux: Nichiren Shoshu Française, 1973, 198 pp.

846.   _____. *The Vision of a New Tokyo--Skyscraping City Among Forests and Fountains*. The Komeito Series, no. 3. Tokyo, 1967.

847.   _____. *The Vision of the Komeito—For a New Society of Happiness and Prosperity*. The Komeito Series, no. 1. Tokyo, 1967, 20 pp.

848.   _____.   *Youth, Let's Advance Towards a New Day.—Lecture by President Daisaku Ikeda at the 31st General Meeting*. 1968, 39 pp. (Japanese text included.)

_____, and TOYNBEE, ARNOLD. See Toynbee (entry 856).

849.   KIRIMURA, YASUJI.   *Fundamentals of Buddhism*.   Translated by Seikyo Times. Tokyo: Nichiren Shoshu International Center, 1977, xi + 180 pp.   ("Essays originally published in the Seikyo Times, January 1974-December 1975. Includes Index.")

850.   MAKIGUCHI, TSUNESABURO. *A Brief Synopsis*. 1953, 28 pp.

+851.   _____. *The Philosophy of Value*. Translated by Translation Division, Overseas Bureau. 1964, xii + 199 pp. [Translation of the 1953 Japanese "Revised and augmented edition" by Josei Toda.] Appendixes. See entries 1021, 1071, 1093.

852.   THE SEIKYO TIMES, ed. and trans. *The Major Writings of Nichiren Daishonin*. Vol. 1. Tokyo: Nichiren Shoshu International Center, 1979, xxxvii + 345 pp.

853.   _____, ed. *Nichiren Shoshu and Soka Gakkai: Modern Buddhism in Action.* 1972, 143 pp. Illus.

854.   TODA, JOSEI. *Essays on Buddhism.* Translated by Takeo Kamio, 1961, 172 pp.

855.   _____. *Lecture on the Sutra—Hoben and Juryo Chapters.* 3d ed., 1968, xii + 305 pp.

856.   TOYNBEE, ARNOLD, and IKEDA, DAISAKU. *The Toynbee-Ikeda Dialogue: Man Himself Must Choose.* Tokyo, New York, and San Francisco: Kodansha International, 1976. Reprinted as *Choose Life: A Dialogue,* ed.   Richard L. Gage (London: Oxford University Press, 1978), 348 pp.

857.   WILLIAMS, GEORGE M. *The Buddhist Tradition (NSA Handbook No. 2).* Compiled by World Tribune Press. [Los Angeles]: World Tribune Press, 1972, 23 pp. Illus.

857A.   _____, comp. *The Gosho Reference.* Los Angeles: World Tribune Press, 1976, 294 pp. Illus.

858.   _____. *NSA Seminar Report 1968-71.* Compiled by World Tribune Press.   Santa Monica, CA: World Tribune Press, 1972, iii + 120 pp. Illus.

859.   _____. *NSA Seminars: An Introduction to True Buddhism.* Santa Monica, CA: World Tribune Press, 1974, 101 pp.

860.   _____. *Origins of Nichiren Shoshu (NSA Handbook No. 3).* Los Angeles: World Tribune Press, 1972, 33 pp. Illus.

861.   _____. *The Practice of Nichiren Shoshu (NSA Handbook No. 4).* Los Angeles: World Tribune Press, 1972, 28 pp. Illus.

862.   _____. *What Is Nichiren Shoshu? (NSA Handbook No. 1).* Compiled by World Tribune Press. [Los Angeles]: World Tribune Press, 1972, iv + 41 pp. Illus.

863.   YANO, JUNYA. "Japan and the Role of the Komeito." *Contemporary Japan* 29, no. 2 (March 1970): 228-44.

864. YOUTH DIVISION OF SOKA GAKKAI, comp.   *Cries for Peace:
      Experiences of Japanese Victims of World War II.* Tokyo: Japan Times,
      1978, 234 pp.

      Periodicals

865. *Argentina Seikyo.* Bi-monthly

866. *L'Avenir* (France). Monthly.

867. *Brazil Seikyo.* Weekly.

868. *Italia Seikyo.* Monthly.

869. *NSA Quarterly.*   Edited by George M. Williams.   Nichiren Shoshu
      Academy.   Santa Monica, CA: World Tribune Press.   Spring 1973-.
      Quarterly. [Includes special issues, such as Volume 4, no. 1 (Spring
      1976), Special Issue, New York Bicentennial Convention.]

870. *Peru Seikyo.* Bi-monthly.

871. *The Seikyo Times* (Tokyo). Monthly.

872. *Seikyo Zeitung* (Germany). Monthly.

873. *The Soka Gakkai News.* Tokyo: International Bureau, Soka Gakkai. 25
      February 1975-. Bi-monthly. [Nos. 1-56 prepared by the Soka Gakkai
      International Bureau, Information Center; nos. 57- by the International
      Bureau.]

874. *Terceira civilização* (Brazil). Monthly.

875. *This Is the Sokagakkai Series.* [Vols. 1-10 are included in the preceding
      denominational materials, listed by specific title; vols. 11-14 consist of
      several short articles.]

876. *World Tribune* (U.S.A.). Tri-weekly.

877. *World Tribune Graphic* (Santa Monica, CA). Spring 1972-. Quarterly.

878. *Komeito Press Releases.* [Although technically separate from Sōka
      Gakkai, this is the political party that speaks for Sōka Gakkai.]

Secondary

Note: many of the titles of works in this section deal more directly with Japanese Buddhism and/or Japanese politics and elections, not mentioning explicitly aspects of Sōka Gakkai and/or Kōmeitō (the Clean Government Party, associated with Sōka Gakkai). Readers may wish to turn to the Topical Index for more convenient access to the many entries of secondary works on Sōka Gakkai. Suggested for first reference are "Kōmeitō" and "Political activity and elections."

879.   ALVAREZ, SILVESTER. "The Soka Gakkai Threat." *Worldmission* 14, no. 3 (Fall 1964): 17-21.

880.   ANZAI, SHIN. "Newly-adopted Religions and Social Change on the Ryukyu Islands (Japan) (With Special Reference to Catholicism)" (entry 8).

*881. AZUMI, KOYA. "Functions of Soka Gakkai Membership." Unpublished paper, Columbia University, 1967. Cited in James Wilson White, *The Sokagakkai and Mass Society* (entry 1087), p. 355.

*882. _____. "Social Basis of a New Religious Party: The Komeito of Japan." Mimeographed copy of a paper read before the Annual Meeting of the American Sociological Association, August 1967. Cited in James Allen Dator, *Sōka Gakkai, Builders of the Third Civilization* (entry 922), p. 152.

883.   BABBIE, EARL R. "The Third Civilization." *Review of Religious Research* 7, no. 2 (1966): 101-21.

884.   _____. "The Third Civilization: An Examination of Sokagakkai." In *Religion in Sociological Perspectives: Essays in the Empirical Study of Religion*. Edited by Charles Y. Glock. Belmont, CA: Wadsworth, 1973, pp. 235-60.

885.   BACH, MARCUS. *Strangers at the Door* (entry 13), pp. 110-15.

886.   BAERWALD, HANS H. "Itto-Nanaraku: Japan's 1969 Elections." *Asian Survey* 10, no. 3 (March 1970): 179-94.

887.   BASABE, FERNANDO M. *Japanese Religious Attitudes* (entry 16), pp. 60-65.

888.   _____; ANZAI, SHIN; and LANZACO, FEDERICO. *Religious Attitudes of Japanese Men: A Sociological Survey* (entry 18), pp. 25-45.

889.   BEALS, DAVID R. "The Soka Gakkai Movement in Modern Japan: The Heritage, Characteristics and Aspirations of One of Japan's New Religions." Th.M. thesis, Berkeley Baptist Divinity School, Berkeley, CA: 1965, 159 pp. Bibliog.

890.   BERNARD, BERNIER. *Breaking the Cosmic Circle: Religion in a Japanese Village* (entry 23). See pp. 120-28, 153-64.

*891.   _____. "The Introduction of Soka Gakkai in a Japanese Rural Region." Unpublished paper. Cited in Bernard Bernier, *Breaking the Cosmic Circle* (entry 23), p. 183.

892.   BETHEL, DAYLE MORGAN. "The Life and Thought of Tsunesaburo Makiguchi: His Contribution to Education." Ph.D. dissertation, Michigan State University, 1971, 176 pp. Abstracted in *Dissertation Abstracts International* 32, no. 12 (June 1972): 6790A. University Microfilms International order no. 72-16,386.

[+]893.   _____. *Makiguchi, The Value Creator: Revolutionary Japanese Educator and Founder of Soka Gakkai.* New York: John Weatherhill, 1973, 174 pp. Illus.

894.   BIRD, FREDERICK. "Charisma and Ritual in New Religious Movements." In *Understanding the New Religions.* Edited by Jacob Needleman and George Baker. New York: Seabury Press, 1978, pp. 173-89.

[+]895.   BLACKER, CARMEN. "New Religious Cults in Japan" (entry 26).

896.   _____. "Le Sōka Gakkai japonais; l'activisme politique d'une secte bouddhiste." *Archives de sociologie des religions* 17 (January–June 1964): 63-67.

897.   BLAKER, MICHAEL K., ed. *Japan at the Polls: The House of Councillors Election of 1974.* Foreign Affairs Study, no. 37. Washington, DC: American Enterprise Institute for Public Policy, 1976, 157 pp. [See index under Komeito for numerous references.]

898. BLOOM, ALFRED. "Observations in the Study of Contemporary Nichiren Buddhism." *Contemporary Religions in Japan* 6, no. 1 (March 1965): 58-74.

899. _____. "The Sense of Sin and Guilt and the Last Age (Mappo) in Chinese and Japanese Buddhism." *Numen* 14 (1967): 144-49. Abstract in *Proceedings of the XIth International Congress of the International Association for the History of Religions*. 3 vols. Leiden: E.J. Brill, 1968. See 2: 175-76.

900. BRAMELD, THEODORE. *Japan: Culture, Education, and Change in Two Communities*. New York: Holt, Rinehart & Winston, 1968, xx + 316 pp. See pp. 7, 12, 65-67, 145, 200-2, 262, 268-69.

901. BRANDFON, JANE HURST. "Becoming a Strong Member: The Commitment Process in Nichiren Shoshu Buddhism." Unpublished paper, Center for the Study of New Religious Movements, 1975.

902. _____. "An Ethic for the Maintenance of Capitalism: The Nichiren Shoshu of America." Paper presented at the 1976 Annual Meeting of the Society for the Scientific Study of Religion, 1976, 21 pp. Cited in Jane Hurst Brandfon, "Becoming a Strong Member" (entry 901); also personal files of H[arry] Byron Earhart.

903. _____. "Pioneer Women in the Nichiren Shoshu Sokagakkai." Unpublished paper, Center for the Study of New Religious Movements, n.d.

904. BRANNEN, NOAH S. "False Religions, Forced Conversions, Iconoclasm." *Contemporary Religions in Japan* 5, no. 3 (September 1964): 232-52.

905. _____, trans. "Happiness and Life's Objective. Chapter 4 of *Shakubuku Kyōten*." *Contemporary Religions in Japan* 8, no. 2 (June 1967): 134-44.

906. _____. "Religion and Politics: Sidelights on Sōka Gakkai." *Japanese Religions* 4, no. 4 (December 1966): 79-99.

+907. _____. *Sōka Gakkai: Japan's Militant Buddhists*. Richmond, VA: John Knox Press, 1968, 181 pp.

908.   _____. "Soka Gakkai: New Religious Sect or Third World Power?"
        Japan Studies 1, no. 2 (1964): 15-20.

909.   _____. "Sōka Gakkai's Theory of Value." *Contemporary Religions in
        Japan* 5, no. 2 (June 1964): 143-54.

910.   _____. "The Teachings of Soka Gakkai." *Contemporary Religions in
        Japan* 3, no. 3 (September 1962): 247-63.

911.   _____. "A Visit to Soka Gakkai Headquarters." *Contemporary
        Religions in Japan* 2, no. 1 (March 1961): 55-62.

912.   _____. "A Visit to Taisekiji." *Contemporary Religions in Japan* 2, no. 2
        (June 1961): 13-29.

913.   "Buddha on the Barricades." *Time* 84, no. 24 (11 December 1964): 38-
        45.

914.   "Buddhist in Japan: Profit and Purity." *Economist* 208 (13 July 1963):
        134.

915.   BURKS, ARDATH W. *The Government of Japan.* 2d ed. New York:
        Thomas Y. Cromwell Co., 1964, xvi + 283 pp. See pp. 16, 84-85.

916.   "The Challenge of Soka Gakkai." *Christianity Today* 12, no. 11 (1 March
        1968): 29.

917.   "Comprehensive Survey: Komeito."   Translated by Universal
        Information Service. *Shori* (March 1968).

918.   "Creative Buddhism." *America* 110, no. 26 (27 June 1964): 857.

919.   CURTIS, GERALD L. *Election Campaigning Japanese Style* (entry 42),
        pp. 198-99.

*920.   DATOR, JAMES ALLEN. "Demographic and Attitudinal Data on
        Sōkagakkai Members." Unpublished paper prepared for presentation at
        annual convention of Association for Asian Studies, March 1968. Cited
        in James Wilson White, *The Sokagakkai and Mass Society* (entry 1087),
        p. 357.

921.   _____. "The Sōka Gakkai: A Socio-political Interpretation."
        Contemporary Religions in Japan 6, no. 3 (September 1965): 205-42.

+922.   ____. *Sōka Gakkai, Builders of the Third Civilization: American and Japanese Members.* Seattle: University of Washington Press, 1969, xiii + 171 pp.

923.   ____. "Soka Gakkai in Japanese Politics." *Journal of Church and State* 9 (Spring 1967): 211-37.

924.   DELIKHAN, GERALD A. "Sokagakkai and Komeito: The Politics of Religion." *Asia Magazine* (26 February 1967).

925.   ____. "Sokagakkai's Startling Success." *Asia Magazine* 4, no. 42 (18 October 1964).

926.   DERZHAVIN, IGOR KONSTANTINOVICH. "Soka Gakkai" [Sōka Gakkai], and "Komeito" [Kōmeitō]. In *Sovremennai IAponnia.* Moscow: Nauka, 566 pp. In Russian.

927.   ____. *Soka-gakkai—Komeito* [Sōka Gakkai—Kōmeitō]. Moscow: Nauka, 1972, 167 pp. In Russian.

928.   DOHERTY, HERBERT J., Jr. "Soka Gakkai: Religion and Politics in Japan." *Massachusetts Review* 4 (Winter 1963): 281-86.

929.   DUGLISS, RODERICK B. "The Foreign Policy of Komeito." In *The Final Report of the Ford Research Project.* Tokyo: International Christian University, 1967. See pp. 845-66.

930.   ____. "The Komeito and the Japanese Elections." *Economic and Political Weekly* (India) (11 February 1967): 377-81.

931.   DUMOULIN, HEINRICH. "Buddhismus im modernen Japan" (entry 48), pp. 330-51.

932.   ____. "Sōka Gakkai." *Die Katholischen Missionen* 83 (January-February 1964): 14-21.

933.   ____. "Soka Gakkai, eine moderne Volksreligion: ein Besuch im Haupttempel Taisekiji." In *Das Moderne Japan: einführende Aufsätze.* Edited by Joseph Roggendorf. Tokyo: Sophia Universität, 1963, pp. 189-200.

934.   EARHART, H[ARRY] BYRON. *Japanese Religion: Unity and Diversity*
       (entry 53); 2d ed., pp. 114-17; 3d ed., pp. 177-82.

935.   _____. "The New Religions" (entry 55), pp. 244-49.

936.   _____. "Recent Publications on the Japanese New Religions" (entry
       57).

+937. _____. "Recent Western Publications on Soka Gakkai." *History of
       Religions* 15, no. 3 (February 1976): 264-88. [Review of entries 893,
       944, 950, 1038, and 1087.]

938.   ELLWOOD, ROBERT S., Jr. *The Eagle and the Rising Sun: Americans
       and the New Religions of Japan* (entry 61), pp. 69-110.

939.   _____. *Religious and Spiritual Groups in Modern America.* Englewood
       Cliffs, NJ: Prentice-Hall, 1972, xvi + 334 pp. See pp. 267-75.

940.   ENDO, YOSHIMITSU. "Soka Gakkai, the Study of a Society for the
       Creation of Value." *Anglican Theological Review* 46 (April 1964): 131-
       41.

941.   FARNSWORTH, LEE W. "Japan: The Year of the Shock." *Asian
       Survey* 12, no. 1 (January 1972): 46-55.

942.   FELDMAN, ALEXANDER. "Buddhist Power." *New Republic* 162, no. 3
       (17 January 1970): 20-22.

943.   FLAGLER, J.M. "A Chanting in Japan." *New Yorker* (26 November
       1966): 37-87.

+944. FUJIWARA, HIROTATSU. *I Denounce Soka Gakkai.* Translated by
       Worth C. Grant. Tokyo: Nishin Hodo Co., 1970, 287 pp.

945.   _____. "Sokagakkai Unmasked." *Far Eastern Economic Review* (12
       February 1970): 19. Reprinted in *Atlas* (May 1970): 60-61.

946.   GARRIGUES, S.L. "The Sokagakkai Enshrining Ceremony: Ritual
       Change in a Japanese Buddhist Sect in America." *Eastern
       Anthropologist* 28, no. 2 (April-June 1975): 133-46.

947.   GITTINGS, J.A. "Politics of Mercy in Sokagakkai." *Japan Christian
       Quarterly* 23 (Summer 1967): 197-99.

*948. GRESSER, JULIAN. "Kōmeitō: An Assessment of Its Political Orientation and Future Course." Unpublished paper, Harvard University, 1966. Cited in James Wilson White, *The Sokagakkai and Mass Society* (entry 1087), p. 358.

949. GROSS, CARL H. "The History of the Sokagakkai Movement and Its Educational Implications." Unpublished paper, 1973, personal files of H[arry] Byron Earhart.

+950. _____. *Sokagakkai and Education.* East Lansing: Michigan State University, College of Education, Institute for International Studies, 1970, 79 pp.

951. HAMMER, RAYMOND JACK. "The Idea of God in Japan's New Religions" (entry 74), pp. 157-60.

952. HAMZAVI, ABDOL HOSSEIN. *The Prophetic Light.* Tokyo: Privately published for the author by John Weatherhill, 1977, 72 pp. See pp. 57-72. (Also in Japanese and Arabic.)

953. "Happy Talk." *Newsweek* 79, no. 23 (5 June 1972): 68.

954. HASHIMOTO, HIDEO. "Soka Gakkai-Komeito: Religion and Politics in Action 1977." *Japanese Religions* 9, no. 4 (July 1977): 23-46.

955. _____, and McPHERSON, WILLIAM. "Rise and Decline of Sokagakkai: Japan and the U.S." *Review of Religious Research* 17, no. 2 (Winter 1976): 82-92.

956. HELTON, W. "Political Prospects of Soka Gakkai." *Pacific Affairs* 38, nos. 3-4 (Fall-Winter, 1965-66): 231-44.

957. HESSELGRAVE, DAVID JOHN. "The Background and Methodology of Soka Gakkai Propagation." In *Studies on Asia, 1966.* Vol. 7, edited by Robert K. Sakai. Lincoln: University of Nebraska Press, 1966, pp. 65-75.

958. _____, ed. "Nichiren Shoshu Soka Gakkai—The Lotus Blossoms in Japan." In *Dynamic Religious Movements: Case Studies of Rapidly Growing Religious Movements Around the World.* Grand Rapids, MI: Baker Book House, 1978, pp. 129-48.

959. _____. "A Propagation Profile of the Soka Gakkai." Ph.D. dissertation, University of Minnesota, 1965, 305 pp. Abstracted in *Dissertation Abstracts* 26, no. 9 (March 1966): 5595. University Microfilms International order no. 65-15,264.

960. _____. "Resurgent Buddhism of the Soka Gakkai." *Christianity Today* 9, no. 16 (7 May 1965): 45-46.

961. _____. "Soka Gakkai's Inner Thrust." *Evangelical Missions Quarterly* 3, no. 3 (Spring 1967): 129-36.

962. HOLTZAPPLE, VICKI REA. "Soka Gakkai in Midwestern America: A Case Study of a Transpositional Movement." Ph.D. dissertation, Washington University, 1977, 348 pp. Abstracted in *Dissertation Abstracts International* 38, no. 12 (June 1978): 7415A. University Microfilms International order no. 7807941.

962A. HUFFMAN, JAMES LAMAR. "Following Nichiren's Trails: A Comparison of Saint Nichiren and the Soka Gakkai." M.A. thesis, University of Michigan, 1967, vi + 153 pp. Available at the Asia Library of the University of Michigan.

963. ICHIKAWA, HAKUGEN. "The Problem of Buddhist Socialism in Japan." *Japanese Religions* 6, no. 3 (August 1970): 15-37. See pp. 29-30.

964. "The Impact of the Soka Gakkai." *Christianity Today* 9, no. 8 (15 January 1965): 54.

965. INGRAM, PAUL O. "Nichiren's three secrets." *Numen* 24, no. 3 (1977): 207-22.

966. _____. "Soka Gakkai and the Komeito: Buddhism and Political Power in Japan." *Contemporary Religions in Japan* 10, nos. 3-4 (September-December 1969): 155-80.

967. *Info, The Spirit of Service.* [Contains many unsigned articles concerning Sōka Gakkai.]

968. INTERNATIONAL INSTITUTE FOR THE STUDY OF RELIGIONS. "Soka Gakkai and Temple Cemeteries." *Contemporary Religions in Japan* 1, no. 1 (March 1960): 94-95.

969. ____. "Soka Gakkai and the Nichiren Sho Sect." *Contemporary Religions in Japan* 1, no. 1 (March 1960): 55-70; no. 2 (June 1960): 48-54.

970. ISHIBASHI, MASAHI. "On the Joint Struggle of All Opposition Parties." *Japan Socialist Review*, no. 269 (15 February 1973): 3-7.

971. ISHIDA, TAKESHI, and ISONO, FUJIKO. "Soka Gakkai." *Correspondent*, no. 31 (March-April 1964).

972. ISHIKAWA, TAIDO. "Has Soka Gakkai Changed?" *Japan Missionary Bulletin* 18 (June 1964): 366-68.

973. ITALIAANDER, ROLF. *Sokagakkai; Japans neue Buddhisten.* Erlangen: Verlag der Evangelisch-Lutherischen Mission, 1973, 423 pp.

974. "Japan's New Church Militant." *Japan Quarterly* 4, no. 4 (October-December 1957): 413-19.

975. JOHNSON, CHALMERS A. "Low Posture Politics in Japan." *Asian Survey* 3, no. 1 (January 1963): 17-30.

976. KAMSTRA, JAKOB H. "Japans grösste Gefahr—die Sokagakkai." *Zeitschrift für Missionskunde und Religionswissenschaft* 44, no. 1 (1960): 41-51; no. 2 (1960): 98-106.

+977. KASAHARA, KAZUO. "Soka Gakkai and Komeito: The Advance of a New Religion into Politics." *Japan Quarterly* 14, no. 3 (July-September 1967): 311-17.

978. KISHI, NOBUSUKE. "Political Movements in Japan." *Foreign Affairs* 44, no. 1 (October 1965): 90-99.

979. KISHIMOTO, KOICHI. *Politics in Modern Japan—Development and Organization.* Tokyo: Japan Echo, 1977, 165 pp. See pp. 120-26.

980. KIYOTA, MINORU. "Buddhism in Postwar Japan: A Critical Survey" (entry 114).

981. KLEIN, NORBERT HANS. "On the Doctrine of Sōkagakkai." *Japanese Religions* 5, no. 3 (July 1968): 63-82.

982.   KOBAYASHI, SAKAE. "Changes in the Japanese Religions after World War II" (entry 115), pp. 92–95.

983.   _____. "Soka Gakkai, a Strange Buddhist Sect." *Japan Christian Quarterly* 24, no. 2 (April 1958): 104–11.

984.   KOESTLER, ARTHUR. "Her Course Is Set." *Life* 57, no. 11 (11 September 1964): 72–74.

+985.   KOHLER, WERNER. *Die Lotus-Lehre und die modernen Religionen in Japan* (entry 118), pp. 203–35.

986.   KÖPPING (KOEPPING) PETER. "Soka Gakkai—die kämpferische neue Religion Japans." *Indo Asia* 11 (July 1969): 247–58.

987.   KUBOTA, TADAO. "What Means the Result of Local Elections?" *Japan Socialist Review*, no. 132 (15 May 1976): 1–6.

988.   KUDO, TAKUYA. "The Faith of Soka Gakkai." *Contemporary Religions in Japan* 2, no. 2 (June 1961): 1–12.

989.   KUMASAKA, Y. "Soka Gakkai: Group Psychologic Study of a New Religio-Political Organization." *American Journal of Psychotherapy* 20 (July 1966): 462–70.

990.   KUWATA, KOICHIRO. "Political Parties in the Next Decade." *Japan Quarterly* 18, no. 2 (April–June 1970): 139–48. See pp. 139–40, 147–48.

991.   LACY, EDWARD F., III. "Soka Gakkai Target: American Negroes." *Negro Digest* 12, no. 12 (October 1964): 20–23.

992.   LANCZKOWSKI, GÜNTER. *Die neuen Religionen* (entry 126), pp. 48–54.

993.   LANGDON, FRANK. "Japan: Multi-Party Drift and Okinawa Reversion." *Asian Survey* 9, no. 1 (January 1969): 40–49.

993A.   LARSON, LYLE E. "Kōmeitō: Japan's Newest Political Party." M.A. thesis, University of Michigan, 1967, 95 pp. Available at the Asia Library of the University of Michigan.

*993B. LATYSHEV, I.A. *The Role of Religion in the Political Life of Japan.* 1964, 34 pp. In Russian. Cited in E. Stuart Kirby, *Russian Studies of*

Japan: An Exploratory Survey (New York: St. Martin's Press, 1981), xvi + 226 pp. See pp. 50-51, 180.

994. LAYMAN, EMMA McCLOY. *Buddhism in America.* Chicago: Nelson-Hall Publishers, 1976, xvii + 364 pp. See pp. 115-39.

995. LEE, JOOINN. "Komeito: Sokagakkai-ism in Japanese Politics." *Asian Survey* 10, no. 6 (June 1970): 501-18.

996. LEE, ROBERT. "Religious Evolution and the Individuation of the Self in Japanese History." Ph.D. dissertation, Harvard University, 1974, 352 pp. Available at the Harvard University Archives, Pusey Library, call no. HU 90.10579.10.

997. LEE, TOSH. "Members of the Soka Gakkai, a Study in Mass Political Behavior." Ph.D. dissertation, University of Wisconsin-Madison, 1970, 413 pp. Abstracted in *Dissertation Abstracts International* 31, no. 11 (May 1971): 6125A. University Microfilms International order no. 71-3472.

998. "Lotus Power." *Newsweek* 75, no. 3 (19 January 1970): 46.

999. McCRIMMON, MARY. "From Christianity to Soka Gakkai." *Japan Missionary Bulletin* 18, no. 6 (July 1964): 397-402.

+1000. McFARLAND, H[ORACE] NEILL. *The Rush Hour of the Gods* (entry 136), pp. 194-220.

1001. McPHERSON, WILLIAM. "Nichiren Shoshu of America, 1972-1977." Unpublished paper, Center for the Study of New Religious Movements, n.d.

1002. MARTINEZ, LUIS S. "Una religion militante en el Japon." *Siglo missiones* 45 (1958): 410-12, 426.

1003. MÉTRAUX, DANIEL ALFRED. "The Last Word: Japan's Sokagakkai." *Soka Gakkai News* 62 (25 January 1978): 7-11.

1004. _____. "The Religious and Social Philosophy of the Sōkagakkai." Ph.D. dissertation, Columbia University, 1978, 341 pp. Abstracted in *Dissertation Abstracts International* 39, no. 1 (July 1978): 418A. University Microfilms International order no. 7811146.

1005.   _____. "The Sokagakkai's Philosophy of Life." In *Proceedings of First International Symposium on Asian Studies, 1979.* Vol. 2, *Japan and Korea.* Hong Kong: Asian Research Service, 1980, pp. 479-87.

1006.   MONSTERLEET, JEAN. "A propos du Sōka Gakkai." *Études* 319, no. 12 (1963): 352-58.

1007.   MOOS, FELIX. "Religion and Politics in Japan: The Case of the Sōka Gakkai." *Asian Survey* 3, no. 3 (March 1963): 136-42.

1008.   MORI, KOICHI. "Study of Makiguchi Tsunesaburō: The Founder of Sōka Gakkai." Th.D. thesis, Graduate Theological Union, 1977, 236 pp. Bibliog., pp. 221-35. Abstracted in *Dissertation Abstracts International* 38, no. 11 (May 1978): 677A-78A. University Microfilms International order no. 7805457.

1009.   MORRIS, IVAN I. "Challenge of Soka Gakkai." *Encounter* 26, no. 5 (May 1966): 78-83.

1010.   _____. *Nationalism and the Right Wing in Japan: A Study of Post-War Trends.* London: Oxford University Press, 1960, 476 pp. See pp. 140-41.

1011.   _____. "Soka Gakkai Brings 'Absolute Happiness.'" *New York Times Magazine* (18 July 1965): 8-9, 36, 38-39.

⁺1012.   MURAKAMI, SHIGEYOSHI. *Japanese Religion in the Modern Century* (entry 153), pp. 107-9, 147-56, 164-66.

1013.   MURAMATSU, TAKESHI. "Die Modernisierung Japans und die Nichirensekte." Translated by Hartmut O. Rotermund. *Kagami* 3, no. 2 (1965): 34-47.

1014.   MURATA, HAJIME. "Soka Gakkai." *Hemisphere* 10, no. 5 (May 1966): 8-12.

⁺1015.   MURATA, KIYOAKI. *Japan'a New Buddhism: An Objective Account of Soka Gakkai.* Foreword by Daisaku Ikeda. New York and Tokyo: Walker/Weatherhill, 1969, xiv + 194 pp. Illus.

1016.   NAGOYA, KAZUHIKO. "Japan's New Political Party." *Atlas* 9, no. 2 (February 1965): 111-13.

1017.   "Namu myoho rengekyo." *Time* 73, no. 24 (15 June 1959): 38.

1018.   "A New Faith Called Soka Gakkai Raises Old Problems in Modern Japan." *Look* 27, no. 18 (10 September 1963): 18-26.

1019.   NISHIO, HARRY K. "Comparative Analysis of the Risshō Kōseikai and the Sōka Gakkai." *Asian Survey* 7, no. 11 (November 1967): 776-90.

1020.   _____. "Extraparliamentary Activities and Political Unrest in Japan." *International Journal* (Canadian Institute of International Affairs) 34, no. 1 (Winter 1968-69): 122-37.

1021.   NITOBE, INAZO. "Preface to the Original." In *The Philosophy of Value*, by Tsunesaburo Makiguchi (entry 851), pp. 187-93.

1021A. NORBECK, EDWARD. *Religion and Society in Modern Japan: Continuity and Change* (entry 168Λ), pp. 164-84.

1022.   NORMAN, W.H.H. "Sokagakkai, Komeito and Freedom of Speech." *Japan Christian Quarterly* 36 (Fall 1970): 258-65.

1023.   *Novas religiões japonêsas no Brasil, por uma equipe de Franciscanos de Petrópolis* (entry 172), pp. 9-17.

1024.   NUKUI, HIROSHI. "Komeito's Drive toward the Lower House and Its Problems—Logic and Facts about the Fiction of a Religious Party." *Japan Socialist Review*, no. 119 (1 November 1966): 3-21.

1025.   O'DONOGHUE, PATRICK FRANCIS. "Nichiren in Modern Buddhism: A Study in Catechetical Adaptation in Japan's Soka Gakkai Leadership." Ph.D. dissertation, Catholic University of America, Washington, DC, 1977, 377 pp. Abstracted in *Dissertation Abstracts International* 38, no. 7 (January 1978): 4221A. University Microfilms International order no. 77-27,718.

1026.   OFFNER, CLARK B. "Soka Gakkai." *Japan Christian Quarterly* 35, no. 3 (Summer 1969): 153-61.

1027.   _____, and STRAELEN, HENRY (HENRICUS J.J.M.) van. *Modern Japanese Religions* (entry 175), pp. 98-109.

1028. OH, JOHN KIE-CH'ANG. "Fusion of Politics and Religion in Japan; the Soka Gakkai-Komeito." *Journal of Church and State* 14 (Winter 1972): 59-74.

1029. No entry.

1030. OKAMOTO, RICHARD. "Japan: A Booming Economy Has Spawned a Militant New Religion with 10 Million Adherents Bent on Dominating the World." *Look* 27, no. 18 (10 September 1963): 15-17.

+1031. OLSON, LAWRENCE. "The Value Creation Society." *American Universities Field Staff* (Reports Service, East Asia Series) 11, no. 6 (1964): 1-24.

1032. OMORI, SHIGEO. "The Okinawa Problem: Controversy between Government and Opposition Parties." *Japan Quarterly* 15, no. 1 (January-March 1968): 22-29.

1033. _____. "The Political Choice of the Komeito Regarding the Security Treaty." *Asahi Journal* 10 (1968): 93-95.

1034. "On Cooperation Among the Opposition Parties after the General Election." *Japan Socialist Review*, no. 339 (February 1977): 11-14.

1035. "On the Results of the 11th Upper House Election." *Japan Socialist Review*, no. 346 (September 1977): 3-12.

1036. "On the Strengthening of Cooperation Among the Socialist, Communist, and Komei Parties." *Japan Socialist Review*, no. 331 (June 1976): 15-17.

1037. PALMER, ARTHUR ARVIN. "Buddhist Politics: Japan's Clean Government Party." Ph.D. dissertation, Claremont University, 1970, 190 pp. Abstracted in *Dissertation Abstracts International* 31, no. 1 (July 1970): 441A-42A. University Microfilms International order no. 70-11,910.

+1038. _____. *Buddhist Politics: Japan's Clean Government Party.* The Hague: Martinus Nijhoff, 1971, xi + 98 pp.

1039. PLANNING SECTION, THE JSP HQS. "Soka Gakkai Decides to Run for Lower House." *Japan Socialist Review*, no. 63 (1 June 1964): 26-30.

1040. "The Power of Positive Chanting." *Time* (17 January 1969): 51.

1040A. PREBISH, CHARLES S. *American Buddhism*. North Scituate, MA: Duxbury Press, 1979, xix + 220 pp. See pp. 12-13, 70-132, 189-90.

1041. "Present Situation of Komeito." *Japan Socialist Review*, no. 88 (15 June 1965): 46-55.

1042. "Publish and Be Damned." *Japan Quarterly* 17, no. 3 (July-September 1970): 241-43.

1043. RAJANA, EIMI WATANABE. "A Sociological Study of New Religious Movements: Chilean Pentecostalism and Japanese New Religions" (entry 190), pp. 79-85, 248-53.

1044. RAMSMEYER, ROBERT L. "The Soka Gakkai and the Japanese Local Elections of 1963." *Contemporary Religions in Japan* 4, no. 4 (December 1963): 287-302.

1045. _____. "The Soka Gakkai: Militant Religion on the March." *Occasional Papers*, no. 9 (Center for Japanese Studies, University of Michigan, 1965), pp. 141-92.

*1046. RASSAT, JOACHIM. "Die Soka Gakkai will Japan moralischer machen." *Die Welt*, no. 158 (July 1962). Cited in Werner Kohler, *Die Lotus-Lehre und die modernen Religionen in Japan* (entry 118), p. 290.

1047. REISCHAUER, EDWIN O. *Japan: The Story of a Nation*. New York: Knopf, 1970, xv + 345 pp. See esp. pp. 309-10. (Also other editions.)

1048. RICCO, MARIO. *Religione della violenza e religione del piacere nel nuovo Giappone* (entry 195), pp. 15-55.

1049. "Ridimensionamenti in seno alla Soka Gakkai?" *Mondo e missione* 100 (1971): 227.

1050. ROSENKRANZ, GERHARD. *Der Weg des Buddha: Werden und Wesen des Buddhismus als Weltreligion*. Basel: Basileia Verlag, 1960, 356 pp. See pp. 314-19.

1051. ROTERMUND, HARTMUT O. "Einführung zum Shakubuku Kyōten der Sōka Gakkai; Bekehrung auf Biegen und Brechen." *Zeitschrift für Religions- und Geistesgeschichte* 24, no. 3 (1972): 227-41.

1052. _____. "Soka-gakkai; ideologie d'une nouvelle secte japonaise." *Revue de l'histoire des religions* 184, no. 2 (October 1973): 137-57.

1053. SAITO, KEN. "Soka Gakkai: Third Force in Japanese Politics?" *Orient/West* 7, no. 11 (November 1962): 33-37.

1054. SASAKI ("CHAIRMAN SASAKI"). "Chairman Comments on the Komeito." *Japan Socialist Review*, no. 125 (1 February 1967): 8-9.

1055. SCALAPINO, ROBERT A., and MASUMI, JUNNOSUKE. *Parties and Politics in Contemporary Japan.* Berkeley and Los Angeles: University of California Press, 1962, ix + 190 pp. See pp. 92-93.

1056. SCHECHTER, JERROLD. *The New Face of Buddha: Buddhism and Political Power in Southeast Asia.* London: Gollancz; NY: Coward-McCann, 1967, xix + 298 pp. See pp. 253-73.

1057. SCHIFFER, WILHELM. "The 'Sōka Gakkai': Its History and Its Claims." *France-Asie* 19, no. 182 (January-March 1964): 1111-18.

1058. SHELDON, CHARLES D. "Religion in Politics in Japan: The Soka Gakkai." *Pacific Affairs* 33, no. 4 (December 1960): 382-87.

1059. SKELTON, T. LANE. "Social Movements and Social Change: The Sōka Gakkai of Japan." Ph.D. dissertation, University of California, Berkeley, 1968, 307 pp. Abstracted in *Dissertation Abstracts International* 30, no. 3 (September 1969): 1246A. University Microfilms International order no. 69-15,001.

1059A. SNOW, DAVID ALAN. "The Nichiren Shoshu Buddhist Movement in America: A Sociological Examination of Its Value Orientation, Recruitment Efforts, and Spread." Ph.D. dissertation, University of California, Los Angeles, 1976, 370 pp. Abstracted in *Dissertation Abstracts International* 37, no. 8 (February 1977): 5374A. University Microfilms International order no. 77-1666.

*1060. "Soka Gakkai Study." Unpublished manuscript, United States Information Service, Tokyo, 1960. Cited in James Wilson White, *The Sokagakkai and Mass Society* (entry 1087), p. 366.

1061. SOLOMON, TED J. "The Response of Three New Religions to the Crisis in the Japanese Value System" (entry 211).

1062. SPAE, JOSEPH J. "Postscript as an Answer." *Japan Missionary Bulletin* 16, no. 8 (October 1962): 507-9.

1063. ____. "Sōkagakkai." *Japan Missionary Bulletin* 14, no. 7 (August-September 1960): 454-57.

1064. "Stamping in Nichiren's Footsteps." *Economist* 214 (20 March 1965): 1250, 1255.

1065. STEINER, KURT. *Local Government in Japan.* Stanford, CA: Stanford University Press, 1965, ix + 564 pp. See pp. 403, 439, 468.

1066. "The Super Missionary." *Time* 102, no. 2 (13 January 1975): 26.

1067. SWEARER, DONALD K. *Buddhism In Transition.* Philadelphia: Westminster Press, 1970, 160 pp. See pp. 58-62, 82, 90-91.

+1068. TAKAGI, HIROO. "The Rise of the New Religions" (entry 224).

1069. ____. "Soka Gakkai Makes Advance into Political World." *Japan Socialist Review* (16 June 1962): 53.

1070. TAKASE, HIROI. "'Sōka-Gakkai.' Gemeinschaft zur Schaffung von (geistigen und sittlichen) Lebenswerten. Über das Geheimnis dieses energievollen Verbandes." Translated by Hartmut O. Rotermund. *Kagami* 2, no. 1 (1963-64): 55-63.

1071. TANABE, SUKETOSHI. "Preface to the Original." In *The Philosophy of Value,* by Tsunesaburo Makiguchi (entry 851), pp. 181-86.

1072. THOMPSON, STEPHEN I. "Religious Conversion and Religious Zeal in an Overseas Enclave: The Case of Japanese in Bolivia" (entry 228).

1073. THOMSEN, HARRY. "Ise or Daisekiji?" *Japanese Religions* 1, no. 2 (1959): 22-30.

1074. ____. *The New Religions of Japan* (entry 233), pp. 81-108.

1075. TSURUMI, SHUNSUKE. "A Brief History of Soka Gakkai." *Japanese Religions* 3, no. 3 (Autumn 1963): 32-40.

1076.   UKAI, NOBUSHIGE.   "The Japanese House of Councillors Election of July, 1962." *Asia Survey* 2, no. 6 (August 1962): 1-8.

1077.   UYTTENDAELE, FRANCIS.   "Sōkagakkai on the March."   *Japan Missionary Bulletin* 16, no. 8 (October 1962): 501-6.

*1078.   VERBA, SIDNEY, et al.   ("Unpub. survey of political attitudes of Japanese made in late 1966 as part of the Cross-National Project for Political and Social Change by associates of Sidney Verba, University of Chicago.") Cited in James Wilson White, *The Sokagakkai and Mass Society* (entry 1087), p. 368.

1079.   "War of the Sects" (entry 241).

1080.   WARD, ROBERT E. *Japan's Political System.* Englewood Cliffs, NJ: Prentice-Hall, 1967, ix + 126 pp. See pp. 39, 72-73. 2d ed., 1978, xi + 253 pp. See pp. 105-9, 117, 124-25, 131-33.

1081.   WEEKS, J. STAFFORD.   "Rissho Kosei-kai: A Cooperative Buddhist Sect."   In *Religious Ferment in Asia.*   Edited by Robert J. Miller. Lawrence: University of Kansas Press, 1974, pp. 156-68.

1082.   WEST, RICHARD.   "Yen Buddhism."   *New Statesman* 67, no. 1735 (12 June 1964): 904-6.

*1083.   WHITE, JAMES WILSON.   "California F-Scale Administered to Sōkagakkai Members in Tokyo, Oct. 1967." Cited in James Wilson White, *The Sokagakkai and Mass Society* (entry 1087), p. 368.

+1084.   _____.   "Mass Movement and Democracy: Sokagakkai in Japanese Politics."   *American Political Science Review* 61, no. 3 (September 1967): 744-50.

1085.   _____.   "Mass Movement, Militant Religion, and Democracy: Sōka Gakkai in Japanese Politics."   Ph.D. dissertation, Stanford University, 1969.   Abstracted in *Dissertation Abstracts International* 305, no. 5 (November 1969): 2100A-2101A.   University Microfilms International order no. 69-17,461.

*1086.   _____.   "Militant Religion in Japan: The Sōka Gakkai."   A.B. thesis, Princeton University, 1964.   Cited in James Wilson White, *The Sokagakkai and Mass Society* (entry 1087), p. 368.

+1087.   ____. *The Sokagakkai and Mass Society*. Stanford, CA: Stanford
          University Press, 1970, xii + 376 pp.

1088.   WILKINSON, STEPHEN L. "Nichiren Shoshu Sokagakkai in America:
          An Analysis of Ultimate Concerns Between 1960 and 1965." Ph.D.
          dissertation, University of Iowa, 1975, 288 pp. Abstracted in
          Dissertation Abstracts International 36, no. 12 (June 1976): 8127A.
          University Microfilms International order no. 76-13,460.

+1089.   WOODARD, WILLIAM P. "The Wartime Persecution of Nichiren
          Buddhism." *Transactions of the Asiatic Society of Japan* 3d Ser. 6
          (November 1959): 99-122.

1090.   WOODROW, ALAIN. *Les nouvelles sectes*. Paris: Éditions du Seuil,
          1977, 187 pp. See pp. 145-46, 188. (See also entry 1090A.)

1090A.   ____. *As novas seitas* [The new sects]. Translated by Celeste Maria
          Jardim de Moraes. São Paulo: Edicoes Paulinas, 1979, 243 pp. See pp.
          164-65, 214-15. In Portuguese. (See also entry 1090.)

1091.   YAMAMORI, TETSUNAO. "Soka Gakkai; a Religious Phoenix."
          Practical Anthropology 19, no. 4 (July-August 1972): 1518-68. Re-
          printed in *Japanese Religions* 8, no. 1 (March 1974): 1-18.

1092.   YANAGAWA, KEIICHI, and REID, DAVID. "Between Unity and
          Separation: Religion and Politics in Japan, 1965-1977." In *Acts, 15th
          International Conference on Sociology of Religion, Venice, 1979*.
          Edited by Jacques Verscheure. Lille Cedex: Secrétariat C.I.S.R., 1979,
          pp. 387-409. Reprinted in *Japanese Journal of Religious Studies* 6, no.
          4 (December 1979): 500-21.

1093.   YANAGIDA, KUNIO. "Preface to the First Edition." In *The Philosophy
          of Value*, by Tsunesaburo Makiguchi (entry 851), pp. 194-97.

1094.   ZARATE, ROBERTO M. GONZALEZ De. "Soka Gakkai: Una religion
          del valor." *Razón y fe* 171, no. 804 (January 1965): 53-66.

Sūkyō Mahikari

Denominational

No publications known.

Secondary

+1095.   DAVIS, WINSTON [BRADLEY]. *Dojo: Magic and Exorcism in Modern Japan.* Stanford, CA: Stanford University Press, 1980, xvii + 332 pp. Illus.

Taireidō

Denominational

1096.   KANTUW, N. *A New Thought: The Doctrine of Tairei, Its Art of Healing.* Tokyo: Yoshusha, 1918. (Articles with separate pagination: "A New Thought," 19 pp.; "The Doctrine of Tairei," 12 pp.; "The Supreme Authority on the Art of Healing," 60 pp. Also contains Japanese original for the second article and translations into Japanese of the first and third articles.)

1097.   TANAKA, MORIHEI. *Taireido; a New Revelation for the Spiritual, Mental, and Physical Salvation of Mankind.* [Tokyo]: Taireido Honin, 1920, 447 pp. Illus. [Library of Congress listing includes: "Printed on double leaves, Japanese style."]

1098.   _____. *Tairedo: A New Revelation Showing the True System of Life; an Outline Only.* [Tokyo? 1919? (as listed in Library of Congress)], 56 pp.

Secondary

1099.   WITTE, JOHANNES. "Eine neue religiöse Bewegung in Japan." *Zeitschrift für Missionskunde und Religionswissenschaft* 33 (1918): 103-4.

Tenkyō-kyō

Denominational

1100. "Tenko-kyo, 'A New Religion for the Coming Era.'" Translated by International Institute for the Study of Religions. *Contemporary Religions in Japan* 3, no. 2 (June 1962): 116-21.

Secondary

No publications known.

Tenrikyō

Denominational

(Unless otherwise specified, published at the city of Tambaichi or Tenri by the Headquarters of Tenrikyo Church, or The Tenrikyo Overseas Mission Dept., or Tenrikyo Central See, or Tenri Jihōsha.)

1101. *Acte de foi Tenrikyo.* 1964, 9 pp.

1102. *Anecdotes of Oyasama, the Foundress of Tenrikyo.* 1962, 159 pp. "Trial" Translation, 26 May 1977, ii + 159 pp. Rev. ed., 1978.

1103. *A propos du sazuke.* 1976. (Also German and Spanish editions.)

1104. *Besseki-Führer.* 1974.

1105. *Catechism of Tenrikyo.* 1979, 42 pp. (Also French, Spanish, and Portuguese [2 vols.] editions.)

1106. *Coisa Emprestada e Tomada Emprestada.* 1977, 54 pp.

1107. No entry.

1108. *Dancing Psalms ("Mikagurauta").* 1950, 24 pp.

1109.   *The Divine Model: The Life of the Foundress of Tenrikyo.* 1958, 12 pp.

1110.   *The Doctrine of Tenrikyo: Preliminary Edition.*   1954, 105 pp.
        (Editions in ten languages.) 2d ed., 1958, 105 pp. Reprint. 1964.

1111.   "The English Glossary of Technics in Tenrikyo." In *Nakanishi Kiyozō
        shū.* Edited by Shunji Katayama. Osaka, 1936, pp. 454–441. (Pages
        numbered from right to left.)

1112.   *Foto (Oyasato).* 1975, 24 pp.

1113.   No entry.

1114.   *A Glimpse of Tenrikyo.* 1953, 18 pp.

1115.   *Guide in Oyasato.* 1968, 17 pp. (Japanese and English text.)

1116.   *Guide to Faith.* Pamphlet series. July 1959–.

1117.   *Guide to Jiba.* 1979, 45 pp.

1118.   *Guide to the Besseki.* Pamphlet. 1974. (Also German, French,
        Porguguese, and Spanish editions.)

1119.   *Guide to the Residence and Historical Sites.* 1976, 27 pp.

1120.   *Hinokishim e tanno* [Hinokishin and Tanno].   1978, 37 pp.   In
        Portuguese.

1121.   *Hinokishim expressão da alegria de viver* [Hinokishin, expression of the
        joy of living]. 1978, 18 pp. In Portuguese.

1122.   *Hinokishin.* 1973, 12 pp. In Spanish. (Also Portuguese edition.)

1123.   *Historia de criação humana* [History of human creation]. 1974, 66 pp.
        In Portuguese.

1124.   *History of Tenrikyo.* 1954.

1125.   *Imagens de Oyassama* [Images of Oyasama].   1973, 39 pp.   In
        Portuguese.

1126.   No entry.

1127. *Instruction No. 2.* 1973, 4 pp. (Also German, Spanish, and Russian editions.)

1128. *Introduccion a Tenrikyo.* 1975, 186 pp. (Also Portuguese edition.)

1129. *An Introduction to Catechism of Tenrikyo.* Translated by Akio Inoue. 1961, 52 pp. Rev. ed., 1967, 47 pp. (French edition, trans. Jacques About, 1965, 50 pp.)

1130. No entry.

1131. *Japan's New Shinto Movement: Tenrikyo.* 1945.

1132. *Jiba terra parental* [Jiba, homeland]. 1978, 45 pp. In Porguguese.

1133. No entry.

1134. *Die Lehre der Tenrikyo.* 1959, 90 pp. Rev. ed., 1975, 95 pp.

1135. *Life of Oyasama, the Foundress of Tenrikyo.* "Trial" ed., 1967, 317 pp.

1136. *The Life of the Foundress of Tenrikyo.* 1964, 25 pp.

1137. *Meditation sur la doctrine.* 1973, 55 pp.

1138. *Mikagura-uta.* 1975, 31 pp. In German. (Also French and Portuguese editions.) See also Nakayama, Miki, *Mikagura-uta* . . . (entry 1227).

1139. *Mikagura-uta: A Trial Translation.* Translated by Forest E. Barber. 1962, 26 pp. ("This translation is a private endeavor and is not to be construed as being authorized by Tenrikyo Headquarters.")

1140. *Mikagura-uta for Teodori Practice.* 1977, 14 pp. (Also French edition.)

1141. *The Mikagura-uta: Practice Manual of Women's Musical Instruments.* 1977, 31 pp.

1142. *Mikagura-uta (Romanized Practice Book for Musical Instruments).* 6 vols. Tenri: Tenri Jihosha, 1973. Vol. 1, *Kozutsumi (Tabor),* 30 pp. Vol. 2, *Surigane (Small Gong),* 30 pp. Vol. 3, *Fue (Bamboo Flute),* 30 pp. Vol. 4, *Champon (Cymbals),* 30 pp. Vol. 5, *Hyoshigi (Wooden Clappers),* 30 pp. Vol. 6, *Taiko (Drum),* 30 pp.

1143.   *Obschii ocherk religioznogo ucheniia "Tenrikio"* [General description of
the religious teaching of Tenrikyō]. Translated by O. Pletnerai and K.
Ida. 1930, 35 pp. In Russian.

1144.   *Ofudesaki: The Holy Scripts.* Translated by Seiichi Yoshida. 1961, 210
pp. (Trial translation.)

1145.   *Oyasato, Guide to Tenrikyo.* 1958, 77 pp. Illus. (Also French, German,
Portuguese, Russian, and Spanish editions.)

1146.   No entry.

1147.   *Résumé de la doctrine et de l'histoire du Tenrikyo.* Translated by
Tatsuo Morishita. 1933, 129 pp.

1148.   *Selections from the Osashizu.* 1976, 101 pp.

+1149.   *The Short History of Tenrikyo.* 1956, 274 pp. Illus. 2d ed. [title
varies: *A Short History of Tenrikyo*], 1958, 272 pp. 3d ed. [listed with
Shōzen Nakayama as author], 1960, 270 pp. Illus. 4th ed., 1967, v +
285 pp. Illus.

1150.   *Shuyoka Handbook.* 1976.

1151.   *Spiritual Maturity Sought for Mankind.* Pamphlet. 1976.

1152.   *The Start for a New Life.* 1977, 14 pp.

1153.   *The Statistical Year Book of Tenrikyo, 1956.* "Compiled by The
Investigating Section." 225 pp. Illus.

1154.   *The Story of Creation.* 1976, 51 pp.

1155.   *Tenrikio.* Translated by Kinzo Tomoda. N.d., 4 pp.

1156.   *Tenrikyo.* 1947, 14 pp.

1157.   *Tenrikyo.* 1975, 3 pp. In German.

1158.   *Tenrikyo: A Religion in Japan.* Tenri: Tenrikyo Administration
Headquarters, 1951, 7 pp. Illus.

1159.   *Tenrikyo: die Offenbarung Gottes und die wahre Erlösung.* Tenri:
Abteilung für Überseeische Mission von Tenrikyo, [1954], 14 pp. Illus.

+1160. *Tenrikyo, Its History and Teachings.* 1966, viii + 324 pp.

1161.   *Tenrikyo: Japan's New Religious Movement.* 1937, 37 pp. Illus.

1162.   *Tenrikyo: Japan's New Shinto Movement: Its Faith, Doctrines,
History, Institutions and Mission World Described with Illustrations.*
1934, 34 pp. Illus.

1163.   No entry.

1164.   *Tenrikyo, New Revelation: Outline of Its Doctrine.* 1946, 27 pp. Illus.

1165.   *The Tenrikyo Religion.* N.d., 4 pp., pages not numbered.

1166.   *Tenrikyo (Religion du vrai salut).* 1973, 46 pp.

1167.   *Tenrikyo—sa foi, ses préceptes et son salut.* 1964, 11 pp.

1168.   *Tenrikyo: Teachings for the Joyous Life.* 1976, 114 pp.

1169.   *Tenrikyo: (Tenrikyo in Outline).* 1945, 18 pp. Illus.

1170.   *Tenrikyo: "Tenrikyo" the Central See.* 1945, 18 pp.

1171.   *Tenrikyo: The Manifestation of God the Parent and the True
Salvation.* 1954, 13 pp. 2d ed., 1957. 4th ed., 1964, 13 pp. Illus. (Also
French, German, and Spanish editions.)

1172.   *Tenrikyō Toshokan-zō Tenrikyō Tosho Mokuroku.* 1959, 133 pp.
[Bibliography of Books on Tenrikyō in the Tenrikyō Library.]   In
Japanese; includes Western-language materials.

1173.   *Tenrikyo: Übersicht der Lehre und deren Entwicklungsgeschichte.*
Translated by Shigeo Yamaguchi. 1932, 80 pp.

1174.   No entry.

1175.   *Tenrikyo Year Book 1975: The 138th Year of Tenrikyo.* 1975, 236 pp.
Illus.

1176.   *Tenrikyo Yearbook 1976: The 139th Year of Tenrikyo.* 1976, 262 pp. Illus.

1177.   *Tenrikyo Yearbook 1977: The 140th Year of Tenrikyo.* 1977, 287 pp. Illus.

1178.   *Tenrikyo Yearbook 1978: The 141st Year of Tenrikyo.* 1978, 285 pp. Illus.

1178A. *Tenrikyo Yearbook 1979: The 142nd Year of Tenrikyo.* 1979, v + 289 pp. Illus.

1179.   *Tenri-Ō-no-Mikoto, What is the Character of God?* 1976, 34 pp. (Also Portuguese edition.)

1180.   *Vida de Oyassama* [The Life of Oyasama]. 1973, 39 pp. In Portuguese.

1181.   *Was lehrt die Tenrikyo.* 1974, 50 pp.

1182.   *The Way to a Happy Life.* Women's Association, 1955, 8 pp.

1183.   No entry.

1184.   *Yoboku Handbook.* 1976, 112 pp. (Also Portuguese edition, *Manual de Yôboku,* 1976, 120 pp.)

1185.   *Yokigurashi. Frohes Leben. Ausstellung über Tenrikyo. Eine Religion in Japan. 12 Mai–15 Juni 1975.* Marburg: Universitätsbibliothek, n.d., 18 pp.

1186.   AKAKI, TOKUNOSUKE. *History, Doctrine and Practice of Tenrikyo.* Osaka: Tenrikyo Senba Daikyokwai, 1911, 52 pp.

1187.   ANDO, TAKATSURA. *Reflections on God, Self and Humanity.* 1968, 119 pp.

1188.   BLACKWOOD, R.T. *Tenrikyo: A Living Religion.* 1964, 14 pp. Reprint. 1968, 23 pp.

1189.   FUKAYA, TADAMASA. *A Commentary on the Mikagura-uta.* Translated by H. Mimoto. 1962, 145 pp.

1190. ____. "The Fundamental Doctrines of Tenrikyo." *Tenri Journal of Religion* 1 (March 1955): 17-30. (Also published separately, 1962, 1978, 18 pp.)

1191. ____. *Introducao ao "Tenrikyo" (Tenrikyo Nyumon)* [Introduction to Tenrikyo]. Translated by Jose Sant'anna do Carmo. 1955, 51 pp. In Portuguese.

1192. ____. *An Introduction to Moto-no-Ri.* 1965, 39 pp.

1193. FUKUDA, YOSHIO. *From Stone to Life: Mattress Prisoner Regains Freedom.* Guide to Faith, no. 5. 10 pp.

1194. HASHIMOTO, MASAHARU. *Rukovodstro dlia posnaniia istinnoi very sekty "Tenrikyo"* [Guidance for learning the true faith of the sect Tenrikyō]. Translated by K.K. Furutani. Kharbin: Manjchzhurskoe propovednicheskoe upravleni, 1928, 18 pp. In Russian.

1195. HASHIMOTO, TAKETO. "The Teaching of Innen in Tenrikyo." *Tenri Journal of Religion* 13 (August 1979): 29-47.

1196. HIRASAWA, HAJIME. "Tenrikyo Followers' Views of Disease Seen From Patients with Malignant Tumors." *Tenri Journal of Religion* 9 (October 1968): 18-31.

1197. IIDA, TERUAKI. "The Concept of Progress in Tenrikyo." *Tenri Journal of Religion* 10 (October 1969): 7-16.

1198. ____. "Idea of Evolution in the Creation of Story of Tenrikyo Doctrine." *Tenri Journal of Religion* 9 (October 1968): 9-17.

1199. ____. "Mikagura-Uta . . . Psalms for the Sacred Dance of Tenrikyo—A Trial Translation in French." *Tenri Journal of Religion* 6 (December 1965): 64-101.

1200. ____. "A Note on Humanism and Tenrikyo." *Tenri Journal of Religion* 8 (May 1967): 28-36.

1201. ____. "Tenrikyo and Humanism." *Tenri Journal of Religion* 4 (June 1962): 36-46.

1202. ____. "Tenrikyo and Humanism—Humanism and the Meaning of Corporality." *Tenri Journal of Religion* 5 (June 1963): 29-40.

[+]1203.   IWAI, TAKAHITO. *The Outline of Tenrikyo.* Nara, 1932, vi + 319 pp.

1204.   KANEKO, KEISUKE. "The Growth and Development of Early Tenrikyo Churches in the Koto District of Shiga Prefecture." *Tenri Journal of Religion* 11 (December 1970): 18-35.

1205.   _____. "On the Returning Home to 'Jiba'—An Aspect of the Pilgrimage through Shrines and Temples in Yamato during the Meiji Era." *Tenri Journal of Religion* 8 (May 1967): 14-27.

1206.   _____. *Only if Breathing Is Done: From a Diary of a Hospital Patient.* Guide to Faith, no. 3. 1958, 6 pp.

1207.   KANEKO, TADASHI. "Preliminary Notes on the Exposition of Ofudesaki." *Tenri Journal of Religion* 10 (October 1969): 37-45.

1208.   KOIZUMI, TAKUZŌ. *Tenrikyō.* Doyusha, 1930, 176 pp.

1209.   KUSUHARA, HISASHI. *A Doctor and Tenrikyo.* 1964, 18 pp. Reprint. 1968, 27 pp.

1210.   MASUNO, MICHIOKI. *Tenrikyo.* Translated by Takuzo Koizumi. 1924, 176 pp. (Includes "The Dancing Psalms composed by The Foundress as translated by Takahito Iwai," pp. 149-76.)

1211.   MATSUDA, TAKETERU. "Obiyayurushi (The Grant of Safe Childbirth)—Taboos in Childbirth in Japan and Relief by God the Parent." *Tenri Journal of Religion* 8 (May 1967): 37-45.

1212.   MATSUMOTO, SHIGERU. "The Idea of Salvation in Tenrikyo." *Japanese Religions* 6, no. 1 (September 1969): 33-40.

1212A. _____. *In Quest of the Fundamental: Tenrikyo Way To Salvation.* Translated by Tamotsu Ogata. 1976, 42 pp.

1213.   _____. "The Meaning of Sacred Places As Phenomenologists of Religion Understand It." *Tenri Journal of Religion* 10 (October 1969): 46-56.

1214.   MOROI, YOSHINORI. *Assertions of a Tenrikyoist.* 1959, 22 pp.

1214A. _____. *Contemporary Thought and Tenrikyo.* Translated by Kosuke Matsumura. 1972, 61 pp. (Also French and Portuguese editions.)

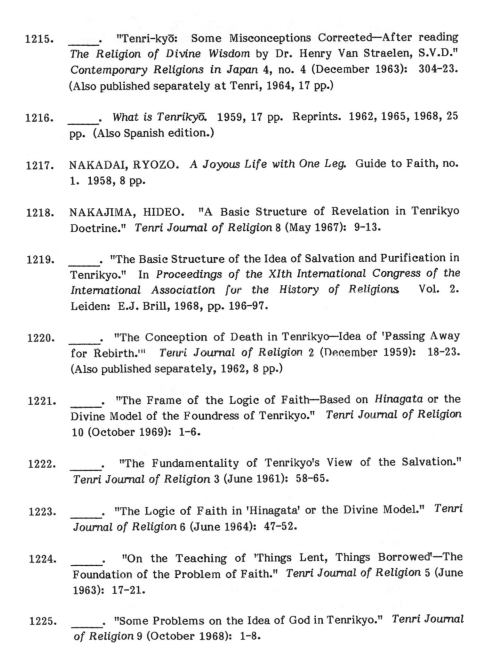

1215. _____. "Tenri-kyō: Some Misconceptions Corrected—After reading *The Religion of Divine Wisdom* by Dr. Henry Van Straelen, S.V.D." *Contemporary Religions in Japan* 4, no. 4 (December 1963): 304-23. (Also published separately at Tenri, 1964, 17 pp.)

1216. _____. *What is Tenrikyō.* 1959, 17 pp. Reprints. 1962, 1965, 1968, 25 pp. (Also Spanish edition.)

1217. NAKADAI, RYOZO. *A Joyous Life with One Leg.* Guide to Faith, no. 1. 1958, 8 pp.

1218. NAKAJIMA, HIDEO. "A Basic Structure of Revelation in Tenrikyo Doctrine." *Tenri Journal of Religion* 8 (May 1967): 9-13.

1219. _____. "The Basic Structure of the Idea of Salvation and Purification in Tenrikyo." In *Proceedings of the XIth International Congress of the International Association for the History of Religions.* Vol. 2. Leiden: E.J. Brill, 1968, pp. 196-97.

1220. _____. "The Conception of Death in Tenrikyo—Idea of 'Passing Away for Rebirth.'" *Tenri Journal of Religion* 2 (December 1959): 18-23. (Also published separately, 1962, 8 pp.)

1221. _____. "The Frame of the Logic of Faith—Based on *Hinagata* or the Divine Model of the Foundress of Tenrikyo." *Tenri Journal of Religion* 10 (October 1969): 1-6.

1222. _____. "The Fundamentality of Tenrikyo's View of the Salvation." *Tenri Journal of Religion* 3 (June 1961): 58-65.

1223. _____. "The Logic of Faith in 'Hinagata' or the Divine Model." *Tenri Journal of Religion* 6 (June 1964): 47-52.

1224. _____. "On the Teaching of 'Things Lent, Things Borrowed'—The Foundation of the Problem of Faith." *Tenri Journal of Religion* 5 (June 1963): 17-21.

1225. _____. "Some Problems on the Idea of God in Tenrikyo." *Tenri Journal of Religion* 9 (October 1968): 1-8.

1226.   _____; OKUBO, AKINORI; and IIDA, TERUAKI. "Yoshinori Moroi's
        Contributions to the Theology of Tenrikyo." *Tenri Journal of Religion*
        4 (June 1962): 1-7 [following page 79 of Vol. 4, new pagination].

1227.   NAKAYAMA, MIKI. *Mikagura-uta: The Songs for the Tsutome.*
        "Trial" ed., 1967. First ed., 1972. 31 pp.

1228.   _____ (NAKAYAMA, MIKI MAEKAWA). *A Study of the Ofudesaki in
        English.* 2 vols. Translated and annotated by Akio Inoue. Tenri-shi,
        Japan: Tenrikyo Doctrinal Translator's Association of *Hon'yaku,* 1971.
        Vol. 1 published as Vol. 7 (220 pp.) and Vol. 2 as Vol. 8 (114 pp.), of the
        periodical *Hon'yaku.*

1229.   NAKAYAMA, SHŌZEN. "The Anniversary of the Tenrikyo Foundress:
        Its History and Significance." *Tenri Journal of Religion* 7 (December
        1965): 1-7.

1230.   _____. *A Collection of Sermons by the Patriarch.* 1953.

1231.   _____. "The Doctrine and Practice of Tenrikyo." *Tenri Journal of
        Religion* 4 (June 1962): 1-5; 5 (June 1963): 1-6; 6 (June 1964): 1-10; 8
        (May 1967): 1-8.

1232.   _____. *The Doctrine of Tenrikyo. Preliminary Edition.* 1954, 105 pp.
        2d ed., *The Doctrine of Tenrikyo,* 1958. Reprint. 1964. 105 pp.

1233.   _____. [*Hitokotohanashi*] *Anecdotes on the Foundress and Her
        Disciples.* Translated by Michio Nishidai. 1964, xiv + 215 pp.

1234.   _____. "The Missionary Spirit of the Foundress of Tenrikyō Manifested
        in the Book of Ofudesaki." In *Proceedings of the IXth International
        Congress for the History of Religions, 1958.* Tokyo: Maruzen, 1960,
        pp. 365-69. Reprinted in *On the Idea of God in Tenrikyō Doctrine*
        (entry 1238).

1235.   _____. "On Sazuke, the Holy Grant in Tenrikyo." In *Proceedings of the
        XIth International Congress of the International Association for the
        History of Religions.* Vol. 2. Leiden: E.J. Brill, 1968, pp. 198-99.

1236.   _____. "On the Doctrine of Tenri-kyō." *Contemporary Religions in
        Japan* 4, no. 4 (December 1963): 325-31. (Also published separately,
        1958, 7 pp.)

1237. _____. *On the Idea of God in the Tenrikyo Doctrine*. 1957, 6 pp. "Read at the 23rd International Congress of Orientalists, Cambridge, 1954." Reprinted in collection of essays by the same title (entry 1238).

1238. _____. *On the Idea of God in the Tenrikyō Doctrine*. 1962, 34 pp.

1239. _____. "The Various Forms of Verbal Evolution in Tenrikyo Doctrine." *Tenri Journal of Religion* 3 (June 1961): 1-7. Abstract in *X. International Kongress für Religionsgeschichte* (Marburg: Kommissionsverlag N.G. Ehvert, 1961), pp. 118-19. (Also printed separately by "Tenrikyō Print. Dept.," 1960, 10 pp.)

1240. _____. "Woman's Position Viewed by Tenrikyo." *Tenri Journal of Religion* 3 (June 1961): 8-12. (Also printed separately by "Tenrikyō Print. Dept.," 1960, 7 pp.)

1241. NAKAYAMA, YOSHIKAZU. *Tenrikyo: Its Origin and History*. 1968, 10 pp. (Also Spanish edition.)

1242. OKUBO, AKINORI. "Counselling in Tenrikyo." *Tenri Journal of Religion* 6 (June 1964): 74-83.

1243. PIETERS, MARY. *A Philosophical Approach to Tenrikyo*. Los Angeles: Tenri Press, 1964, 6 pp.

1244. SAWAI, YUICHI. "A Memorandum on the Danjiai or 'Discussion.'" *Tenri Journal of Religion* 11 (December 1970): 11-17.

1245. _____. "The Methods and Task of Sermon." *Tenri Journal of Religion* 10 (October 1969): 17-25.

1246. *Sectarian Shinto (The Way of the Gods)* (entry 205), pp. 58-62.

1247. SERIZAWA, SHIGERU. "On 'Osatoshi'—A Problem of Conveying Teachings." *Tenri Journal of Religion* 5 (June 1963): 22-28.

1248. _____. "Systematic Description in the *Ofudesaki*." *Tenri Journal of Religion* 11 (December 1970): 1-10.

1249. _____; NAGAO, HIROMI; and NAKAJIMA, HIDEO. "An Introduction to the Tenrikyo Canons: Ofudesaki, Mikagurauta, Osashizu." *Tenri Journal of Religion* 4 (June 1962): 69-80.

1250. SHINOZAKI, TOMIKI. *Misfortune Turned into a Blessing.* Guide to
Faith, no. 6. 5 pp.

1251. SHIONOYA, SATOSHI. "Tenrikyo's Future Missionary Work." *Tenri
Journal of Religion* 13 (August 1979): 48-58.

1252. SUGIYAMA, SOKICHI. *A Surgical Operation on the Mind: A
Reflection on my Day of Revival.* Guide to Faith, no. 2. 1958, 4 pp.

1253. TAKANO, TOMOJI. "I Want to Become such a Man of the Belief:
Memories of Some Predecessors of Tenrikyo." *Tenri Journal of
Religion* 4 (June 1962): 19-24.

1254. TENRIKYŌ HAWAII DENDŌ-CHŌ. *Tenrikyō Hawaii Dendō shi* [A
history of the missionary work of the Tenrikyo in Hawaii]. Honolulu,
1957, 365 pp. (In Japanese and English.)

1255. TOMINAGA, MIKITA, ed. *Bibliography of Tenrikyo.* Typescript. 1935,
130 pp. Available at Tenri University, Tenri, Japan.

1256. UEDA, YOSHINARI.   *The Outline of Tenrikyo Doctrine and Its
History.* 1955.

1257. [YAMAMOTO, GISUKE.] *Relying on God the Parent: The Coffeehouse
Grows Big Like a Snowball.* Guide to Faith, no. 4. 8 pp.

1258. YAMAMOTO, KUNIO. "On 'a Thing Lent, a Thing Borrowed'—with
Reference to Disease." *Tenri Journal of Religion* 3 (June 1961): 66-74.

1259. YAMAMOTO, YOSHIO. "Tenrikyo and Religion—the Idea of Salvation
in Our Religion." *Tenri Journal of Religion* 7 (December 1965): 25-35.

1260. YAMAZAWA, TAMESUKE. *La doctrine de Tenrikio.* Translated by
Kiyoshi Mizutani and Tsuneji Takeuchi. 1931, 29 pp.

1261. _____. *Tenrikyō, a New Shintō Movement.* 1933, 39 pp. Illus.

1262. _____. *The Tenrikyo Doctrine.* Translated by Hisaichi Ikari and Kenji
Watanabe. [1930], 29 pp.

1263. YUINE, TAIJIRO. *Catechism on Tenrikyo.* 1925, 29 pp.

Periodicals

1264. *Tenri Journal of Religion.* March 1955-. (Contents of vols. 1-13, August 1979, are included in the preceding denominational materials.)

1265. *Tenri, Y.P. News* (Los Angeles).

1266. *Tenrikyo.* Los Angeles: Tenrikyo Mission Headquarters in America, 1955-.

1267. *Tenrikyo Hawaii Monthly.* Honolulu: Tenrikyo Mission Headquarters in Hawaii, 1957-.

1268. *Tenrikyo Newsletter* (Los Angeles). Monthly.

1269. *Tenrikyo; religio divini parentis nostri.* Monthly. (Nos. 1-124/5: 26 October 1932-20 December 1940; new no. 1:   26 January 1962.) Semimonthly: 26 October 1934-20 January 1935. Monthly: 10 March 1935-. (In English, French, and German.)

Secondary

1270. ANESAKI, MASAHARU. *History of Japanese Religion* (entry 3), pp. 313-14, 371-72.

1271. ASTON, WILLIAM GEORGE. *Shinto: The Way of the Gods.* London: Longmans, Green & Co., 1905, ii + 390 pp. See pp. 375-76.

1272. BACH, MARCUS. *Strangers at the Door* (entry 13), pp. 118-21.

1273. BALET, L. "Le Tenrikyō, religion de la raison céleste." *Mélanges japonais* 6, no. 23 (July 1909): 291-323; no. 24 (October 1909): 439-66.

1274. BECKER, CARL B. "Concepts and Roles of God in Tenrikyo." *Tenri Journal of Religion* 13 (August 1979): 1-28.

1275. BELLESSORT, ANDRÉ. *La société japonaise (Voyage au Japan).* 9th ed. Paris: Perrin et Cie., 1926, xvi + 412 pp. See pp. 225-28.

1276. BERNIER, BERNARD. *Breaking the Cosmic Circle: Religion in a Japanese Village* (entry 23), pp. 116-20, 149-53.

+1277.   BOWNAS, GEOFFREY. "Tenri and Yamato." In *Japanese Rainmaking and Other Folk Practices.* London: George Allen & Unwin, 1963, pp. 131-40.

1278.   _____. *Tenrikyo.* Typescript. Tenri University Library, n.d., 118 pp. In the files of Tenrikyō headquarters.

1279.   BRUMBAUGH, THOBURN T. "Young Sect Shows Rapid Growth." *Christian Century* 50 (3 May 1933): 605.

+1280.   CHINNERY, THORA E. *Religious Conflict and Compromise in a Japanese Village. A Firsthand Observation of the Tenrikyo Church.* Vancouver: University of British Columbia Press, 1971, x + 62 pp. (A published version of the M.A. thesis of Thora Elizabeth Hawkey [entry 1303], apparently the maiden name of Chinnery.)

1281.   CLEMEN, CARL. *Die nichtchristlichen Kulturreligionen in ihrem gegenwärtigen Zustand* (entry 38), pp. 29-33.

1282.   EARHART, H[ARRY] BYRON. *Japanese Religion: Unity and Diversity* (entry 53); 2d ed., pp. 111-14; 3d ed., pp. 172-77.

1283.   _____. "The New Religions" (entry 55), pp. 238-44.

1284.   ECKEL, PAUL E. "The History and Development of Tenrikyo." M.A. thesis, University of Southern California, 1936, 118 pp.

1285.   ELLWOOD, ROBERT S., Jr. *The Eagle and the Rising Sun: Americans and the New Religions of Japan* (entry 61), pp. 37-68.

1286.   EVERMEYER, FLORENCE E. "How Some Orientals Worship in America." *Missionary Review of the World* 57, no. 6 (June 1934): 271-73.

1287.   FARR, KATHARYN. "Tenrikyo: Teaching of the Heavenly Reason." M.A. thesis, University of Washington, 1935, 90 pp.

*1288.   FOXLEY, C. "Tenrikyo, a New Japanese Sect." 1918. Cited in Mikita Tominaga, ed., *Bibliography of Tenrikyo* (entry 1255).

*1289.   FUJISHIMA, UTA. *History of the Enlightened Period of Meiji.* Taisho Kyokwai, 1915, pp. 436-37. Cited in Mikita Tominaga, ed., *Bibliography of Tenrikyo* (entry 1255).

1290. GERLITZ, PETER. *Gott erwacht in Japan: Neue fernöstliche Religionen und ihre Botschaft vom Glück* (entry 69), pp. 45-74.

1291. GOWEN, HERBERT H. "The Religion of Heavenly Reason." *Anglican Theological Review* 17: 156-65.

1292. _____. "Tenrikyō, the Religion of Heavenly Reason." *Religion: the Journal of the Society for the Study of Religions* 12 (June 1935): 42-44, 52.

1293. GREENE, DANIEL CROSBY. "Tenrikyō; or the Teaching of the Heavenly Reason." *Transactions of the Asiatic Society of Japan* 22 (1895): 24-74. Reprinted in abridged form in *Japan Evangelist* 3 (1896): 156-59, 199-205.

1294. GUARIGLIA, GUGLIELMO. "Prophetismus und Heilserwartungs-Bewegungen" (entry 71), pp. 249-50.

1295. GUNDERT, WILHELM *Japanische Religionsgeschichte* (entry 72), pp. 132-36.

1296. HAAS, HANS. "3 Religionen der Japaner." *Archiv für Religionswissenschaft* 17 (1914): 255-95. See pp. 270-71.

1297. _____. "Die Tanzpsalmen der Tenrikyo-kwai." *Zeitschrift für Missionskunde und Religionswissenschaft* 25 (1910): 162-73, 193-205.

+1298. _____. "Tenrikyo: Ein neues synkretistisches Religionsgebilde in Japan unserer Tage." *Zeitschrift für Missionskunde und Religionswissenschaft* 25 (1910): 129-45.

1299. HÄCKER, P. "Tenrikyō, eine japanische Religion mit weltreligiösem Einschlag." *Sonne der Wahrheit* 11 (1931-32), no. 7: 81-82; no. 8: 91-92.

1300. HAHN, THOMAS KITAI. "Tenrikyo and Education." Ph.D. dissertation, Michigan State University, 1974, 208 pp. Abstracted in *Dissertation Abstracts International* 35, no. 9 (March 1975): 5946A. University Microfilms International order no. 75-7179.

1301.   HAMMANN, LOUIS J. *The Puzzle of Religion: the Parts and the Whole*. Washington, DC: University Press of America, 1977, 175 pp. See pp. 69–79.

1302.   HAMMER, RAYMOND JACK. "The Idea of God in Japan's New Religions" (entry 74), pp. 80–93.

1303.   HAWKEY, THORA ELIZABETH. "Conflict and Compromise in a Japanese Village." M.A. thesis, University of British Columbia, 1963, 136 pp. See also entry 1280.

*1304. HEISE, R. *Über die Religionen in Japan: Shinto, Konfuzianismus, Buddhismus*. 1931. Cited in Mikita Tominaga, ed., *Bibliography of Tenrikyo* (entry 1255).

1305.   HERBERT, JEAN. *Dieux et sectes populaires du Japon* (entry 82), pp. 153–66.

+1306. HOLTOM, DANIEL C. *The National Faith of Japan* (entry 85), pp. 267–86.

1307.   HUNTER, LOUISE H. *Buddhism in Hawaii: Its Impact on a Yankee Community* (entry 91), p. 194.

1308.   "Inspired Tenrikyo Teachings: Grand Sale of Religious Endeavors." *Japan in Pictures* 1, no. 9 (August 1933): 46–47.

1309.   JEAN-JOSEPH. "A travers la presse religieuse." *Mélanges japonais*, no. 22 (1909): 256–62.

1310.   JORDAN, DAVID K. *Gods, Ghosts, and Ancestors: The Religion of a Taiwanese Village*. Berkeley: University of California Press, 1972, xviii + 197 pp. See p. 29.

1311.   KATO, GENCHI. *A Study of Shinto: The Religion of the Japanese Nation*. Tokyo: Meiji Japan Society, 1926, ix + 250 pp. See pp. 210–12. 2d ed., 1937, ix + 255 pp. See pp. 253–54. Reprints. London: Curzon; New York: Barnes & Noble, 1971.

1312.   KOBAYASHI, SAKAE. "Changes in the Japanese Religions after World War II" (entry 115), pp. 41–52.

1313.   KOHLER, WERNER. *Die Lotus-Lehre und die modernen Religionen in Japan* (entry 118), pp. 50-58.

1314.   LANCZKOWSKI, GÜNTER. *Die neuen Religionen* (entry 126), pp. 15-23.

1315.   LANTERNARI, VITTORIO. *The Religions of the Oppressed* (entry 127), pp. 225-27.

1315A.   LAUBE, JOHANNES. "Die Gottesbezeichnungen und die Gottesverständnisses der Tenrikyō auf dem Hintergrund der religiösen und politischen Geschichte Japans." In *Der Religionswandel unserer Zeit im Spiegel der Religionswissenschaft.* Edited by Gunter Stephenson. Darmstadt, Germany: Wissenschaftliche Buchgesellschaft, 1976, pp. 109-22.

⁺1316.   _____. *Oyagami: Die heutige Gottesvorstellung der Tenrikyo.* Studien zur Japonologie. Monographien zur Geschichte, Kultur und Sprache Japans, vol. 14. Wiesbaden: Otto Harrassowitz, 1978, 322 pp.

1317.   _____. "Zur Bedeutungsgeschichte des Konfuzianistischen Begriffs 'Makoto' ('Wahrhaftigkeit')." In *Fernöstliche Kultur.* Edited by Helga Wormit. Marburg: N.G. Elwert Verlag, 1975, pp. 100-57. See pp. 147-57.

1318.   LOFTIN, MARION T. "The Japanese in Brazil: A Study in Immigration and Acculturation" (entry 129), pp. 256e-256i.

1319.   McALPINE, W.A. "At Tenri." *Japan Quarterly* 5 (1958): 363-67.

1320.   MacCAULEY, C. "The Present Religious Condition of Japan." *American Journal of Theology* 6, no. 2 (April 1902): 209-35. See pp. 218-19.

1321.   McFARLAND, H[ORACE] NEILL. "The New Religions of Japan." *Contemporary Religions in Japan* 1, no. 2 (June 1960): 35-47. See pp. 39-43.

⁺1322.   MARUKAWA, HITOO. "Religious Circumstances in the Late Tokugawa and the Early Meiji Periods: Religious Backgrounds in the Cradle Years of Tenrikyo" (entry 139).

1323.   MINAMI, HIROSHI. *Psychology of the Japanese People.* Translated by
        Albert R. Ikoma. [Honolulu]: East-West Center, 1970, xii + 189 pp.
        See pp. 120-23.   Tokyo: University of Tokyo Press; Toronto:
        University of Toronto Press, 1971, xvii + 177 pp. See pp. 115-17.

1324.   MIYAMOTO, SHOTARO FRANK.   "Social Solidarity Among the
        Japanese in Seattle." *University of Washington Publications in the
        Social Sciences* 11, no. 2 (December 1939): 57-130. See p. 99.

1325.   MOCHIZUKI, KOTARO, ed. "The Tenrikyo (A Sect of Shintoism)." In
        *Japan To-day: A Souvenir of the Anglo-Japanese Exhibition Held in
        London, 1910.* [A Special Number of *Japan Financial and Economic
        Monthly*]. Tokyo: Liberal News Agency, 1910, 772 pp. See pp. 699-
        702.

+1326. MURAKAMI, SHIGEYOSHI. *Japanese Religion in the Modern Century*
        (entry 153), pp. 13-15, 44-45, 48-49, 70-72, 75-76, 85-86, 100-1.

+1327. NEWELL, WILLIAM, and DOBASHI, FUMIKO.   "Some Problems of
        Classification in Religious Sociology as Shown in the History of *Tenri
        Kyōkai.*" In *The Sociology of Japanese Religion.* Edited by Kiyomi
        Morioka and William H. Newell. Leiden: E.J. Brill, 1968, pp. 84-100.
        Printed simultaneously as *Journal of Asian and African Studies* 3, nos.
        1-2 (January-April 1968): 84-100.

1328.   "Newly Born Religions of Japan." In *Dai Nippon.* Vol. 2. Tokyo:
        Bummei Kyokwai, 1931, pp. 179-83.

1329.   *Novas religiões japonêsas no Brasil, por uma equipe de Franciscanos de
        Petrópolis* (entry 172), pp. 18-26.

1330.   OFFNER, CLARK B., and STRAELEN, HENRY (HENRICUS J.J.M.)
        van. *Modern Japanese Religions* (entry 175), pp. 41-59.

+1331. OGUCHI, IICHI, and TAKAGI, HIROO.   "Religion and Social
        Development" (entry 179), pp. 313-51.

1332.   OSAKA, MOTOKICHIRO. "Tenrikyō, One of Japan's New Religions."
        Japan Christian Quarterly 5 (October 1930): 363-70.

1333.   OSTWALD, MARTIN. "Tenrikyō oder 'Die Lehre von der Himmlischen
        Vernunft.'" *Zeitschrift für Missionskunde und Religionswissenschaft* 22
        (1907): 196-210.

1334. PETTAZZONI, RAFFAELE. *La confession des péchés.* Vol. 2. Translated by R. Monnot. Paris: Librairie Ernest Leroux, 1931-32. See pp. 18-21. First published as *La confessione dei peccati* (Bologna: N. Zanichelli), 1929.

1335. PIERSON, D. "Missionary Problems in Japan." *Missionary Review of the World* (New York), 1912.

1336. RAJANA, EIMI WATANABE. "A Sociological Study of New Religious Movements: Chilean Pentecostalism and Japanese New Religions" (entry 190), pp. 57-63.

1337. RICCO, MARIO. *Religione della violenza e religione del piacere nel nuovo Giappone* (entry 195), pp. 57-101.

1338. ROSENKRANZ, GERHARD. *Fernost—wohin?* (entry 198), pp. 119-27.

1339. SCHINZINGER, ROBERT. "Peculiarities of the Japanese Character." *Orient/West* 8, no. 5 (September-October 1963): 30-41.

1340. SEIDENSTICKER, E.D. Review of *The Religion of Divine Reason* by van Straelen (entry 1346). In *Monumenta Nipponica* 13 (1957): 368-71.

1341. SHIMIZU, T., and UNNO, K. *Modern Japan.* Tokyo, 1933, pp. 363-64.

1342. "Sind die Japaner religiös? (aus der Praxis der Tenrikyō–Sekte)." *Deutsche Japan-Post* 7, no. 2 (1908-1909): 7.

1343. STEIN, GÜNTHER. "Japan's Next Sect (the Tenrikyō)." *Spectator* (August 1935): 317-18. Also in *Living Age* 349 (1935): 142-44.

1344. STRAELEN, HENRY (HENRICUS J.J.M.) van. "Japan's Most Powerful Religious Movement." *Missionary Bulletin* 6 (1953): 1-7, 50-57, 76-85, 115-19, 129-34.

1345. _____. "Un messianisme japonais contemporain: La religion de la sagesse divine. *Archives de sociologie des religions* 4 (July-September 1957): 123-32.

+1346. ____. "The Religion of Divine Wisdom, Japan's Most Powerful Religious Movement." *Folklore Studies* 13 (1954): 1-165. Published in revised form as a book. Kyoto: Veritas Shoin, 1957, 236 pp. See Seidensticker (entry 1340) and Moroi (entry 1215) for reviews.

1347. ____. "Tenrikyō, die Religion der Himmlischen Weisheit, Japans grösste religiöse Bewegung." In *X. International Kongress für Religionsgeschichte.* Marburg: Kommissionsverlag N.G. Ehvert, 1961, pp. 121-23.

1348. ____. "Tenrikyō, le plus dynamique des mouvements religieux du Japon contemporain." In *Missionsstudien.* Edited by Karl Muller. Kaldenkirchen: Steyler, 1962, pp. 22-47.

1349. ____. "Le Tenrikyo, un syncretisme dynamique au Japon contemporain." In *Devant les sectes non chrétiennes: Rapports et compte rendu de la XXXIe semaine de missiologie.* Louvain, Museum Lessianum, Section Missiologique, no. 42. [Paris]: Desclée De Brouwer, [1961], pp. 210-24.

1350. SUGAI, TAIKA. "The Soteriology of New Religions" (entry 221), pp. 34-38.

1351. "Tenrikyō." *Japan Magazine* 23 (1933).

1352. THOMSEN, HARRY. *The New Religions of Japan* (entry 233), pp. 33-60.

1353. UEHARA, TOYOAKI. "A Study of Tenrikyo: With Special Reference to the Teaching of God and Man." M.A. thesis, University of Southern California, 1955, 248 pp.

1354. WARREN, F. "Tenrikyo, a Study in Religious Methods." *Japan Christian Quarterly* 7, no. 1 (January 1932): 30-38.

1355. WITTE, JOHANNES. "Eine Werbeschrift der Tenrikyo einer japanischen Shinto-Sekte." *Ostasien Jahrbuch* 6 (1928): 42-61.

1356. YAMAMOTO, K. "The Religion of the Japanese Masses." *Japan Christian Intelligencer* 1, no. 1 (5 March 1926): 26-34.

1357. YAMAZAKI, F. "Tenrikyō." *Japan Magazine* 6, no. 4 (August 1915): 235-38.

Tenshō-Kōtai-Jingū-Kyō

Denominational

(Unless otherwise specified, published at Tabuse by Tenshō-Kōtai-Jingū-Kyō.)

+1358. *Divine Manifestation: Ogamisama's Life and Teaching.* 1970, 154 pp. (Spanish edition, 1975, 151 pp.; German edition, 1976, 247 pp.)

1359. *Kami no Kuni (Kingdom of God).* 1966, 200 pp. Illus.

1360. *Key to Heaven: A Concise Explanation of God's Teaching.* 1965, 185 pp.

1361. *Mioshie: An Introduction to Ogamisama's Teaching.* 1966, 19 pp. (Also German and Spanish editions.)

1362. *Mioshie, the Divine Teaching.* 1950, 33 pp. 1952, 35 pp.

1363. *The Paradise of Tabuse.* 1953, 58 pp. Illus. In Japanese. ("Explanation of Pictures" in English.)

1364. *Prescription for Happiness.* 1966, 51 pp. (Also Esperanto, French, German, and Spanish editions.)

+1365. *The Prophet of Tabuse.* 1954, 183 pp. (Greek edition, 1967, 199 pp.; Spanish edition, 1967, 243 pp.; German edition, 1971, 339 pp.)

1366. *The Road to God.* 1952, 6 pp.

1367. *Teachings of God Through Sayo Kitamura.* 1964, 20 pp.

1368. *30 Years of Ogamisama's Sacred Task.* 1975, 32 pp. (Also Spanish edition.)

1369. INTERNATIONAL INSTITUTE FOR THE STUDY OF RELIGIONS. "Tensho Kotai Jingu-kyo (The testimony of believers)." *Contemporary Religions in Japan* 2, no. 3 (September 1961): 43-47.

1370.   KITAMURA, SAYO. *Guidance to God's Kingdom*. 1956, 1958, 1961, 21 pp.

1371.   _____. *Ogamisama Says . . . Religious and Philosophical Teachings of the Japanese Prophetess of Tabuse*. 1963, 48 pp. (Also Esperanto, German, and Spanish editions.)

1372.   _____.   "Tensho   Kotai   Jingu-Kyo   (The   Dancing   Religion)." *Contemporary Religions in Japan* 2, no. 3 (September 1961): 26-42.

Periodicals

1373.   *Ogamisama's World-Wide Newsletter* (Tabuse).   Published from Fall 1965 (no. 1) to November 1976 (no. 43).   Quarterly.   (Also Spanish edition.)

1374.   *The Voice From Heaven.* 1963-. (Also Spanish edition.)

Secondary

1375.   ANDERSON, MYRDENE.   "Impact of the death of a charismatic leader: Incorporating an Ethnography of Tensho-Kotai-Jingu-Kyo." B.A. honors thesis, University of Hawaii, 1968, viii + 148 pp. Available in The Hawaiian Collection, Thomas Hale Hamilton Library, University of Hawaii at Manoa.

⁺1376.   BLACKER, CARMEN. "New Religious Cults in Japan" (entry 26).

1377.   EYDE, DAVID B.   "A Study of the Japanese Dancing Religion." Unpublished paper.   The Hawaiian Collection, Thomas Hale Hamilton Library, University of Hawaii at Manoa. 1954, 19 pp.

1378.   GUARIGLIA, GUGLIELMO.   "Prophetismus und Heilserwartungs-Bewegungen" (entry 71), p. 249.

1379.   HAMMER, RAYMOND JACK.   "The Idea of God in Japan's New Religions" (entry 74), pp. 166-72.

1380.   HERBERT, JEAN. *Dieux et sectes populaires du Japon* (entry 82), pp. 203-9.

1381. JABBOUR, MILLARD E. "The Sect of Tensho-Kotai-Jingu-Kyo: The Emergence and Career of a Religious Movement." M.A. thesis, University of Hawaii, 1958, 128 pp.

1382. JOYA, MOCK. *Quaint Customs and Manners of Japan.* Vol. 2. Tokyo: Tokyo News Service, 1951, pp. 105-6.

1382A. KERNER, KAREN. "Building God's Kingdom: Society and Order in a Japanese Utopian Community." Ph.D. dissertation, Columbia University, 1979, ii + 365 pp. Abstracted in *Dissertation Abstracts International* 42, no. 12, pt. 1 (June 1982): 5173A-74A. University Microfilms International order no. DA 8211110.

1383. _____. "Japan's New Religions" (entry 107).

1384. _____. "The Malevolent Ancestor: Ancestral Influence in a Japanese Religious Sect." In *Ancestors.* Edited by William H. Newell. The Hague: Mouton, 1974, pp. 205-17.

1385. KOBAYASHI, SAKAE. "Changes in the Japanese Religions after World War II" (entry 115), pp. 104-7.

+1386. KOHLER, WERNER. *Die Lotus-Lehre und die modernen Religionen in Japan* (entry 118), pp. 98-117.

1387. KÖPPING, KLAUS-PETER. *Religiöse Bewegungen im modernen Japan als Problem des Kulturwandels* (entry 122), pp. 49-76.

1388. LANCZKOWSKI, GÜNTER. *Die neuen Religionen* (entry 126), pp. 38-43.

1389. LANTERNARI, VITTORIO. *The Religions of the Oppressed* (entry 127), p. 225.

+1390. LEBRA, TAKIE SUGIYAMA. "An Interpretation of Religious Conversion: A Millennial Movement Among Japanese-Americans in Hawaii." Ph.D. dissertation, University of Pittsburgh, 1967, 449 pp. Abstracted in *Dissertation Abstracts* 28, no. 3 (September 1967): 1134A-35A. University Microfilms International order no. 67-11,391.

1391. _____. "Logic of Salvation: The Case of a Japanese Sect in Hawaii." *International Journal of Social Psychiatry* 16 (1969-70): 45-53.

1392.   _____. "Reciprocity-Based Moral Sanctions and Messianic Salvation."
         American Anthropologist 64, no. 3 (June 1972): 391-407.

1393.   _____. "Religious Conversion and Elimination of the Sick Role: A
         Japanese Sect in Hawaii."   In *Transcultural Research in Mental
         Health.* Mental Health Research in Asia and the Pacific, vol. 2, edited
         by William P. Lebra. Honolulu: University Press of Hawaii, 1972, pp.
         282-92. Reprinted in *Culture, Disease, and Healing: Studies in Medical
         Anthropology,* ed. David Landy (New York: Macmillan, 1977), pp. 408-
         14.

1394.   _____. "Religious Conversion as a Breakthrough for Transculturation; a
         Japanese Sect in Hawaii." *Journal for the Scientific Study of Religion*
         9, no. 3 (Fall 1970): 181-96.

1395.   MAY, L.C. "The Dancing Religion: A Messianic Sect." *Southwestern
         Journal of Anthropology* 10 (Spring 1954): 119-37.

1396.   MURAKAMI, SHIGEYOSHI. *Japanese Religion in the Modern Century*
         (entry 153), pp. 139-40.

+1397.   NAKAMURA, KYOKO MOTOMOCHI. "No Women's Liberation: The
         Heritage of a Woman Prophet in Modern Japan." In *Unspoken Worlds:
         Women's Religious Lives in Non-Western Cultures.* Edited by Nancy A.
         Falk and Rita M. Gross. San Francisco: Harper & Row, Publishers,
         1980, pp. 174-90.

1398.   OLSON, RONALD. "Mioshie: A New Messianic Cult." In *Papers of the
         Kroeber Anthropological Society* 8-9 [The Walter Buchanan Cline
         Memorial Volume]. Berkeley: University of California, 1953, pp. 78-
         81.

1399.   RAJANA, EIMI WATANABE. "A Sociological Study of New Religious
         Movements: Chilean Pentecostalism and Japanese New Religions"
         (entry 190), pp. 63-68.

1400.   REPS, PAUL. *Square Sun, Square Moon: A Collection of Sweet Sour
         Essays.* Rutland, VT: Charles E. Tuttle Co., 1967. 2d printing, 1968,
         100 pp. See pp. 44-48.

1401.   SPAE, JOSEPH J. "Odorikyō, The Dancing Religion."   *Missionary
         Bulletin* 12, no. 6 (July 1958): 440-44.

1402.   THOMSEN, HARRY. *The New Religions of Japan* (entry 233), pp. 199–219.

Tōdaiji of Hawaii

Denominational

1403.   HIRAI, TETSUSHO. *Todaiji of Hawaii.* Honolulu: Todaiji Hawaii Bekkaku Honzan, n.d.

Secondary

1404.   DeFRANCIS, JOHN. *Things Japanese in Hawaii* (entry 44), pp. 52–54, 72–77.

1405.   HUNTER, LOUISE H. *Buddhism in Hawaii: Its Impact on a Yankee Community* (entry 91), pp. 195–96.

1406.   MULHOLLAND, JOHN F. "Todaiji Hawaii, Bekkaku Honzan." *Hawaii's Religions* (entry 152), pp. 259–60.

*1407.   ROBINSON, BARBARA B. "Todaiji of Honolulu, Survey of a Regressive Religious Group." Hawaiian and Pacific Collection, Sinclair Library, University of Hawaii. Cited in Louise H. Hunter, *Buddhism in Hawaii* (entry 91), p. 249, n. 40.

Zenrin-kai

Denominational

No publications known.

Secondary

1408.   SPAE, JOSEPH J. "Tenchi Kōdō Zenrinkai." *Japan Missionary Bulletin* 13, no. 8 (October 1959): 514–17.

UTOPIAN GROUPS

General Discussions

+1409.   FAIRFIELD, RICHARD, ed. *Communes, Japan.* Special issue of *The Modern Utopian.* San Francisco: Alternatives Foundation, 1972, 134 pp. See pp. 3-94. ("Material on Japanese communes was compiled from personal experience and interviews in the communes themselves with added material and insights from other writers and visitors. . . ." Includes information on Atarashiki Mura, Ittōen, Shinkyō, Yamagishi-kai, and several small communal groups.)

1409A.   MATSUBA, MOSHE, ed. *The Communes of Japan: The Kibbutz on the Other Side of the World.* Imaichi-shi, Tochigi-ken, Japan: Japanese Commune Movement, 1977, 235 pp. [Includes general comments on kibbutz and Japanese communes, as well as brief articles on Ittōen, Atarashiki Mura, Yamagishi-kai, Shinkyō, and other Japanese communal groups and farms.]

Atarashiki Mura

Denominational

No publications known.

Secondary

1410.   ANESAKI, MASAHARU. *History of Japanese Religion* (entry 3), pp. 402-3.

+1411.   PLATH, DAVID W. "The Fate of Utopia: Adaptive Tactics in Four Japanese Groups" (entry 187).

+1412.   _____. "Modernization and Its Discontents: Japan's Little Utopias" (entry 188).

Ittōen

Denominational

(Unless otherwise specified, published at Kyoto by Ittōen Publishing House.)

1413. *General Information about Ittoen.* N.d., 1 p.

1414. KUROKAWA, COLBERT N., ed. *What is Itto-en? Its Theory and Practice.* 1959, 90 pp. Illus.

1415. NISHIDA, TENKO (ITTOEN TENKO-SAN). *A New Road to Ancient Truth.* "Being extracts from his writings translated by Makoto Ohashi in collaboration with Marie Beuzeville Byles with an introduction by Marie Beuzeville Byles." London: George Allen & Unwin, 1969, 183 pp. Illus. New York: Horizon Press, 1972.

1416. _____. *One Fact of Light.* Translated by Colbert N. Kurokawa. 1958, 6 pp.

1417. _____. *Selflessness: Selected Sayings of Tenko Nishida.* 1958, 26 pp. Illus.

1418. _____. *What is Itto-en? Its Theory and Practice.* Kyoto: Itto-en Publishing House, 1959, 90 pp. Illus.

Periodicals

1419. *Light.* English Supplement to *Hikari* [Light], a monthly organ of the Itto En in Japanese. 1919-. Occasional.

Secondary

1420. ANESAKI, MASAHARU. *History of Japanese Religion* (entry 3), pp. 400-1.

1421. BACH, MARCUS. *Strangers at the Door* (entry 13), pp. 96-104.

1422. BYLES, MARIE BEUZEVILLE. *Paths to Inner Calm.* London: George Allen & Unwin, 1965, 208 pp. See pp. 131-34, 160-75, 183-92.

+1423. DAVIS, WINSTON. "Ittoen: The Myths and Rituals of Liminality, Parts
        I–III." *History of Religion* 14, no. 4 (May 1975): 282-321; "Parts IV–
        V." *History of Religion* 15, no. 1 (August 1975): 1-33.

1424.   DEED, MARTHA L. "Itto En: Compound of One Light." *Journal of
        Religious Thought* 23, no. 1 (1966-67): 61-73.

1425.   GERLITZ, PETER. *Gott erwacht in Japan: Neue fernöstliche
        Religionen und ihre Botschaft vom Glück* (entry 69), pp. 129-38.

1426.   HAMMER, RAYMOND JACK. "The Idea of God in Japan's New
        Religions" (entry 74), pp. 173-76.

1427.   HAVENS, JOSEPH. "A Month in the Itto-En Religious Community."
        Inward Light 24 (Fall-Winter 1961): 32-34.

1428.   HAVENS, TERESINA ROWELL. "Itto-en: Reconstruction by
        Penitence." *Friends Intelligencer*, 4 August 1945, pp. 491-93.

1429.   IWAHASHI, TAKEO. "Ittoen: The New Religious Movement in
        Japan." *The Friend* (London) 67 (1927): 14.

1430.   McFARLAND, H[ORACE] NEILL. "The New Religions of Japan."
        Contemporary Religions in Japan 1, no. 3 (September 1960): 33-36.

1431.   "Peace and War in Japan." *Catholic Worker* (March 1941): 5.

+1432. PLATH, DAVID W. "The Fate of Utopia: Adaptive Tactics in Four
        Japanese Groups" (entry 187).

+1433. _____. "Modernization and Its Discontents: Japan's Little Utopias"
        (entry 188).

1434.   REICHELT, KARL L. *The Transformed Abbot*. Translated by G.M.
        Reichelt and A.P. Rose. London: Lutterworth Press, 1954, 157 pp.
        See pp. 31-33.

1435.   THOMSEN, HARRY. "Ittoen, the Park of One Light." *Japanese
        Religions* 1, no. 3 (1959): 16-24.

1436.   _____. *The New Religions of Japan* (entry 233), pp. 221-34.

1437.   ZIMMERMANN, WERNER. *Licht im Osten* (entry 259), pp. 51-64.

Shinkyō

Denominational

+1438. SUGIHARA, YOSHIE, and PLATH, DAVID W. *Sensei and His People: The Building of a Japanese Commune.* Berkeley: University of California Press, 1969, xvii + 187 pp. Illus.

Secondary

+1439. PLATH, DAVID W. "A Case of Ostracism—and Its Unusual Aftermath." *Trans-action* (January-February 1968): 31-36.

+1440. _____. "The Fate of Utopia: Adaptive Tactics in Four Japanese Groups" (entry 187).

1441. _____. "Modernization and Its Discontents: Japan's Little Utopias" (entry 188).

1442. No entry.

_____, and SUGIHARA, YOSHIE. See Sugihara (entry 1438).

1443. REPS, PAUL. *Square Sun, Square Moon: A Collection of Sweet Sour Essays.* Rutland, VT: Charles E. Tuttle Co., 1967. 2d Printing, 1968, 100 pp. See pp. 38-39.

*1444. YAMANE, TSUNEO. "Formation of a Communal Settlement in Japan—a Case in Shinkyō." Unpublished paper. Cited in David W. Plath, "The Fate of Utopia" (entry 187), p. 1162.

Yamagishi-kai

Denominational

No publications known.

Secondary

[+]1445.   PLATH, DAVID W. "The Fate of Utopia: Adaptive Tactics in Four
          Japanese Groups" (entry 187).

[+]1446.   _____. "Modernization and Its Discontents: Japan's Little Utopias"
          (entry 188).

[+]1447.   _____. "Utopian Rhetoric: Conversion and Conversation in a Japanese
          Cult." In *Essays on the Verbal and Visual Arts: Proceedings of the
          1966 Annual Spring Meeting, American Anthropological Society*, pp. 96-
          108.

APPENDIXES

BIBLIOGRAPHICAL SUGGESTIONS FOR FURTHER READING

A. Suggestions for Locating Western–Language Materials on the Japanese New Religions

The materials in this bibliography are quite diverse in character, ranging from popular religious tracts to scholarly tomes. It is unfortunate, but not surprising, that such a wide range of materials is not housed in any single library. In fact, one of the purposes of compiling this bibliography has been to bring together citations of the disparate writings by and about the Japanese New Religions. The next step for the user of a bibliography, of course, is to obtain the actual materials cited; the following suggestions are intended to help the reader or librarian pursue leads and obtain materials.

The general and secondary works in this bibliography present the least difficulty in searching. Many books and articles in these two sections can be found in a large public library, or a college or university library. More specialized works must be obtained from research libraries. In this bibliography two kinds of specialized publications abound: those in Japanese (or Asian) studies, and those in religion and theology. For my own convenience, I searched Japanese and Asian titles at The University of Michigan, which has a graduate program in Japanese Studies; similar research libraries related to graduate programs in Japanese (or Asian) Studies would give the reader access to most specialized works on Japan. I searched specialized works on religion at The University of Chicago, for me the closest research library in the field of religion; other research libraries related to graduate programs in religion should hold most of the specialized books and articles on religion. Two important exceptions should be mentioned for missionary publications. For Roman Catholic missionary publications, the library of Notre Dame University turned up some publications not available elsewhere. Protestant missionary publications were searched at Union Theological Seminary in New York, which houses the collection of the former Mission Research Library. The social science works in this bibliography will be found in most college libraries, although some works will have to be obtained from research libraries.

For those who have access to the Library of Congress, of course, this is the most comprehensive collection in the United States, and the best single source for locating materials cited in this bibliography. A small, specialized center with probably the best collection of materials on religious movements in the United

States is the Program for the Study of New Religious Movements, Graduate Theological Union, 2465 LeConte Avenue, Berkeley, California 94709. This program focuses on American movements and files materials on several hundred groups, of which Japanese (or Japanese-derived) groups are a minority. A unique feature of this program is that it collects both the ephemera published by the New Religions and also unpublished articles by scholars (for example, see entries 901-903). See also the Newsletter of this program, *New Religious Movements*, listed in Appendix D. Another American center, which I have not had the opportunity to visit, is the Institute for the Study of American Religion, P.O. Box 1311, Evanston, Illinois 60201. From the files of this institute has been published *A Directory of Religious Bodies in the United States* (entry 142A), including Japanese New Religions. On p. 76 of this work it is stated that "ISAR will, for cost, be happy to supply information on these groups from its files."

Unpublished materials present greater difficulties. For the reader's convenience, doctoral dissertations have been cited with the microfilm order number. Master's theses should be available at the respective universities where they were submitted. Some unpublished materials are to be found in special collections. For example, entry 1375 is housed in The Hawaiian Collection, Thomas Hale Hamilton Library, University of Hawaii at Manoa. Searching special collections dealing with Asia, Japan, or religion may turn up not only obscure publications of a secondary nature, but also some of the denominational publications by the New Religions.

Denominational publications are difficult to obtain, both in Japan and elsewhere. Among the more recent publications by New Religions, some have been prepared in a more scholarly format for Western readers, and some have been released through commercial publishers. These works are more likely to find their way into research libraries as well as college libraries. On the other hand, denominational publications that are more nearly direct translations of Japanese works and more focused on devotional practice are less likely to be found in college and university libraries.

Two American sources for denominational works have already been mentioned: Library of Congress and the Program for the Study of New Religious Movements. These institutions are more concerned with cataloging and keeping what other libraries may discard as ephemera. Readers who are interested enough to seek their own materials may want to write directly to the offices of New Religions. California addresses of five Japanese New Religions are listed on pp. 215-16 of Robert S. Ellwood, Jr., *The Eagle and the Rising Sun* (entry 61). Addresses for a number of additional movements are found in J. Melton Gordon (with James V. Geisendorfer), *A Directory of Religious Bodies in the United States* (entry 142A). Those who have the time to wait for a reply may want to write directly to Japan, using addresses in Ichirō Hori, ed., *Japanese Religion* (entry 89A) or "Statistics on Religious Organizations in Japan 1947-1972" (entry 216A).

The larger New Religions have prepared price lists of their publications and are able to send recent publications upon payment. These New Religions have special staff for translation of Japanese works and for foreign missions (outside Japan) and will be quicker to respond. The smaller New Religions do not always have special staff for dealing with Western-language inquiries and will be slower to respond. Older materials are not always kept by these headquarters, and pre-World War II materials are very hard to find.

Except for the headquarters of New Religions, there is no one library in Japan that can be recommended for Western-language materials on the New Religions. The Diet Library and university libraries in Japan tend to focus on scholarly works and do not attempt to acquire devotional and denominational works. Until recently the best repository for materials published by the New Religions was the small library of the International Institute for the Study of Religions (Kokusai Shūkyō Kenkyūjo). This institute was of considerable help in compiling both the first and second editions of this bibliography, but after I left Japan in early 1980 the office of the institute closed and the library was scattered. (The institute continues as a foundation and still publishes *Japanese Journal of Religious Studies*.)

To the best of my knowledge, the only international repository for materials on New Religions or "new religious movements" is the Project for the Study of New Religious Movements in Primal Societies, headed by Dr. Harold W. Turner, Department of Religious Studies, King's College, University of Aberdeen, Aberdeen AB9 2UB, Scotland. This project focuses on the encounter of primal or tribal societies with more complex cultures, especially modern African religious movements arising out of the interaction of Christianity and African traditions. Turner himself has already published the first two volumes of a projected four-volume work, *Bibliography of New Religious Movements in Primal Societies*, listed in Appendix D. (Turner kindly contributed many European citations for the first and present edition of this work.)

Until a central repository for materials on Japanese New Religions exists, the interested reader has no alternative but to explore the aforementioned possibilities.

B. Western-Language Materials on Japanese Religion

This list of bibliographies provides access to both specialized monographs and general surveys; therefore, no specific studies are mentioned.

BANDŌ, SHŌJUN, et al. *A Bibliography on Japanese Buddhism*. Tokyo: Cultural Interchange Institute for Buddhist Press, 1953, 180 pp.

1660 items classified by Buddhist sect and subdivided topically. Index of authors and subjects.

EARHART, H[ARRY] BYRON. *Japanese Religion: Unity and Diversity*. 3d ed. Belmont, CA: Wadsworth Publishing Co., 1982, xii + 272 pp. See pp. 213-54.

Includes annotated bibliography, arranged by religious tradition, with separate sections for Japanese history and culture, and general works on Japanese religion.

HECKEN, JOSEPH van. *The Catholic Church in Japan Since 1859*. Translated and revised by John Van Hoydonck. Tokyo: Enderle, 1963, vi + 317 pp.

Includes bibliographical materials from 1859-1959.

HERBERT, JEAN. *Bibliographie du shintô et des sectes shintôïstes*. Leiden: E.J. Brill, 1968, 72 pp.

Lists 1,182 Japanese and Western publications alphabetically. Subject index.

IKADO, FUJIO, and McGOVERN, JAMES R., comps. *A Bibliography of Christianity in Japan--Protestantism in English Sources (1859-1959)*. Tokyo: Committee on Asian Cultural Studies, International Christian University, 1966, 125 pp.

Materials arranged alphabetically with separate indexes for title, author, and subject.

KATO, GENCHI, et al. *A Bibliography of Shinto in Western Languages from the Oldest Times till 1952*. Tokyo: Meiji Jingu Shamusho, 1953, 58 pp. "Appendix, Books and Articles on Shinto Published 1941-1952," 7 pp. Index.

Includes 1,138 items in 58 pages arranged alphabetically.

KITAGAWA, JOSEPH M. "The Religions of Japan." In *A Reader's Guide to the Great Religions*. Edited by Charles J. Adams. 2d ed. New York: Free Press, 1977, pp. 247-82.

A bibliographical essay discussing materials historically and topically.

_____. *Religion in Japanese History.* New York: Columbia University Press, 1966, x + 475 pp.

For bibliography see pp. 373-407, "Works in Western Languages," and pp. 407-56, "Works in Japanese"; arranged alphabetically. See also pp. 341-59, "Chronological Table," and pp. 361-72, "Glossary."

C. Japanese-Language Materials on the New Religions

Included herein are three kinds of works: (1) Western-language descriptions of Japanese materials; (2) general studies of the New Religions in Japanese; and (3) reference and bibliographical works on the New Religions in Japanese. For the person with no knowledge or beginning knowledge of Japanese, works in category (1) such as Holzman and the *K.B.S. Bibliography* are most useful. For those who read Japanese, works in category (2) such as Inui, et al., Saki, and Takagi provide general treatments, while Murakami and Tsurufuji take up more specialized topics within the New Religions. Except for some documentation of special problems, each of these books mentions the leading Japanese works on the New Religions. For those entering special research, works in category (3) such as the publications of the Ministry of Education, Science and Culture (Shūmuka, Religious Affairs Section) are indispensable; the bibliography by Morioka and Yanagawa is a useful tool. The recent "handbook" for the study of Japanese New Religions by Inoue, et al., is a convenient synthesis of information and insights, the best single volume for introducing the reader to this subject. The comprehensive bibliography for Tenrikyō is apparently the only such work completed covering one New Religion. For Japanese materials on other New Religions, see the monographs listed under Secondary materials for that New Religion in Part II.

HOLZMAN, DONALD, et al. *Japanese Religion and Philosophy: A Guide to Japanese Reference and Research Materials.* Ann Arbor: University of Michigan Press, 1959, vii + 102 pp. Reprint. Westport, CT: Greenwood Press, 1975. Author index and subject index.

See esp. items 915-44 for "Sect Shinto and the New Religions," with brief annotations.

INOUE, NOBUTAKA, et al. *Shinshūkyō Kenkyū Chōsa Handobukku* [Handbook for study and field research of the New Religions]. Tokyo: Yūzankaku, 1981, 307 pp. Bibliography, pp. 259-306 (mostly Japanese, but including some Western-language materials).

The best Japanese work on the subject, by a team of younger specialists in Japanese New Religions; features separate chapters on aspects of the New Religions (origins, social organization, etc.), basic literature by and about the New Religions, and research methods; also included are a derivation chart for most groups, a vocabulary for major organizations, and a list of statistics for forty New Religions.

THE INTERNATIONAL INSTITUTE FOR THE STUDY OF RELIGIONS. *Directory of the Sectarian Shinto Federation and the Principal Shinto Shrines of Japan.* Directory no. 5. Tokyo: International Institute for the Study of Religions, 1957, 40 pp.

Lists official bulletins for sectarian Shinto.

_____. *New Religions, Bahai, Islam and the Japan Free Religious Association.* Directory no. 4. Tokyo: International Institute for the Study of Religions, 1958, 75 pp.

Lists official bulletins for the New Religions.

INUI, TAKASHI; OGUCHI, IICHI; SAKI, AKIO; and MATSUSHIMA, EIICHI. *Kyōso—Shomin no Kamigami* [Founders—the gods of the people]. Tokyo: Aoki Shoten, 1955, 273 pp. Illus.

A general study of the founders of eight major New Religions; several useful charts of chronology are included.

K.B.S. Bibliography of Standard Reference Books for Japanese Studies with Descriptive Notes. Vol. 4, Religion. Tokyo: Kokusai Bunka Shinkokai (The Society for International Cultural Relations), 1963, iii + 181 pp. Reprint. Tokyo: University of Tokyo Press, 1971.

See items 26-30, 91-94 for New Religions and sectarian Shinto. Annotations.

KOKUGAKUIN DAIGAKU NIHON BUNKA KENKYŪSHO, ed. *Shintō Rombun Sōmokuroku* [Comprehensive index of articles on Shinto]. Tokyo: Meiji Jingū Shamusho, 1963, 755 pp.

See pp. 53-57 for articles on Sect Shinto and p. 160 for New Religions.

MORIOKA, KIYOMI, ed. *Hendōki no Ningen to Shūkyō* [Man and religion in times of social change]. Tokyo: Miraisha, 1978, 242 pp.

Features a general chapter on social change and religion by the editor, followed by four specific studies of New Religions (one of which appears in English as entry 759 in the present bibliography) and several other studies on change and religon.

MURAKAMI, SHIGEYOSHI. *Kindai Minshū Shūkyōshi no Kenkyū* [Studies in recent popular religious history]. Rev. ed. Kyoto: Hōzōkan, 1963, 248 pp.

Chart of derivation of recent popular religions. Critical essays on the origin and development of Sect Shinto out of the peculiar socioreligious situation of late Tokugawa and early Meiji times. Extensive documentation in footnotes.

_____. *Kindai Nihon no Shūkyōsha* [Religious leaders of recent Japan]. Tokyo: Asoka Shuppansha, 1967, 242 pp. Chronology of Japanese recent religious history.

A general study of twenty-seven religious leaders, most of them founders of New Religions. Brief list of references after each chapter.

_____. *Nihon Hyakunen no Shūkyō: Haibutsu Kishaku kara Sōka Gakkai made* [A century of Japanese religion: From the persecution of Buddhism to Sōka Gakkai]. Tokyo: Kōdansha, 1968, 208 pp. See pp. 204-8 for bibliography.

Chart of derivation of recent popular religions. Interpretation of the conditions during the century when the New Religions arose and analysis of major New Religions. See the translation of this book, entry 153.

OGUCHI, IICHI. *Nihon Shūkyō no Shakaiteki Seikaku* [The social characteristics of Japanese religion]. Tokyo: Tokyo Daigaku Shuppankai, 1953, 209 pp.

See pp. 72-103 for brief comments on the New Religions.

SAKI, AKIO. *Shinkō Shūkyō—Sore o Meguru Gendai no Jōken* [The New Religions—the contemporary conditions surrounding them]. Tokyo: Aoki Shoten, 1960, 240 pp. See p. 240 for bibliography.

Analysis of the major characteristics of the New Religions and the social conditions that gave rise to the New Religions.

Shinshūkyō no Sekai [The world of the New Religions]. 5 vols. Tokyo: Daizō Shuppan, 1978-79.

The first volume treats "general problems" concerning the New Religions; the remaining volumes provide popular overviews of more than twenty major New Religions.

SHIN-SHŪ-REN. *Shin-shū-ren Yōran* [Union of New Religions directory]. Revised and enlarged edition. Tokyo: Shin-shū-ren, 1966, 94 pp.

Information concerning Shin-shū-ren (Shin Nihon Shūkyō Dantai Rengō-kai, Union of New Religious Organizations of Japan) and its member organizations. See Table 1 in the present volume for the list of membership in Shin-shū-ren.

SHŪMUKA, BUNKACHŌ, MOMBUSHŌ [Religious Affairs Section; Ministry of Education, Science and Culture], ed. *Shūkyō Nenkan* [Religion yearbook].

Published annually (successor to several earlier titles), valuable source of statistical and other current official information. See also the periodical *Shūmu Jihō*, especially Kiyomi Morioka and Keiichi Yanagawa, "Sengo no Shūkyō Jijō—Bunken Mokuroku" [The postwar religious situation—a bibliography].

TAKAGI, HIROO. *Nihon no Shinkō Shūkyō* [The Japanese New Religions]. Tokyo: Iwanami Shoten, 1959, viii + 209 pp. Illus. See pp. 207-9 for bibliography.

Interpretation of the New Religions as mass movements.

Tenrikyō Toshokan-zō Tenrikyō Tosho Mokuroku [Bibliography of books on Tenrikyō in the Tenrikyō Library]. Tenri Jihōsha, 1959, 133 pp.

Comprehensive bibliography of Japanese books on Tenrikyō, also including some Western-language materials (all the Western-language materials have been searched and inserted in the present bibliography, especially under the *Secondary* entries for Tenrikyō).

THOMSEN, HARRY. *Bibliography on the New Religions.* Kyoto: Christian Center for the Study of Japanese Religions. 1960, 2 + 37 pp.

Includes Japanese (especially denominational) materials for sixteen New Religions.

TSURUFUJI, IKUTA. *Kyōha Shintō no Kenkyū* [A study of Sect Shinto]. Osaka: Taikōsha, 1939, 443 pp. See appendix, pp. 1-4 for bibliography of Sect Shinto.

A prewar survey of the thirteen original members of Sect Shinto.

WATANABE, BAIYŪ. *Gendai Nihon no Shūkyō* [Contemporary Japanese religion]. Tokyo: Daitō Shuppansha, 1951, 346 pp. Illus.

Analysis of the New Religions in the context of Japanese religion.

D. Comparative Materials for the Study
of New Religious Movements

According to Wallace ("Revitalization Movements," p. 264), "Our files now contain references to several hundred religious revitalization movements, among both western and nonwestern peoples, on five continents," and a more thorough search for these movements "would without question gather in thousands." Whatever the total number of such movements, they are much too numerous to be treated individually. Therefore, no attempt is made to list materials for separate movements, since the following works contain references to major movements and relevant materials. The vast range and number of comparative materials is suggested by the kinds of publications listed here. There are some bibliographies, such as those of Turner and Leeson, that deal with new religious movements in specific areas. Other works have been included that pursue the problem of religious movements historically, as that of Cohn, and regionally, as those of Clark, Fuchs, La Barre (*The Peyote Cult*), and Worsley. Bibliographies within these works afford abundant materials. Some works have been listed because of their attempt at comparative study and synthetic interpretation: those of Guariglia, Lanternari, and Mühlmann. Theoretical arguments and relevant bibliographies can be found in La Barre, ("Materials . . ."), Robbins, et al., Smelser, Wach, Wallace, and Wilson.

CLARK, ELMER T. *The Small Sects of America*. Rev. ed. New York: Abingdon Press, 1949, 256 pp. See pp. 236-40 for bibliography; also appendixes, index, and "Index of Religious Bodies in the United States," pp. 241-46.

Briefly describes many American sectarian movements according to several types; excludes non-Christian groups.

COHN, NORMAN. *The Pursuit of the Millennium: Revolutionary Messianism in Medieval and Reformation Europe and Its Bearing on Modern Totalitarian Movements*. 2d ed. New York: Harper & Row, 1961, xvi + 481 pp. See pp. 435-68 for bibliography of original sources and modern works.

A study of the historical origins and nature of medieval and later European millenarian movements.

ELLWOOD, ROBERT S., Jr. *Religious and Spiritual Groups in Modern America*. Englewood Cliffs, NJ: Prentice-Hall, 1972, xvi + 334 pp.

Provides brief introductions to and selected documents from various groups, including some Japanese movements.

FUCHS, STEPHEN. *Rebellious Prophets: A Study of Messianic Movements in Indian Religions*. New York: Asia Publishing House, 1965, xiv + 304 pp.

Traces messianic movements in India regionally and tribally, with "Literature" cited at the end of sections.

GLOCK, CHARLES Y., and BELLAH, ROBERT H., eds. *The New Religious Consciousness.* Contributions by Randall H. Alfred et al. Berkeley: University of California Press, 1976, xvii + 391 pp.

A volume of essays on new religious movements based on field work in the Oakland Bay area.

GUARIGLIA, GUGLIELMO. "Prophetismus und Heilserwartungs-Bewegungen als völkerkundliches und religionsgeschichtliches Problem." *Wiener Beiträge zur Kulturgeschichte und Linguistik* 13 (Horn-Wien: Verlag Ferdinand Berger, 1959), pp. 1-322. See pp. 278-305 for bibliography.

A worldwide comparative and typological study of prophetic movements discussed regionally.

JULES-ROSETTE, BENNETTA, ed. *The New Religions of Africa.* Norwood, NJ: Ablex Publishing Corporation, 1979, xxii + 248 pp.

Includes eleven chapters on aspects of various African New Religions, as well as a general introduction and conclusion, and a bibliography, pp. 231-40.

LA BARRE, WESTON. "Materials for a History of Studies of Crisis Cults: A Bibliographic Essay." *Current Anthropology* 12, no. 1 (February 1971): 3-44.

A bibliographical essay valuable for its theoretical clarification of "crisis cults" (and viewed from the standpoint that culture and symbols are "adaptive man-made artifacts"); it also provides some materials by geographical area.

_____. *The Peyote Cult.* 4th enlarged ed. [Hamden, CT]: Archon Books, 1975, xix + 296 pp.

A 1938 doctoral dissertation on the diffusion and religious use of peyote among Native Americans, this work is also valuable for its original bibliography, pp. 175-88, and for three more recent bibliographic essays: pp. 195-210, 213-50, and 251-85.

LANTERNARI, VITTORIO. *The Religions of the Oppressed: A Study of Modern Messianic Cults.* Translated by Lisa Sergio. New York: Knopf; London: MacGibbon & Kee, 1963, xix + 343 pp. Bibliography, pp. 323-39. New York: New American Library, 1965, xvi + 286 pp. Bibliography, pp. 255-71. First published as *Movimenti religiosi di libertà e di salvezza dei popoli oppressi* (Milan: Feltrinelli, 1960), 365 pp. Also published as *Religiöse Freiheits- und Heilsbewegungen unterdrückten Völker,* trans. Friedrich Kollmann (Neuwied: Luchterhand, 1960), 538 pp.

A worldwide comparative study of messianic and prophetic movements, discussed by region, including mention of some Japanese New Religions; the bibliography is conveniently arranged by region.

LEESON, IDA. *Bibliographie des 'Cargo Cults' et autres mouvements autochtones du Pacifique Sud.* Document technique no. 30. Sydney: Commission du Pacifique Sud, 1952, 16 pp. (Also English edition.)

Materials arranged according to geographical region within the South Pacific.

MÜHLMANN, W(ILHELM) E. *Chiliasmus und Nativismus—Studien zu einer Psychologie, Soziologie und historischen Kasuistik der Umsturzbewegungen.* With contributions by Alfons M. Dauer, et al. Berlin: Dietrich Reimer Verlag, 1961. 2d printing, 1964, 472 pp. See pp. 445-51 for bibliography.

Separate indexes for subjects, personal names, names of founders and prophets, tribal groups, and names of religious movements.

"Regional" papers by other contributors in Part 1, with analysis and interpretation by the main author in Part 2.

New Religious Movements Newsletter. No. 1- (October 1978-).

A publication of the Program for the Study of New Religious Movements in America, located at the Graduate Theological Union, 2465 LeConte Avenue, Berkeley, California 94709. Provides current information about new religious movements, legal questions, and ongoing research; it focuses mainly on movements in the United States, including those of Asian origin such as Japanese New Religions. The program has developed a file of published and unpublished materials by and about such movements and also has released some bibliographies such as Robbins's, listed in Appendix C.

PALMER, SPENCER J., ed. *The New Religions of Korea. Transactions of the Korea Branch, Royal Asiatic Society* (Seoul) 43 (1967), 180 pp.

Includes one general introduction and five specialized articles on Korean New Religions.

ROBBINS, THOMAS. *Civil Liberties, "Brainwashing," and "Cults": A Select Annotated Bibliography.* Berkeley, CA: Center for the Study of New Religious Movements, Graduate Theological Union, 1981, 48 pp.

Deals mainly with the legal, psychological, and sociological aspects of "brainwashing" and deprogramming; articles and books focus on movements in America, especially the Unification Church ("Moonies").

_____, and ANTHONY, DICK, eds. *In Gods We Trust: New Patterns of Religious Pluralism in America*. New Brunswick, NJ: Transaction Books, 1981, 338 pp.

A collection of descriptive, interpretive, and theoretical articles focusing on the recent religious ferment in the United States; it does not deal with Japanese groups, but does treat Unification Church ("Moonies") and other "Eastern" groups.

_____; ANTHONY, DICK; and RICHARDSON, JAMES. "Theory and Research on Today's 'New Religions.'" *Sociological Analysis* 39, no. 2 (Summer 1978): 95-122.

Review of recent literature of New Religions, especially American movements or branches in America, focusing on the diversity of theoretical arguments; pp. 114-22 provide a convenient bibliography of recent literature.

SMELSER, NEIL J. *Theory of Collective Behavior*. New York: Free Press of Glencoe, 1963, xi + 436 pp. Illus. See pp. 388-427 for bibliography.

See esp. pp. 313-81 for analysis of "The Value-Oriented Movement," a more lengthy abstract treatment of the same phenomena covered in Wallace, "Revitalization Movements"; extensive documentation of historical and theoretical materials.

THRUPP, SYLVIA L., ed. *Millennial Dreams in Action: Essays in Comparative Study*. Comparative Studies in Society and History, Supplement 2. The Hague: Mouton & Co., 1962, 229 pp. Index for personal names, place names, and subjects.

Seventeen papers dealing with millenarian and messianic themes in various areas and periods.

TURNER, HAROLD W. *Bibliography of New Religious Movements in Primal Societies*. 4 vols. Boston: G.K. Hall, 1977-. Vol. 1, *Black Africa*, 1977, x + 277 pp. Index of authors and sources; select thematic guide. Vol. 2, *North America*, 1978, x + 285 pp. Indexes for authors and sources; films, records and tapes; main movements; and Indian individuals. Vols. 3 and 4, forthcoming.

Vol. 1: 1,906 annotated items arranged by geographical subregions of Africa, with separate sections for theoretical and general works.

Vol. 2: 1,608 annotated items arranged by three subregions of North America, with separate sections for theoretical and general works.

Vol. 3 will treat Asia and Oceania; Vol. 4 will treat Latin America and the Caribbean.

_____. *Religious Innovation in Africa: Collected Essays on New Religious Movements*. Boston: G.K. Hall, 1979, x + 354 pp.

These essays by Turner cover his earlier and more recent work on the methodology and typology appropriate for the study of African movements, with several historical and biographical treatments.

WACH, JOACHIM. *Sociology of Religion*. Chicago: University of Chicago Press, 1944. 1949, xi + 418 pp. See pp. 391-95 for bibliography of materials published 1943-48, supplementing documentation in the footnotes.

See pp. 109-205 for "Specifically Religious Organization of Society," esp. pp. 156-205 for the distinction between protest and secession; also pp. 306-9 for "Typology II: The New Faith."

WALLACE, ANTHONY F.C. *The Death and Rebirth of the Seneca*. New York: Alfred A. Knopf, 1970, xiii + 384 pp.

A detailed description and interpretation of one North American "revitalization movement" ("the Old Way of Handsome Lake") featuring an extensive bibliography, pp. 369-84.

_____. "Revitalization Movements." *American Anthropologist* 48 (1956): 264-81.

A theoretical treatment of the concept of revitalization as inclusive of all cultural innovations such as nativistic movement, reform movement, cargo cult, religious revival, messianic movement, utopian community, and other forms. For elaboration of this theory of revitalization see his *Religion: An Anthropological View* (New York: Random House, 1966), 300 pp. See esp. pp. 30-39, 157-66, 209-15.

WILSON, BRYAN R. *Magic and the Millennium. A Sociological Study of Religious Movements of Protest among Tribal and Third-World Peoples*. New York: Harper & Row, Publishers, 1973, xi + 547 pp. Bibliography. Index of Authors. Index of Subjects. Index of Principal Movements, Tribes, and Persons.

A comprehensive sociological interpretation of religious movements among tribal peoples from the viewpoint that "thaumaturgical (or . . . magical) preoccupations are the fundamental orientation of new religious movements among simpler peoples. . . ."

WORSLEY, PETER. *The Trumpet Shall Sound. A Study of "Cargo" Cults in Melanesia*. 2d augmented edition. New York: Schocken Books, 1968, lxix + 300 pp. See bibliography, pp. 277-88, with "Supplementary Bibliography of Literature on Melanesian Cargo Cults 1957-67, compiled by D.A. Heathcote," pp. 389-93.

A study of "millenarism" in various areas of Melanesia with analysis of underlying factors.

INDEXES

AUTHOR INDEX

This index includes all entries with a specific author, and also some entries listed by translator or editor. Some entries are listed in the name of the headquarters or institute that issued them. A number of entries without specific authors are not included. All references are to entry numbers (not page numbers). Some concrete details explaining the handling of names are as follows.

Pseudonyms are cross-referenced to actual names (when known); entry numbers are given under the actual name. Explanation of pseudonyms (when known) is given within entries.

Cross-references are also supplied for the maiden name and married name of several women.

Japanese names often appear in Western languages in somewhat different transliterations, making consistency difficult for the bibliographer. The solution in this bibliography has been to list all works by one author under the customary transliteration for this name, indicating where necessary the alternate transliteration used in the article or book cited. For example, entries 484–488 are listed under Deguchi, Onisaburo, the customary transliteration for this name. (Technically, the given name should be Onisaburō, with a long vowel indicated by a macron, but the principle herein is to provide macrons in the bibliography only when they are used in the citation.) In entry 485 the author's name is given as Onisabro Deguĉi; in entry 487 Deguchi is transliterated as Degutshi: each alternate reading is placed in parentheses in the respective entry. In this author index, alternate readings of names (such as Deguĉi and Degutshi) are not given entry numbers but cross-referenced to the customary transliteration (in this case Deguchi).

Western names are given in their most complete form, with all works by the author listed under the complete form of the name.

For other tips on efficient location of materials, see also Suggestions for Convenient Use of The Bibliography.

TOPICAL INDEX

This index includes the major topics found in most items. Some lengthy or important materials are indexed by several topics, while briefer materials, especially those in the category of "History and analysis of individual New Religions," are not included. Some entries either are indexed according to the subject indicated in the title or are not included because they were not available to the compiler. Entries from all sections of the bibliography are indexed together, but certain topics tend to accumulate entries primarily from one section. Topics such as "New Religions, definition of," "Historical development of the New Religions," and "Japanese religion, relationship of New Religions to" come mainly from Part I, General Bibliography. Topics such as "Doctrine," "Manuals, catechisms, guides, and outlines of religious teaching," "Prayers, prayer books, liturgies," and "Scriptures and commentaries" are drawn mainly from denominational materials in Part II, Bibliography of Individual New Religions. Topics such as "Comparative studies of Japanese New Religions with non-Japanese movements," "History and analysis of individual New Religions," and "Political activity and elections" are taken mainly from secondary materials in Part II. These general topics have been treated loosely in order to group many entries for the reader. Materials with more specialized focus have been listed under narrower topics with fewer items. All references are to entry numbers.

All topics are subdivided according to the format of the bibliography: first come "General" references, if there are any, and then entries for each New Religion, arranged alphabetically (with "Utopian Groups" last).

For other tips on efficient location of materials, see also Suggestions for Convenient Use of The Bibliography.

MICHIGAN PAPERS IN JAPANESE STUDIES

No. 1. *Political Leadership in Contemporary Japan*, edited by Terry Edward MacDougall.

No. 2. *Parties, Candidates and Voters in Japan: Six Quantitative Studies*, edited by John Creighton Campbell.

No. 3. *The Japanese Automobile Industry: Model and Challenge for the Future?*, edited by Robert E. Cole.

No. 4. *Survey of Japanese Collections in the United States, 1979-1980*, by Naomi Fukuda.

No. 5. *Culture and Religion in Japanese-American Relations: Essays on Uchimura Kanzō, 1861-1930*, edited by Ray A. Moore.

No. 6. *Sukeroku's Double Identity: The Dramatic Structure of Edo Kabuki*, by Barbara E. Thornbury.

No. 7. *Industry at the Crossroads*, edited by Robert E. Cole.

No. 8. *Treelike: The Poetry of Kinoshita Yūji*, translated by Robert Epp.

No. 9. *The New Religions of Japan: A Bibliography of Western-Language Materials*, by H. Byron Earhart.